Teach EFL

For my mother and late father, Mary and Jim Riddell

Teach EFL

David Riddell

First published in Great Britain in 2001 by Hodder Education. An Hachette UK company.

First published in US in 2001 by The McGraw-Hill Companies, Inc.

This edition published 2014

Paperback ISBN 978 1 473 60115 4

eBook ISBN 978 1 473 60117 8

10 9 8 7 6 5 4 3 2 1

The publisher has used its best endeavours to ensure that any website addresses referred to in this book are correct and active at the time of going to press. However, the publisher and the author have no responsibility for the websites and can make no guarantee that a site will remain live or that the content will remain relevant, decent or appropriate.

The publisher has made every effort to mark as such all words which it believes to be trademarks. The publisher should also like to make it clear that the presence of a word in the book, whether marked or unmarked, in no way affects its legal status as a trademark.

Every reasonable effort has been made by the publisher to trace the copyright holders of material in this book. Any errors or omissions should be notified in writing to the publisher, who will endeavour to rectify the situation for any reprints and future editions.

Cover image © Alhovik / Shutterstock

Typeset by Integra Software Services Pvt. Ltd., Pondicherry, India.

Printed and bound in Great Britain by CPI Group (UK) Ltd., Croydon, CRO 4YY.

John Murray Learning policy is to use papers that are natural, renewable and recyclable products and made from wood grown in sustainable forests. The logging and manufacturing processes are expected to conform to the environmental regulations of the country of origin.

John Murray Learning
338 Euston Road
London NW1 3BH
www.hodder.co.uk

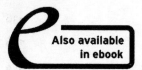

Also available in ebook

Contents

Acknowledgements

For this edition I would like to thank my colleagues at International House London, and especially:

David Carr, Fiona Johnston, Ifthaquar Jamil, Jessica Luby, Jan Madakbas, Harry Van Manen, Jo Ridd, Dominique Vouillemin and Vicki Willson

Meet the author

I grew up wanting to be a DJ, and I particularly wanted to have the breakfast show on Radio 1. Well, such are childhood dreams. Instead I ended up teaching English, and training others to do the same – not quite the same thing, but it is a job that has never been dull, and never been predictable.

I have met wonderful students from around the world in my classrooms, several of whom have become long-lasting and close friends. I have had some fantastic colleagues. I have worked in some great schools.

Of course, it's not all good. You never get rich teaching English, and some students can try your patience (and some colleagues, too). But I have had so many happy times teaching, learnt so much from my students about different cultures, and seen so many success stories. At its best, it's a great job; full of variety and unpredictability.

And it has been so satisfying to train so many others to teach over the years. And this book is part of that process ... a chance for me to share some of the things that I believe help people to be good teachers, based on over 30 years' teaching experience. I hope it helps! But if a radio station comes calling for me...

Introduction

Despite the title of this book, I do not think it is possible for someone to 'teach' himself or herself how to teach, without actually doing it, just as you cannot learn from a book how to use a computer if you do not have a computer to use. However, I do know from my experience as a teacher trainer that there are EFL/ESL teachers who have no qualifications or training. This is not good for the profession, and it is certainly not good for the students. However, it is a fact. I also know that even those people who do undertake a training course need as much practical help and support as they can get, not only during the course, but also – and maybe particularly – after the course, as they begin their first teaching assignment. So, you cannot teach yourself to be a teacher, but you can learn and improve your skills as you go along.

This book, therefore, is intended for these three types of reader:
- ▶ teachers teaching without having had any training
- ▶ teachers who have recently trained and who lack experience
- ▶ trainee teachers doing a training course

By 'teachers' I refer to those in any country, teaching to monolingual and multilingual classes, to students whose first language is not English, and to students who are classified as adult learners (generally defined as 16+). Since the book has such a broad focus it inevitably deals with the general, rather than the specific, teaching context. This is no bad thing. The book's purpose is to provide new teachers with the basic teaching skills, background knowledge and awareness that will subsequently enable them to develop and fine-tune what they do in the classroom.

I have seen situations where too much is expected of new/trainee teachers. Many of my ex-trainees have complained about the lack of support and help from some first-time employers who sometimes seem to expect students to know everything from having done a four-week training course, or similar. This is unrealistic. Equally, tutors on training courses should not forget that most of their trainees have never been in front of a class before in their lives and that they need support and encouragement as well as expert training.

Fortunately, most employers and tutors do provide such support. However, they are not always available when needed by the new or trainee teacher. I hope this book will fill that space.

This book should not be seen as the be-all and end-all of EFL/ESL teaching. To many experienced teachers reading the book (a book not intended for such readership) much of what I have written will be seen as prescriptive, just as the typical training course and most course books are prescriptive. I will always argue, from long experience, that a level of prescriptiveness is needed (and welcomed by trainees) at the beginning of their teaching career. I make no apologies for being prescriptive in this book – once teachers have more experience and confidence, they can develop their awareness and methodology. The models of teaching that I outline here can be applied successfully in most contexts, giving new teachers a much-needed degree of security. Please note, when referring to teachers in general, I have used 'she'/'her' throughout; students are referred to as 'he', 'she' or 'they' (singular and plural).

This book is not intended for experienced teachers or for those teaching young learners. It is not intended to apply in all parts to all teaching contexts. It certainly does not cover all aspects of teaching. Instead, it aims to raise awareness of the role of teachers and students teaching and learning English, and to give practical ideas for teaching English as a foreign or second language to adults.

This is effectively a teaching 'handbook' which can be referred to at short notice for suggestions, examples and reassurance. It is just the beginning of the long process of becoming an effective and successful teacher. It has been written to provide help and encouragement. I hope it does.

Good luck, and enjoy the ride! It won't be dull.

David Riddell (davi77@hotmail.com)

1 Being a student

My own memories of my schooldays and the teachers that taught me are very vivid. As a learner of French I experienced two very different styles of teaching – one where I was taught primarily in English, and one where I was taught mostly in French. I found the second much more intimidating, but also much more effective. The first was safe, comparatively easy, but did little to make me a competent user of the language. Just as it was no good for someone to **show** me how to change a spark plug (I had to **do** it to learn), so it was no good for me to learn a new language without getting more opportunity to use it. That is one reason why our students in EFL are mostly taught entirely in English, regardless of their level. Allow a couple of students to start using their own language and you will quickly hear loud complaints from the other students – they know that this is not helping their learning.

Teachers have differing views on the use of L1 (the student's mother tongue) in the classroom, and it depends to an extent on whether you are teaching a monolingual or a multilingual class. In a multilingual class, lessons are taught almost entirely in English, partly for the reason already given, and partly because this 'total immersion' approach encourages real communication as opposed to rule learning and the completion of exercises. Of course, there may be times when the occasional quick translation may be helpful, but if either the teacher or other students start using non-English to any extent beyond this, the students are very likely to become unhappy.

In a monolingual class it is inevitable that the students will speak their own language more, and perhaps the teacher will too (if she knows it!). But if the teacher starts teaching in that language rather than English, the **authenticity** of the target language will be lost.

All teachers, especially of 'General English', know that different students prefer to learn in different ways. Let's be honest here – as much as teachers believe in the effectiveness of the 'communicative approach', there are still many students who prefer to listen to explanations of grammar, learn rules, and do practice exercises. It is safer – just as when my French teacher taught in English. On the other hand, there are those students who only want to 'talk', being more concerned with fluency than with accuracy. There are students who want learning to be 'fun', and those who perceive 'fun' as 'not learning'.

It is obvious, then, that 'being a student' is a complicated existence. We, as teachers, have to appreciate this and be as aware as we can of our students' different attitudes to learning.

TASK

Here are some questions I used in a survey done with some of my students. Before I report the findings, answer the questions yourself based on your own experience of new-language learning.

1 **What makes a good student?**

2 **What helps you when you are learning a new language?**

3 **How important is learning grammar when you are learning a language?**

4 **Should learning be communicative, or should you learn from explanations, rules, and practice exercises?**

5 **How important is it for a student to have some responsibility for their own learning and not to rely exclusively on the teacher?**

6 **Is it a good thing to be in a class with students from your own country (of course, in non-English-speaking classes students will all be from the same country, so this question does have rather limited value!)?**

7 **Is it a good thing for the teacher to use your language?**

STOP here and consider your answers before reading on.

The students I asked were from eleven different countries – Japan, Mexico, Brazil, Russia, Turkey, Italy, Israel, France, Korea, Algeria, and Spain. They were intermediate and upper intermediate level students studying in London with ages ranging from 18 to 45. Most had experience of learning another language besides English, and all had experienced more than one learning style.

I also put the same questions to Thomas Grossmann, a Swiss German teacher who passed his Proficiency in the month of December. Six months later, he was a qualified EFL teacher and was teaching shortly after that. This remarkably quick transformation made Thomas an ideal person to ask about both learning and teaching.

But first the student reactions:

1 What makes a good student?

'respect your teacher'

'know that you're not the only student in the class'

'you must have a desire to study'

'listen'

'respect other students'

'be interested'

'socialize with other students and teachers'

'speak in class'

'pay attention'

'do your homework'

'spend time outside class using English'

'go over what you have learnt in class'

'know why you are learning English'

'respect the culture of the country'

'be attentive, disciplined, active in class'

'Respect' is a word that came up several times, and some cultures are especially respectful of the role of the teacher. Others have had strained relationships with teachers from their own schooldays and are perhaps still a little suspicious of teachers in general. Most, however, have opinions about what the role of the teacher should be, something we will look at in the next unit.

Having a 'desire to study' – an 'interest' in what is being learnt – is crucial, in my view. The inquisitive student, the one who wants to know 'why?' and 'how?' and who asks lots of questions, may be the student that new and learning teachers dread the most, but in the long run these are the students who thrive and make visible progress and who keep the teacher challenged and rewarded.

'Pay attention' and 'listen' are very important points, too. 'Listen' should be followed by 'respond' because to listen is not enough. Think of any conversation you have had with a person who, you know full well, is not really listening to what you are saying. It is frustrating. Their thoughts are elsewhere and you do not have their attention. Students whose minds wander, or who are content only to listen (back to that 'safe' option!)

suggest that their desire to study, to learn, is limited. This was certainly the view of the students I spoke to, some of whom were themselves 'guilty' of this at times!

'Go over what you've learnt', 'do your homework', 'use English outside class' are points which cannot be emphasized too much. I should add that all my students stressed the ideal of learning English in an English-speaking country, if possible. This obviously makes it much more possible to use English outside school, as well as making the learning process more authentic. But, of course, this is not always possible.

However, it is important for students not to perceive their lessons as the be-all and end-all of their learning. Yes, they should do their homework. Yes, they should revise what they have studied. But most of all they should take whatever opportunity they can to use their English – speaking, listening, reading, writing. As teachers we should not only encourage them to do so, but also tell them **how** to do it (e.g. suggesting English newspapers, both online and printed, as well as English radio and TV, which can also be accessed online, plus magazines, books, etc. to read). The student who limits his 'learning' to inside the classroom will make very little real progress.

2 What helps you when you are learning a language?

'be in the country of the language'

'don't be shy'

'watch TV'

'a balance and variety'

'use only English when possible outside class'

'have a part-time job if possible'

Most of these have already been mentioned. The point made about the part-time job only applies to work in an English-speaking country, but this situation certainly plunges the student into using English authentically.

Watching TV (equally, watching films, listening to the radio, reading newspapers, etc.) underlines what has already been said about using English outside class.

3 How important is learning grammar when you are learning a language?

'grammar, grammar, grammar is very boring'

'quite important'

'very important'

'gives meaning to conversation'

'not too much'

'it is important because if you learn grammar you can speak properly'
(whatever 'properly' means!)

Predictably, different views were expressed, reflecting, in part, students' own language-learning experiences from earlier education. The very word 'grammar' has negative connotations for most people, and can be a real turn-off in the classroom, much as the word 'homework' can. But it is a word with an undeserved reputation! Ask most people what they understand by 'grammar' and they will usually come up with 'rules', 'exercises', 'copying from the board', 'boring', 'not useful', etc. Say to a class 'now we're going to do grammar' and you won't be greeted with a sea of smiling faces – though some students still view the learning of rules as 'real learning'.

4 **Should learning be communicative, or should you learn from listening to explanations and making notes and doing practice exercises?**

'beginners need more practice exercises, after that learning should be communicative'

'it should be more communicative because if French schools did that we would speak better English'

'communicative, otherwise it is boring'

This 'communicative' approach is partly the result of using only English in the classroom, but more than this, it is giving students the opportunity to use the language they are learning in authentic contexts. We will look at this much more later, but it is the overwhelming view of students I have taught that this communicative approach is more successful, more real than the approach of rule learning.

5 **How important is it for a student to have some responsibility for their own learning and not to rely on the teacher alone?**

'very important'

'teacher helps to show you the right way'

'trains you for "real life"'

'it is important to have some responsibility for your own learning'

'a good student has some responsibility outside the class, but they have to be guided'

The student who comes to class but never uses his English outside it (more likely when they are learning in their own country), or who never studies outside it, will make very little genuine progress. The classroom is not 'real life' (as mentioned above). It is *artificial*. Everything is controlled by the teacher and how she has planned the lesson.

We have to encourage our students to read English, speak English, hear English, write English. We also have to encourage learner independence within the classroom.

6 **Is it a good thing to be in a class with students from another country? (This is mostly relevant to classes in English-speaking countries.)**

'more interesting'

'different cultures'

'yes, it makes you use English'

'it is good to open your mind, and we have to speak English'

7 **Is it a good thing for your teacher to use your language some of the time when teaching?**

'teacher must first try and explain in English'

'never, never'

'only with low-level students'

'it is not necessary'

These comments support the views expressed at the start of this unit and show how aware most students are of the need to immerse themselves in English in the classroom.

Comments from Thomas Grossmann, from his perspective of a student who became a teacher, are also very relevant. His views on what helped him gain the Cambridge Proficiency of English in a relatively short time cover many of the points already mentioned, as well as one or two others:

'a positive attitude towards the language, the country where it is spoken, and its people'

'absorbing as much language as possible (especially vocabulary, phrasal verbs and idioms) by watching TV, talking with native speakers, listening to audiobooks'

'reading books, magazines, newspapers'

'discussions in class'

'being able to figure out a grammar rule for oneself' (described by Thomas as the 'aha' effect!)

'not being afraid of making mistakes'

'a good reference book'

'trying to get the "feel" and "rhythm" of the language'

'copying the pronunciation from native speakers and slightly exaggerating it'

'the iron will to learn the language (motivation)'

'keeping penfriends'

Thomas also says: 'I think an advantage I had was that I learnt English in England where I could use it every day. I imagine that if I had learnt it in Switzerland it would have been much harder and less close to my heart. My views on effective learning since becoming a teacher haven't altered much. Every person has his or her individual way and pace of learning and, whatever that is, it should be encouraged. Another point which I think is very important (especially if one doesn't learn English in a country where it is spoken), is to use as much **real** language as possible.'

Summary

Our students usually have different favoured learning styles, influenced by their previous learning experiences.

▶ Most prefer, or accept the advantages of, a mostly communicative approach to their learning.

▶ Students have to accept some responsibility for their own learning and not rely only on the teacher.

▶ Learning has to include authentic practice, and has to continue outside the classroom.

▶ Students need motivation and commitment.

▶ Students prefer – and expect – English to be the only language spoken in the lessons, except with very low-level classes.

Everything which has been mentioned in this unit inevitably affects the role of the teacher and how she plans her teaching, and this is what the next unit will look at.

2 Being a teacher

Most people remember at least some of their teachers from schooldays, whether positively or negatively. Teachers make an impression. And students have expectations. If being a student is a 'complicated existence', then being a teacher is trying to meet the many varying expectations that students have, and that the teacher herself has, of the teacher's role. Perhaps we should say 'roles' because 'teaching' is only part of what the teacher has to do inside – and outside – the classroom.

TASK

1 **Think back to your own schooldays and the teachers you had. Which ones did you consider to be 'good' and which were 'bad'? Why?**

2 **If you studied a language at school, how did that teacher approach her lessons? What was effective and not effective and why? How did you learn? Was anything lacking in your lessons?**

3 **On the basis of your previous answers, what do you think constitutes an effective and popular teacher of English to speakers of other languages? Make a list of the most important qualities.**

STOP – do this task before reading on.

Many people have experienced the 'listen and take notes' approach to language learning, followed by doing practice exercises from a book, and with a strong emphasis on remembering what has been learnt, as opposed to using the language. It must be stated that some students do prefer this approach (which is not necessarily to say that it is an effective approach). This method implies a very limited responsibility for the teacher whereas, in reality, the effective and popular teacher has a multitude of responsibilities.

The survey I did with students highlighted not only this multitude of responsibilities, but also the expectations that students have of their teacher. Students, of any subject, are a critical and discerning audience, which can make a teacher's job hard. However, if teachers can respond to their students' personalities, attitudes, needs and backgrounds, they will become better teachers.

What makes a good teacher?

I asked the same students featured in Unit 1 'What makes a good teacher?' Of all the questions I asked, it was this one that produced the most opinions. In no particular order, these are some of the qualities mentioned in their replies:

'they must be passionate about teaching, and patient, adapting to the level of the students'

'a good teacher must be strict, friendly, interesting'

'should be passionate and intelligent'

'should teach grammar clearly'

'should not rely on the course book only'

'must know students' individual needs'

'help students make progress'

'give interesting lessons'

'be kind'

'not show a distance'

'be funny'

'have an original teaching style'

'have energy'

'have lots of patience'

'adapt the course book'

'treat students as individuals'

'be stimulating'

'know the students' names'

'you must know your students'

'must care'

'it is not enough to know your subject'

'Knowing your subject is not enough'

Just from these comments it is obvious that a teacher has to be more than a 'teacher'. That last comment – 'it is not enough to know your subject' – underlines the point that it is not enough for a teacher to go into a classroom and effectively 'give a lecture' while students make notes. Of course, the teacher has to know her subject – this is essential – but it is not enough.

For new or trainee teachers, however, 'knowing your subject' feels more than enough! What strikes terror into new teachers' hearts is the 'G-word' – grammar. The most common cry I hear is 'I don't know grammar – I never did it at school.' Or, if grammar was learnt at school, it was in the form of so-called rules of language, and terminology that has all been forgotten. Well, 'grammar' is, or should be, much much more than this. We will see in a later unit what is involved in learning 'grammar', and how it can be 'taught'. However, that is the 'teaching' not the 'knowing'. Yes, as teachers we do have to know how the present perfect simple is formed and how it is used. We need to know what a phrasal verb is and the different kinds that exist. We need to know why we can say 'if I *left* now' rather than 'if I *will* leave now', and we need to know why *may* has different meanings in the sentences 'You *may* leave now if you want' and 'Luc's late, he *may* have missed the bus'. The 'mistake' new or trainee teachers sometimes make is to think that they have to know everything straight away. Well, relax. First, no teacher knows everything about the language they are teaching and never will.

Second, teachers starting out are students themselves, students of the language they are teaching. You learn as you go along and you build up your knowledge. This is how it has to be. So don't read a grammar book from cover to cover. Instead, concentrate on understanding the language that you are going to be focusing on next in the classroom. Little by little your confidence will grow.

The teacher also has to know **how** to teach. She has to have an awareness of effective and successful methodology. The comments about the teacher not relying on the course book, giving interesting lessons, having an original teaching style, and being stimulating, all confirm that students want – expect – their teacher to teach in a much more challenging and interesting way than simply setting them work from the course book. The main part of this book deals with this very area – the methodology.

'Give interesting lessons'

Students get bored easily. They expect the teacher to plan her lessons so that learning becomes interesting, challenging and varied. They expect the teacher to teach in a way that is appropriate to the level being taught, and to the individuals in the class. They expect the teacher to adapt and supplement the course book being used and definitely not to rely on it as the sole resource. In short, they expect the teacher to know **how** to teach effectively, and for the teacher to 'be stimulating'.

We saw in Unit 1 that students generally respond better, and benefit most, from a communicative approach to learning, and it is this approach that we will focus on here. Very frequently, people who have undertaken training courses in teaching English in the communicative way have told me they wish they had learnt a language in the same way. I certainly wish I had.

'Know your students'

But still that is not enough. A teacher may know her subject. She may know how to teach it, but she has to know the people that she is teaching – and I don't just mean 'know their names', though that is important, too. So, find out about the students – the people – that you are teaching: what they like and are interested in; and what they don't like and are not interested in. Find out about their previous learning experiences. Find out what their expectations are of the course you are going to be teaching. Find out what their aims are. Ask them about themselves: their country, their culture, their interests. Speak to them outside class. Speak to them inside class. **Listen** to them. Show an interest in what they are saying. Show an interest in them as human beings. Be approachable. Help and support them. Be friendly. **Respond** to their needs. Be tolerant. Be patient.

In my opinion, no teacher is complete if they do not go beyond 'teaching the lesson'. The personal qualities required by the teacher described here can be summed up in the phrase 'show an interest'. If you do not want to show an interest in students as human beings, you will only have limited success as a teacher.

'Be passionate and patient'

Thomas Grossmann, remember, can look at the roles of the teacher from both perspectives. When he gave me his views on being an English teacher he had only recently started his first job, and only a short time before that had passed his Cambridge Proficiency of English exam. He trained in England and went on to teach in his home country, Switzerland. This is what he says:

> I think to be a successful teacher you have to like the job. One should be able to motivate the students and make lessons fun. A dash of humour would be good, too. The ability to explain something complicated in a clear way is important. Having patience, creativity, and good communication skills are an advantage, too.

> I started teaching and it's great fun. I was really nervous before the first lesson but everything went smoothly. The worst thing that has happened to me as a teacher was that I wanted to teach them too much – I had three 50-minute lessons and prepared a lesson plan for each lesson. But after two lessons I was still doing material which I had prepared for the first and in the end I hurried them just to get through everything. Looking back, I think that was a mistake.

You have to 'like the job'. Yes, you do. Of course, at times all teachers want to scream and do anything but go and teach their 25th hour of the week. But there are few jobs, if any, which are always positive. With this job, you meet people from all over the world; you have the scope for creativity (mentioned by Thomas), and can have a very good time. As one of my students said, a teacher needs to have energy – you have to always appear enthusiastic about what you are doing, even at 9 a.m. on Monday. If the teacher appears uninterested, the students will become that way themselves.

But, as Thomas says, you do need enormous patience at times. And when, inevitably, the time comes when you do want to scream, just think back to how difficult you found it to learn a new language, or to remember it the next day. In other words, keep thinking of how the student is feeling – maybe tired, maybe frustrated, maybe stressed – and if you then show impatience, how will that affect them thereafter?

Thomas also mentions humour. This doesn't mean the teacher has to be an entertainer, but that they should inject some fun, some light relief from time to time. Most humour arises naturally from the different situations that occur with the various students in your class. The sound of students laughing is (usually!) a very welcome sound, so encourage it when appropriate.

'Help students make progress'

Teachers must know how to plan their lessons appropriately (see Units 18–21), and how to assess objectively the strengths and weaknesses of their own teaching in general, and of specific lessons. This is all part of professional development (Unit 27).

If there is not this critical self-evaluation, there will be no development or progress. New or trainee teachers have a tendency to dismiss most of their lessons as 'disasters', but this usually revolves around something terribly minor like 'I forgot to give the instructions before handing out the papers'. As we shall see later, one of the first questions the teacher should ask herself is 'Did I achieve my aims?' The better the planning, the more likely the lesson will be effective.

Summary

▶ Teachers have many different roles inside and outside the classroom.
▶ They need to know their subject.
▶ They need to use appropriate teaching methodology.
▶ They need to find out about their students; know them; respond to them.
▶ They need to demonstrate various personal qualities.
▶ They need to show interest in their work and their students, and they must have limitless energy!
▶ They need to plan lessons according to the needs of their class.
▶ They need to know how to properly evaluate the success of a lesson, and evaluate their own strengths and weaknesses.

As this whole book is about 'being a teacher', this unit has been no more than an introduction. One point not mentioned in this unit – but another vital aspect of the teacher's role – is classroom manner and management. This is what we will focus on in the next unit.

3 Classroom management and manner

We saw in the previous unit that a teacher has many roles, including managing her classroom and students. We shall look at how she does this, and at the manner she adopts when teaching. Effective classroom management is an essential ingredient in successful teaching. For the purposes of this unit we will focus on the following:

Teacher talk	the grading of the teacher's language and the amount spoken, instruction-giving, directions
Gestures	how gestures can help to clarify what a teacher wants her students to do
Interaction and management	factors to consider, depending on who is interacting with whom in the classroom and in the teacher's management of the class
Manner	the importance of an appropriate teaching manner

Teacher talk

The teacher has to use a level of language which will be understood by the students in the class. This level will be influenced, of course, by the level of the students. This does not mean speaking at an unnaturally slow pace, or raising your voice – do not patronize your students. If a student has a poor level of English this does not mean they lack intelligence, so never give that impression to them. Instead, **simplify** the language being used. For example, rather than saying 'work in pairs', to a very low-level class, say 'work in twos' (accompanied by a gesture pairing students off). There is no point in saying 'work in pairs' when they might not know what 'pairs' means.

Rather than just saying 'underline' (e.g. 'underline the correct answer'), **demonstrate** visually or by a gesture what you mean.

The same applies to the teacher's language in general conversation. Rather than saying 'What did you get up to last weekend?', say 'What did you do...?' And rather than saying 'Do you want me to go through your job application with you?', say 'Do you want me to look at...?' So, simplify your language.

When teaching, this grading of language needs to be accompanied by an appropriate level of **Teacher Talk Time** (**TTT**). This does not mean 'try not to talk' (I have seen new teachers struggling desperately to avoid speaking at all having been told to keep their TTT low). It means 'don't use too much unnecessary language, because the more you say, the more likely you are to be misunderstood. There are times when the teacher has to do a lot of talking. There are times when lessons need to be teacher-centred. But what we should be aiming for is economy of language coupled with appropriate grading. It's a little like the advice for packing a suitcase. First pack it, then reduce the contents by half to what you really need. As a teacher, it is easy to start saying far more than you have to, and to run the risk of confusing your students. This is especially the case the lower the level of the class. Clearly, a class of advanced students will understand most of what you say, and you can be less careful with your language, but if you are teaching an elementary class, for example, you need to think about everything you say.

TASK 1

Look at the following examples of teacher talk. They are a combination of instructions, directions, and general chat (either as part of the lesson or before or after it) given to an intermediate level class. Try to simplify the language, and reduce the TTT to an appropriate amount. In some cases you might also want to question how the teacher's choice of words may impact on the students' motivation level. When you're done, check the Key.

Look at the following examples of teacher talk and identify the problem:

1 'I want you to do this exercise in which you have to answer ten questions. You can do it by yourself if you prefer, or work with your partner. When you finish I'll put you in larger groups for you to check your answers.'

2 'I want you to do a mingling activity now, which I'm sure you're going to hate!'

3 'No, erm, make that threes … wait a minute, there's thirteen of you, better make it threes and one four. Javier, do you want to work in a '3' or a '4'?'

4 'That's a jolly nice scarf. It must have cost you a bomb.'

5 'I'm handing out a piece of paper ...'

6 'This is going to be boring but it has to be done.'

7 'This is going to be easy ...'

8 'Did you enjoy that?'

9 'I want you to go through Exercise 1 and work out the answers. You must also justify your answers.'

10 'Would you like to stand up, please?'

TIPS FOR SUCCESSFUL INSTRUCTION GIVING

1 Plan your instructions – even script them at first if you feel it will help you.

2 Having planned them, review them and edit as necessary.

3 Only say what you have to.

4 Use simplified language, but do not over-simplify for the level.

5 Don't patronize (e.g. talking unnaturally slowly or loudly).

6 If you are getting blank faces, it probably means they haven't understood. So adjust your language as you speak, if necessary.

7 When giving instructions, make sure the students are looking at you and listening to you.

8 Don't give out papers before your instructions unless you have to – you will lose the students' attention.

9 Stand front and centre. Keep still.

10 Project your voice *slightly* so your instructions stand out.

11 Maintain eye contact.

12 Break up the instructions: 'Do questions 1–5. Say if the sentences are true or false. Give reasons for your answers. Work together. You have five minutes. Go.'

13 Only give instructions for what they have to do at that time, not later.

14 Give an example of what they have to do / do Question 1 with them.

15 Give a rough idea of how long they have.

16 Make it clear if you want them to work individually, in pairs, or in groups.

17 Don't ask lower-level students 'So, what do you have to do?' – they haven't got the language for this, and confusion will result. Once your instructions are over, tell them to begin, then check everyone is doing the activity correctly and deal with individual problems.

18 If one person says 'I don't understand', help that person individually. Don't hold up the rest of the class, and the lesson.

19 Don't *invite* the students to do something; politely *tell* them. So, don't say 'Would you like to stand up?', say 'Stand up, please'.

20 Students like – and expect – the teacher to be polite but direct in her language. They need to be told clearly what they have to do and how you want them to do it. Don't be afraid to do this! But don't tell the students they are going to find the activity boring, or difficult, or interesting, or easy!

Gestures

Everyone uses their hands and face to express or clarify meaning. Teachers do it more than most because they quickly realize how much meaning their body language can add to the words they are using. At the beginning, you may have to remind yourself to do a 'writing' gesture with your hand when you say 'I want you to write ...' to a low-level class; but after a while you will use gestures all the time quite automatically. You can work out for yourself what appropriate gestures you can use to clarify meaning – but make sure your choice is clear, appropriate, and consistent. You will find that your students' understanding will be greater as a result. You will also find yourself gesticulating more than you need to when you are outside the teaching context!

TASK 2

Consider what gestures you could use to indicate the following. There are no 'right' answers; the aim of this task is to get you thinking what gestures *you* might use in the classroom.

1 'Work in pairs / threes.'
2 'Get in a circle / straight line.'
3 'Stand up / sit down.'
4 'Listen / Read / Write / Speak.'

5 'Tick the right answer.'

6 'Think about ...'

7 'Look at me.'

8 What gesture could you use to indicate the student is wrong in his answer? Only partly right?

9 'Past tense' / 'Now' / 'In the future.'

10 What type of gesture could you use to clarify the meaning of word/sentence stress?

TIPS

1 Be clear/unambiguous.

2 Be consistent.

3 Don't over-exaggerate to the extent that you appear patronizing.

4 Don't use inappropriate gestures (e.g. pointing is considered rude by most people).

Interaction

There is a huge variety of different teaching contexts worldwide. Whether you are teaching a class of six sitting together in a semi-circle ('horseshoe') formation in a multilingual class, or a monolingual class of 50 students sitting behind rows of desks, you must consider how best to manage your classroom and the people in it. Because there is a huge range of possibilities, there are very few 'rights and wrongs', but lots of questions for the teacher to consider.

Here is a selection of questions to think about. The answers sometimes depend upon the situation. With some questions, you may have no choice (e.g. seating arrangements). With other questions, it is possible to give general answers.

▶ Where do you want the students to sit for a particular activity?

▶ Do you want them to work individually? In pairs? In groups?

▶ If you need them to work in pairs, what will you do if there is an odd number of students?

▶ If you are teaching a multilingual class, do you want to separate students who speak the same language?

▶ Where are you going to place yourself? What does it depend on?

- Will you always stand?
- How can you try to be sure all the students can hear you?
- Where will you stand when you use the board?
- How does your distance and position affect your 'relationship' with the class?
- How important is eye contact and why?
- How important is it to use your students' names?
- What will you be doing when the students are working individually/together?
- Should every activity last until all students have finished it?
- How can you attract the class's attention at the end of an activity?
- How can you politely stop two students from talking when they should be listening to you?
- What should you check in your classroom before the lesson begins?

TIPS

1 **Plan in advance what type of interaction you want for each stage of the lesson (teacher to class / pairs / groups etc.).**

2 **If you need even numbers (A working with B) and you get an odd number of students, two students can work together as 'one' (A, A and B). Don't participate yourself because then you will not be able to monitor other students.**

3 **In a multilingual class try, if possible, to have students from different nationalities working together to encourage only English in the lesson. In any case, vary who works with whom from time to time.**

4 **If you are doing 'teacher to class' work, stand where you can be seen by everyone (usually front and centre). If students are working together, go around and monitor their work, helping individuals as necessary and generally just 'keeping an eye' on how everyone is doing. If someone finishes an activity quickly, give them something else to do. You should aim to keep everyone busy all of the time, otherwise pace drops and students get bored (especially at higher levels).**

5 **Sometimes it might seem more appropriate to sit – if you have a smallish class and are just 'chatting', for example. This would not be appropriate, though, if you have a class where students are forced to sit in rows.**

6 When using the board, try not to block students' view. Stand to one side. If you are still blocking someone's view, move out of their way as often as you can so they can see what you are writing.

7 Writing on the board is not easy ... it needs practice. Make sure your board looks neat, well organized and clear. Students copy what you write so it needs to be a proper 'record' for them to copy and refer to in the future.

8 Maintain eye contact with your class. This will keep you aware of how students are reacting to each part of your lesson (for example, you can usually tell if someone is not understanding what you are saying just from their facial expression). This will help you to remain in control of the lesson. Also, as in any conversation, it is polite to look at the person you are talking to.

9 Learn your students' names as quickly as you can and use them. Again, this is just polite, but it is very difficult to attract a student's attention in class if you do not know their name. 'Excuse me, you ...' (or equivalent) is simply not acceptable. Students will expect you to know who they are and show an interest in them. For the first two or three lessons it is perfectly understandable if you cannot remember all the names, but after that it gets embarrassing. Do a 'name-game' activity on the first day, perhaps. If the class is all new, they too will want to learn names.

10 If students are working together or individually on an activity for which you have given them 'ten minutes', this does not mean literally ten minutes. It is just a rough idea of how long they have. Maybe they only need five minutes, or maybe you realize they are having unexpected difficulty and need a few extra minutes. So be flexible. Do not feel that you have to wait for every single person to finish what they are doing before you stop the activity – very rarely does everyone have time to finish. Otherwise, you are running the risk of bored students sitting twiddling their thumbs, waiting for the lesson to continue. Do not be afraid, then, to say 'OK, stop there. Don't worry if you haven't finished; we'll go through the answers together.'

11 Devise a way, which works for you, to attract the attention of the class when you want them to stop working together and listen to

you again. **Projecting your voice (not shouting!) may be enough; tapping the board with a pen works for some; perhaps raising your hand. The bigger the class, the more important this will be.**

12 **If two students are chatting to each other when they should be listening (to you or another student), stop them, otherwise it becomes very distracting. If you are teaching adults, treat them as adults – so just a gentle and polite request for them to listen.**

13 **Before the lesson begins, check you have everything you need – board pens/chalk, books/photocopies, audio material. Check you have any technology that is required – CD player, overhead projector, IWB etc. – and that you know how to use it. Do not wait for the lesson to begin to check all this since if you hit a problem you will appear unprofessional.**

Manner

In my opinion, however good you might be at teaching, however well you might know your subject, however popular you might be with you colleagues, if you do not treat your students with personal respect then you are not a good teacher. I have seen and heard teachers shouting at adult students before (for being late to class, for example). I have seen teachers tell students to go away and not disturb them during their tea break. I have seen teachers treating students with remarkable rudeness, and I am always shocked when I witness this (only very occasionally, thank goodness). I would rather employ an 'average teacher' who is friendly and kind to students, than a highly skilled teacher who shouts at students or has no patience with them. Yes, it can be a very frustrating job. Yes, some students will want to make you scream at times. Yes, you will teach students with very different cultures from your own. But if you have limited patience or tolerance levels, then this isn't the job for you. If you are not friendly and patient with your students then they will not respect you, whatever the standard of your teaching.

So, be friendly. Show an interest in the students as people. Be patient. Be tolerant. Be understanding. Have a joke with them. Never shout at a student. Talk to your students outside class. If you genuinely like them, all the better. Think of how you want to be treated by a teacher if you were learning a language in a foreign country, and of how you expect others to behave towards you in daily life.

Key to Task 1

1 *'Answer the ten questions. Work together.'*

   Avoid unnecessary talk ('in a moment'), unnecessary instructions ('when you've finished') which can be saved for later, complex words ('avoid').

2 *'Stand up and walk around ...'* (accompanied by a gesture).

   'Mingling' is teacher language, avoid it. If you say 'you're going to hate it' then they probably will.

3 *'Work in twos'* (plus gesture).

   These were clearly unplanned instructions from a teacher who hadn't thought about how the activity was going to work.

4 This is the teacher chatting outside class. Poor grading ('jolly'), inappropriate and overly-colloquial language ('cost you a bomb') even for a high-level class.

5 Don't give a running commentary. You don't need to tell them that you are handing out paper. Also, never give instructions while doing something else at the same time.

6 Again, don't be negative when setting up an activity.

7 If you tell them it's going to be easy and it isn't, how will they feel? If it is easy they may wonder why you gave it to them in the first place.

8 And if they say 'No'?

9 Avoid phrasal verbs ('go through'). Say 'do'. And 'justify' is too difficult. Say 'give reasons'.

10 *'Stand up, please.'*

   If you ask them if they want to stand up and they say 'No', then what?

Summary

▶ Teachers need to adjust their language to suit the level of the class they are teaching.

▶ This is done not by talking loudly or unnaturally slowly, but by simplifying the language they use.

▶ With lower levels especially, teachers should restrict the amount of language they use.

- Meaning can be clarified by the use of gestures and other body language.
- Instructions should be clear, relevant and precise – planned in advance if necessary.
- Class management is an important part of the teacher's responsibility and it needs to be thought about before and during the lesson.
- Teachers should adopt a supportive, friendly and encouraging manner.

4 Focusing on language via a situational presentation

What is grammar?

'An abstract system of rules whereby a person's mastery of their native language can be explained.' (Adapted dictionary definition)

Different dictionaries define 'grammar' in different ways, but they all effectively talk about the 'rules of the language'. I don't think it really matters what definition we give the word, anyway, as we all have an idea in our minds of what the word means to us. However, do not assume, as many do, that 'grammar' equals only 'tenses' or verb forms (e.g. present perfect, past continuous/progressive). Grammar is language and how we use it; tenses are just a fraction of our language.

Personally, I don't like the word 'grammar' as it has too many negative connotations. For many it implies the rather dry learning of rules and then controlled practice of these rules with little or no communicative practice. Grammar doesn't have to be like this, and it shouldn't be. For this reason, in this and subsequent units we need to think about focusing on 'language' rather than purely 'grammar', though it is a term we still need to refer to.

What is much more important than a definition of the word 'grammar' is knowing what students need to know when they are learning language. We also need to know different ways to 'teach' language. And there's another awkward word: 'teach'. 'Teach', like 'grammar', has connotations. It implies a lot of teacher talk and explanations, initial student ignorance of what is being covered, a beginning and an end (they didn't 'know' it before, they did after), and it implies a completeness (they now know everything there is to know about this). You don't hear a teacher going into class saying 'I'm going to teach them relative clauses today', but teachers do know what their aims are in any lesson. I prefer 'clarification' of language to 'teaching' of language, but like 'grammar', 'teach' is a useful, all-embracing word that has to be used, and will continue to be used here. But do not think that language is just a series of unrelated items that can be dealt with one by one!

There are other words and terms that are, let us say, controversial in the profession, but at this stage of your career it is more important to concentrate on how to 'teach' than to be concerned with terminology.

WHAT DO STUDENTS NEED TO KNOW WHEN LEARNING NEW LANGUAGE?

▶ They need to understand **meaning** of the 'target language' within the given context.
▶ They need to know how to **form** the language (how it is constructed).
▶ They need to know the natural **pronunciation** of this language.

This is often referred to as **MFP**. As well as knowing the MFP, students need to use the language – **practice**.

This is a simplistic answer to the question, but for new and training teachers it is a very helpful one, especially when it comes to assessing if the lesson you have just taught was successful in terms of your language aims. We will look at each of the MFP areas in the remaining part of this and later units.

Situational presentations

'Presentation' is another controversial word. For many it implies, as does 'teach', that language can be broken up into convenient chunks which can be taught in isolation and built upon brick by brick until students 'know English'. Of course, it does not work this way. Experienced teachers know how best to develop a student's awareness of the language without falling into the 'Today we're going to do conditional sentences' approach, but until experience has been gained, it is very difficult to avoid dealing with language in chunks. Too much should not be expected of a trainee teacher, but it often is. Certainly, no person can become a teacher in four weeks – but they can develop their teaching skills and awareness sufficiently to be able to go in and deliver a reasonably successful lesson. That is where the real training begins.

So I make no apologies for talking about 'situational presentations', or 'a lesson on the 2nd conditional', or whatever. Rightly or wrongly this is what trainees are exposed to on training courses, and this is how the majority of course books deal with teaching and language. Once you gain real experience, you will be able to re-evaluate your approach.

Language needs context because context provides meaning. One way to illustrate meaning is via a situation. This can be done in a number of ways, including pictures. This situational presentation tends to be quite controlled by the teacher, at least initially, but with the students involved at all times. Let's take the word *should* – a modal auxiliary verb which, like other modals, can have different meanings depending on the context. If a student asks 'What does *should* mean?' you cannot usefully answer them. In isolation it is meaningless. If we put the word into a sentence – *You should wear a suit* – this is better because the word now fits in grammatically to a sentence – the form is illustrated. But meaning is still very limited. We don't know who is speaking, who they are speaking to, and why they are speaking. In short, there is no situation, thus no context, thus no meaning.

One way to provide context whilst maintaining student involvement is as follows. This is for an elementary / pre-intermediate class (A2).

STAGE 1

Spend a few minutes on a class discussion about unemployment in the students' countries, how people go about finding work, the stages of applying for a job – leading to tips for a successful interview. The teacher asks questions and maximizes student talking time.

STAGE 2

The teacher says she has a friend, Jason, who is going for an interview tomorrow for a job at the bank. She elicits from the students how Jason should appear when he goes for the interview (appropriate clothes, shaved, hair combed, etc.). She then shows a picture of how Jason typically appears and asks if this would be appropriate for his interview. She highlights his dirty shoes, uncombed hair, unshaven face, and casual clothes.

STAGE 3

The teacher says she saw Jason earlier. She emphasizes that Jason is her friend and she really wants him to get this job but is not confident because the interviewer is likely to expect interviewees to be dressed in a certain way. So, pointing to Jason's casual clothes the teacher asks if the students think it would be a good idea for Jason to go to the interview dressed in this way. Having established that it wouldn't, and still pointing to Jason's clothes, the teacher says 'So what did I say to Jason when I saw him?' If possible, the teacher could also have a picture of someone wearing a suit to make the contrast with Jason's clothes and to make it clearer to the students what she is thinking. At this point, the teacher is testing to see if any students are familiar with the language being presented, wondering if anyone will reply *You should wear a suit*. This is the teacher's model/marker sentence containing the language being targeted. Maybe someone will know it, or may say the sentence with mistakes. Or maybe no one has any idea. This is not important, you are just seeing if anyone knows it. If no one does, the teacher says the sentence to the class, making sure everyone is listening.

At this stage of the lesson the main focus has been on meaning. The model sentence *You should wear a suit* now has a context, and the 'function' of 'giving friendly advice'. The function is basically the reason for speaking – other examples being 'inviting', 'apologizing', 'refusing', 'expressing surprise', etc. What the teacher has therefore done is to **illustrate** meaning by means of a pictorial situation and introduced a **model sentence** containing the **target language** (subject + *should* + base verb – this is the form). The function of giving friendly advice has been established via the situation. Depending upon the precise level of the class and what you have taught them before, you may need to have begun this lesson by checking they understood essential vocabulary (*suit, polish, shave, comb, suggest*) so as not to have the lesson 'stall' at a critical point. See Unit 8 for ways of focusing on vocabulary / lexis.

So far in this lesson the only aim that has been achieved is that meaning has been illustrated. However, it is essential that the teacher checks that the students really have understood the meaning. The fact that one student, maybe, has given you your model sentence does not mean that everyone has understood its meaning in the given context. Before you go any further in this unit, therefore, you should read Unit 9, then return to complete this unit.

Read Unit 9 now.

Now you have read about how to check students' understanding of new language, the **meaning** of **MFP** has been covered for this example lesson. As for the **pronunciation**, you should later read Unit 10, but for now it is enough to say that the students must hear you say the model sentence several times naturally and then be given the chance to say it themselves.

This is not as straightforward as it may sound, as we shall see later, but if we are teaching language for active use then the students need to know how to say it.

The **form** of the language has already been implicitly established via the giving and repetition of the model sentence, but this needs to be checked, just as the meaning needed to be checked. In the 'Jason' lesson it is easy to elicit further examples of *should*: *You should polish your shoes, You should comb your hair, You should shave.* These sentences can then be put onto the board (keeping the students participating by getting them to tell you what to write). Form can be highlighted by using different colour pens, if possible, and/or a substitution table:

		wear a suit.
		polish your shoes.
You	**should**	comb your hair.
		shave.
	shouldn't	wear those clothes.

You is not unnecessarily repeated, nor is *should*. This way the form is further highlighted. Notice the same subject is used – the sentence *He should wear a suit*, for example, is not giving advice and therefore has a different meaning.

You could, if you feel it appropriate, label the respective parts of the sentence (subject / *should(n't)* / base verb). You could include your concept questions and answers. You could also mark sentence stress and intonation. Whatever degree of detail you decide is necessary, students need to have some 'takeaway' record of the form that is being covered in the lesson – the above illustration is probably the minimum requirement.

We will come back to form and pronunciation elsewhere, but the initial 'presentation' via pictures is an approach which is very commonly used, especially at lower levels.

Because it is primarily 'teacher-led' it is a method more suitable for students whose level of English is not high rather than for more advanced students, who need a greater learning challenge (see next two units).

TIPS

1 If you are using pictures, make sure they are clear, simple and appropriate.

2 If necessary, check essential vocabulary at the start of the lesson.

3 Build the context slowly, carefully and clearly – *guide* the students and keep them involved throughout. Don't tell them what they can tell you. By continually asking them questions you are also checking they understand.

4 Have an obvious 'target' – a model sentence which will be a logical conclusion to your context build. In my example, *You should wear a suit* was a logical 'conclusion' to the storyline.

5 Try to elicit the sentence if you can; otherwise just tell them. If they have never come across this language before, it just tells you the extent of your task. It does not mean your context wasn't clear!

6 If possible, show your context to a colleague or friend beforehand to see if they think it is clear and appropriate.

You should also research the language yourself so you know everything you need to know about it. You need to anticipate possible problems your students might have with this language. These could include:

▶ confusion about the time reference
▶ a desire to refer to it as a tense (e.g. present simple) which it isn't
▶ incorrectly adding a *to* – *You should to wear a suit*
▶ thinking that by changing the person (e.g. from *you* to *I*) the function remains the same – it doesn't

See Unit 20 for more on anticipating language problems.

TASK

For each of the sentences below:

a Try to work out the form. In simple terms, what is the fixed structure that never changes? Refer to the *should* example earlier. Another example is '*I wish I hadn't done it*' = subject + *wish* + subject + *had / hadn't* + past participle. It sounds a bit complicated and 'grammatical' but it helps you, and students, know how a sentence is built.

b Think of a possible **context** and establish the **function** (e.g. 'giving advice') and meaning, including the time reference.

c Think about, or even prepare, a possible picture(s) to illustrate your meaning.

Do not worry about the level of the class these sentences might be aimed at, but none would be for a very low-level class, so assume that your students have a reasonable level of English.

1 **I shouldn't have done it.**

2 **I'm going to France next week.**

3 **Would you mind helping me?**

4 **Let's go to a concert.**

5 **I've worked here for ten years.**

Do this now, and check it later!

Key to task

1 **I shouldn't have done it.**

Form:	subject + *should / shouldn't have* + past participle
Function:	maybe 'expressing regret about past action'
Context:	student copies from another student in an exam, tells a friend about it the next day and expresses regret.

2 **I'm going to France next week.**

Form:	Subject + *is / am / are* + verb-*ing* = present continuous (progressive)
Function:	maybe 'giving information about future schedule'
Context:	two busy friends with diaries trying to arrange to go out, one explains that the next week is impossible.

3 **Would you mind helping me?**

Form:	would you mind + -*ing* form of verb
Function:	maybe 'polite request for help' – asking now, but for help in near future.
Context:	person at airport struggling with heavy cases, asks a passer by for help.

4 Let's go to a concert.

Form	*let's* + base verb (NOT '*let us*' as this is unnatural in spoken English).
Function:	maybe 'making a suggestion' – suggesting now what you could do later.
Context:	two friends wanting to go out later, not sure where to go. One looks in the entertainment guide to see what's on, notices a concert and suggests that.

5 I've worked here for ten years.

Form:	subject + *has / have* + past participle
Function:	maybe 'giving reason for wanting to find a new job'. Time reference is past to present (from ten years ago to now) and maybe continuing into the future, at least for a while.
Context:	employee to employer explaining why they have decided to leave the company – wanting a new challenge.

For each of the above **contexts**, meaning can be illustrated either with visuals or some other way (e.g. a recorded dialogue), but in each case there is a situation which illustrates the **meaning**. How much detail you give the students about the **form** will depend on their level. Higher-level students are normally comfortable and confident using terminology, lower-level ones much less so – it is pointless referring to 'subject' if they do not know what a 'subject' is.

Summary

▶ The meaning, form and pronunciation of new language needs to be covered, and communicative practice should be given, too.
▶ Situational presentations are controlled and effective ways to introduce language at certain levels.
▶ They can be done via visuals as long as these are clear and appropriate.
▶ Teachers need to be clear in their own minds of the meaning of the target language, how it is formed, and how it is spoken.

- ► This type of presentation is usually teacher-led, but with student involvement throughout. Let them do as much of the 'storytelling' as possible.
- ► Have a model sentence to work towards – elicit it if you can; give it if you can't.
- ► Check they really have understood the meaning (Unit 9).

This approach makes language more real than just a series of rules and explanations. The students see the language in a situation that is real and that provides the meaning. The teacher, therefore, starts with meaning and then introduces the language. In a sense, it is grammar in disguise, useful if you have students who are demotivated by thinking they are about to do a grammar lesson. If it works well, the presentation is interesting, even enjoyable. Above all, it is much better than giving an 'explanation' of a language point.

Some other ways to approach language teaching will be covered in the next three units.

5 Focusing on language via a text or recording

The 'presentation' approach featured in the previous unit involved the teacher supplying a situation, possibly using visuals, in order to build a context with her students and eventually leading to a 'model sentence' containing the target language. It was very teacher controlled, though with full student participation, and rather contrived. It is a method which is effective, especially with lower levels, but no one method can, or should, be used exclusively or else it becomes predictable and boring. In addition, the method described is not especially challenging for higher-level groups. What we will look at in this unit, then, is another approach which provides variety from the previous one, a greater challenge, more learner autonomy, and a more realistic context.

TASK 1

Look at the reading texts below and answer the following questions:

a **Does the language seem relatively simple, or high level for an intermediate class?**

b **Does the text seem authentic ('real') or 'made-up'?**

c **What specific language point appears to be potentially the most difficult/useful to focus on in class?**

1 BERTRAND'S SAN FRANCISCO EXPERIENCE

Bertrand is French and he lives and works in the north of France. His English is very good because he studied it at school and uses it in his job. A few months ago, he went to San Francisco for the first time to visit some friends he met in France a few years ago. He stayed for a week and in that time Bertrand and his friends had a very busy time – they visited Fisherman's Wharf, rode in the cable cars, saw the sea lions by Pier 39, ate in a different restaurant every day, walked up the steep hills, and did lots of shopping in the fantastic department stores. And, of course, they took lots of photographs.

At dinner one evening Bertrand and his friends – Marie, Myrianne and Norbert – were having dinner when the fire alarm sounded, but the waiters didn't seem to be worried, they just carried on working. Everyone around them carried on eating. They thought it was so weird, everyone carrying on with their meals even though the fire alarm was sounding. Bertrand and his friends decided to get out quickly, but just as they went out of the door they saw a sign by the entrance warning customers that there was going to be a fire alarm test that evening and they should ignore it. Bertrand and his friends quietly sat back down again to continue their meal feeling a bit embarrassed.

The friends continued to tour San Francisco and sample the different food at all the many restaurants in the city, and not listening to any more fire alarms! They had a wonderful time and had a lot of fun. They didn't know when they might meet again but this had been a great experience for them all. Bertrand was sad to leave his friends, especially as he knew he had to go back to work three days later.

2 A SPECIAL OFFER

Abibus have been producing top-class cars with unbeatable value for 12 years. We have been talking to you, our customers, a lot recently to find out if there was any way of making our cars even better than before and you told us that our product is as good as it gets. The only way to make Abibus cars even more attractive would be to reduce the price, but that can't be done ... or can it? Well, yes it can! From the beginning of next year, for a period of six months, we are cutting the cost of all our Abibus cars by 10% – yes, 10%! So from January 1 next year, Abibus cars will be 10% cheaper, but still top class. We have been doing business with you for 12 years. Now for the next 12!

3 LIVING IN FRANCE

When I left my country a few months ago to work in France, I was very excited – I still am! But it hasn't been easy! For a start, there's the language. I used to study French at school, but that was a long time ago, so when I moved to Paris I knew it would be difficult because I had forgotten most of what I'd learnt. And I knew that driving would be a problem because I'm used to driving on the left, but in France they drive on the right! So, the first few times I drove here, it was really strange and difficult. It's still not easy, but I'm getting used to it – slowly! I really like the life here, though, – it's fast and exciting. The food is very different – it's generally great, but I'll never get used to eating frogs' legs. I was told that it tastes like chicken, but I don't agree! But the wine is great, and there are so many different types of cheese, I love it!

There are so many places to visit, and things to do, but a lot of people who visit France only come to Paris. Paris is great, but France is a fantastic country – the south of France is beautiful, and with great weather. And the north of France has some great places to visit – Lille is really pretty and is a friendly area. Yes, I'm really glad I live in this country now!

Key to task 1

1 Bertrand's San Francisco experience

<u>Level of language</u>

Although this is the longest of the texts, the language is quite simple for intermediate students. *Steep hills*, *sample*, *embarrassed*, and maybe *department stores* are the only items of vocabulary that could cause problems, and the grammatical forms should mostly be familiar.

<u>Authenticity</u>

Definitely made up! It has the feel of having been specially written and graded (in terms of language) and the 'fire alarm' situation is somewhat contrived. This contrasts with authentic or near authentic texts. An authentic text is a 'real' one, e.g. a newspaper article. A near authentic text is one which is not real, but appears real – maybe something adapted from its original form, or an authentic-sounding made up text. The 'Bertrand' text is neither authentic nor near authentic. This does not mean that it is not valid to use, as we will see. What is important about this text, which makes it OK to use, is that the use of the target language is authentic. There is only one example of the target language, and it is surrounded by other language. So the text, while sounding a little contrived, is valid for classroom use.

<u>Language to focus on</u>

They were having dinner when the fire alarm sounded.

In this example from the text, we are using two verb forms – the past progressive (continuous), and the past simple. The progressive is **were having** and the simple is **sounded**. In the sentence, they started dinner **before** the fire alarm sounded, and may or may not have continued after. Thus, the simple **interrupts** the progressive.

This language point is a very useful one to focus on, and appropriate for the level.

How this can be done, we will see later.

2 A special offer

Level of language

Higher than in the previous text, though not significantly (*top class, unbeatable value, cutting the cost, to do business*) – certainly not so high that meaning is unclear.

Authenticity

Again, this is not an authentic text. However, it is near authentic because it was adapted from a real text and it sounds more real.

Language to focus on

Present perfect progressive, e.g. *Abibus have been producing cars for 12 years*. This describes an activity which started at a definite point in the past and continues to the present, with the likelihood of it continuing into the future. The present perfect tense, both simple and progressive, is a particularly difficult one for students, and there are differences between British and American use.

3 Living in France

Level of language

The vocabulary would be reasonably straightforward for intermediate students, but there is a variety of verb forms used with some complex time references (see below).

Authenticity

Not authentic, but adapted from an article about people working in different countries, so near authentic.

Language to focus on

Different uses of *used to*:

> *I used to study French at school.*
>
> *I'm used to driving on the left.*
>
> *I'm getting used to it (driving on the right).*
>
> *I'll never get used to eating frogs' legs.*

You may not focus on all four uses at the same time, but with a higher-level class you could. Consider for yourselves how these differ in meaning and time reference!

Using texts to illustrate meaning

Before we look at the advantages of using texts to illustrate the meaning of language that you want to focus on, we need to consider possible methodology. If we refer to the 'Bertrand' text above and assume we are teaching an intermediate group of multilingual adults, we could follow the stages below:

1 Ask the class if anyone has been to / would like to go to San Francisco. If anyone has, they can tell the others about it. If no one has then they can tell you what they imagine San Francisco to be like. Alternatively, show pictures of San Francisco (steep hills, cable cars, Fisherman's Wharf, etc.) to get the class talking about it.

2 Tell students they are going to read about Bertrand, who visited San Francisco. They will have to read the text quickly and answer the questions:

Why did Bertrand visit San Francisco?

How many people was he with?

Why did they stop eating?

Did they finish their meal later?

Students read the text, and then work together to answer the questions. You then check the answers.

3 Highlight the sentence from the text *They were having dinner when the alarm sounded* and focus on the language (MFP).

From this point on, you could follow the procedure described in the previous unit (concept questions, pronunciation work, highlighting the form on the board, eliciting further examples). This is a crucial part of the lesson as it is where you need to focus on the target language and check understanding.

4 Provide students with varied activities such as practice of the progressive / simple 'interrupted' action. See Unit 11 for more on practice activities.

Stage 3 above might appear a 'quick check' which almost gets in the way of everything else, but it is, in fact, the most important part of the lesson because this is where you are checking meaning, form and pronunciation. This is not a 'reading' but a 'grammar' lesson, so Stage 3 must not be a 'rush job' to get on to some fun practice activity that you have planned; students cannot have practice of something which they do not first understand.

So what is the purpose of the Reading part of the lesson? The text does what the picture of Jason in the previous unit did (*you should wear a suit*) – it provides a context, and the context illustrates meaning. However, it is important that the Reading text/tasks are not so demanding that students end up spending much more time trying to understand the text than working on the grammar. The tasks that you provide, therefore, need to be relatively straightforward (as above in Stage 2). They should serve to check basic understanding of the context, as well as directing students towards the specific language that you will focus on later. The lesson effectively starts as a Reading, but the text is there primarily to provide a later language focus (compare this with a Reading comprehension lesson – see Unit 12).

There are, of course, many variations to the stages listed above. But what we have looked at here is one way of dealing with grammar via a text, keeping a basic approach similar to that of the previous unit, but adapting the way meaning is illustrated.

TASK 2

Look at Texts 2 and 3 above and the language focus suggested. How might you stage each lesson (following a similar pattern to the first text)? There is no key for this task, but it will help you to come up with possible ideas for yourself.

The three texts above are all 'made-up', though two are adapted from authentic sources. Sometimes it is easier and more convenient to devise your own texts to suit your requirements, but if you do, ensure that the level is appropriate for the students you are teaching, and that there is enough 'other language' in the text, not just a very unnatural over-use of the target language. Even with the 'Bertrand' example above, unauthentic as it is, there is plenty of 'other language' – with only one example of the target language.

Ideally, however, it is better to use authentic texts if possible. Course books (and you are likely to be using one) will usually 'present' language via authentic / near authentic material, but sometimes you may find, for example, a **newspaper article** which contains a piece of language that you want to focus on in class. Similarly, you might introduce language via a **recording**. Have a look at this conversation from a recording. What piece of language do you think the teacher wanted to focus on later?

Jill	Hello.
Guy	Hello, er, Jill?
Jill	Yes, speaking.
Guy	It's Guy here.
Jill	Oh, hello Guy. How are you?
Guy	Fine, thanks. Er, I was wondering if you could, er, babysit for us tonight?
Jill	Yeah, sure, what time?
Guy	Er, we're going out at about 7.30.
Jill	7.30? Yeah, fine, what time do you want me to come round?
Guy	About 7?
Jill	Fine.
Guy	We'll leave some food for you.
Jill	Great. That would be lovely.
Guy	And some wine, if you like.
Jill	Cool.
Guy	See you later, then ... and thanks again.
Jill	No problem, see you later. Bye.

Despite the 'script', this is an authentic recording – what you have above is merely the transcript. The two teachers were given a situation ('Guy – you want Jill to babysit tonight / Jill – you are available to babysit tonight / Guy – call Jill') and from that they improvised a telephone call. This was recorded, and the transcript written up afterwards for the teacher's benefit. So on the recording it sounded like a natural conversation. Most of the time, however, teachers don't need to go to all this trouble because the course book you will be using will have many recordings to introduce language, just as they have many texts, but sometimes you might prefer to prepare your own. If you do, don't script it, and make sure the recording is clear to use in class. And, as with the texts, make sure it is, at the very least, near authentic in sound and contains 'other language'.

The piece of language that the teacher wanted to focus on from the recording was the very hesitant and polite request *I was wondering if you could* + base verb, as a means of introducing other forms of request. The possible procedure could be the same as with the text. For more on Listening comprehension lessons, see Unit 13.

It is important to stress, though, that you will rarely want to make up your own texts or recordings when course books use this approach so much, and when there is so much authentic material available to use.

Advantages of this approach

The previously described situational presentation using pictures is a largely teacher-centred approach, albeit with student involvement. It is, as we saw, an approach particularly effective with lower levels, primarily because there is very little 'other language' for them to deal with. With the approach described in this unit, however, there is a great deal of 'other language'. How much, and at what level, will be influenced by who you are teaching (you can, for example, edit a newspaper article if you feel it is too long and the reading part of the lesson would take up too much time). Also you shouldn't allow students to get concerned by unknown vocabulary in the text/recording if they don't actually need to know it for this lesson. As we saw before, the principal aim in such a lesson is language-related, not skills-related.

With the right level, therefore, this approach has a number of advantages, if executed properly:

▶ It is more challenging.
▶ Various skills are required.
▶ There is generally greater variety/stimulation.
▶ It is less teacher-centred.
▶ Students are exposed to the target language in an authentic/ near authentic setting.
▶ Consequently, they see/hear the target language before having to focus on it.
▶ The target language is surrounded by 'other language'.
▶ Students should be encouraged to read/listen in English in their everyday lives, to be exposed to 'real English' – using this approach in the classroom encourages them to do so.
▶ The whole approach becomes more natural, less contrived.
▶ Course books use this approach a lot, making preparation easier for the teacher.

POSSIBLE DANGERS
▶ The text/recording part of the lesson may go on too long, leaving inadequate time for the language focus/practice (unintentional language neglect).

- It is sometimes tempting for new teachers to devote too little time to the language focus part of the lesson (intentional language neglect).
- The text/recording may be inappropriate in terms of level.
- The tasks provided may be inappropriate in terms of level, or just too time consuming.
- If the text/recording is made up, it may contain too unnatural use/ over-use of the target language.

Overall, the approach is very realistic and stimulating.

Summary

- Texts and recordings can be a very effective way of illustrating meaning of particular language.
- The approach involves a greater challenge for higher-level students.
- Skills work and language focus are integrated.
- Target language is surrounded by other language, which is more 'real'.
- Students are exposed to the target language before having to focus on it.
- There is greater variety and interest.
- The teacher should ensure that the language focus part of the lesson is given adequate time.
- Texts/recordings can come from course books, authentic sources, or be made up.
- Made-up texts/recordings need to be 'near authentic' (e.g. recordings should not be scripted).

6 Focusing on language via Test Teach Test

We have looked at two different ways of focusing on grammar in the classroom; via a situational presentation, and via a text or recording – the latter usually from a set course book. Another approach is what is often referred to as **Test Teach Test**. In very simple terms, this approach begins with the teacher giving the students some kind of task relating to a particular piece of language with the basic aim of seeing how much the students already know, or do not know, about this language. So let's do it! Have a go at this:

TASK

Complete these sentences using *the / a / an*:

1 I really like _____ actor who plays Johnny Redway.

2 I'm just calling to say how much I enjoyed _____ concert.

3 I hope you'll give her _____ gift on her birthday.

4 _____ unemployed receive money from the government.

5 Last week I went to buy _____ book for my trip, but when I got to the end of _____ book I discovered some pages were missing!

Why did you choose these answers? Can you think of any rules?

Now complete these sentences with *the, a,* or add nothing:

6 The bus can carry _____ 45 passengers.

7 I wasn't born in _____ England. I was born in _____ United States.

8 _____ politicians are not generally respected by society.

9 I spent the evening in _____ bar drinking _____ beer.

10 On _____ last evening of his vacation, Zsigmond and his girlfriend went on _____ beach. They looked at _____ moon and talked about _____ love! He thinks he's so romantic!

Why did you choose these answers?

The object of this exercise, given to the students at the start of the lesson, is to discover how much they know or don't know about articles (*a / an / the*), and to allow the students to discover the same facts for themselves! It gives the students some immediate responsibility for their own learning, especially if they can work on this task together in pairs or groups sharing their knowledge. Assuming you are giving this task to, say, an intermediate class, then your students are likely to get most of the answers correct. What they might have more trouble with is the 'why?'

This part of the lesson is the first **Test** in 'Test Teach Test'. But 'test' is a somewhat misleading and intimidating word as it gives the impression that students are under pressure and need to provide correct answers. In fact, it is a discovery task – but somehow 'Discovery Teach Test' doesn't have the same ring to it, although some people do prefer 'Task Teach Task'.

By having the students work together on the task, the Test element is reduced. If they are told to work in silence and not to compare answers afterwards, then they will feel pressure. Of course, it is perfectly valid for them to work individually at first, as long as they then get a chance to compare their answers before the teacher goes through it with them.

The teacher, having set up the task, should now be monitoring and evaluating as she observes how much / how little the students seem to know, and what the particular problems are that will need to be clarified later. Also, she may be able to deal with some individual problems while the class is working.

It is important, too, not to think that this first Test must be 'grammatical' in its presentation, such as the above one on articles. It can also be communicative and unstructured, supposing some prior exposure to the language you are to focus on.

For example, for a lesson on prepositions of place and position (*in the corner, on the shelf, under the table*, etc.) you might begin by asking students to describe to each other a room in their accommodation, or the classroom you are teaching in. Or you might provide a picture of a room and give them the same task.

As they work, you listen to see how accurately or inaccurately they use prepositions in their descriptions.

Another example: for a lesson on the second conditional sentence (e.g. *If I won the lottery, I'd buy a house*), you might ask your students to tell each other what they would do if they won a huge amount of money. Better still, give them a greater variety of 'What if?' type questions to discuss.

For experienced teachers and high-level classes, you can also throw open the lesson and ask the students to tell each other everything they know, or think they know, about the language in question. But this really should not be tried by newer teachers, and certainly not by those on training courses.

Having done this first Test the teacher now has to do the **Teach** part of the lesson. To be honest, this is a tricky stage in this kind of lesson for a new or trainee teacher, for the simple reason that you do not know until the lesson is underway exactly what you are going to have to spend most time on. If your students have completed the first task very well (going back to our task on articles), or if they have used the target language reasonably accurately in communication (e.g. the prepositions), then your own task at this stage will be less demanding. However, if they have been very inaccurate and confused in their use of the language, then you are going to have to do a lot of clarification, but if they have done a conventional grammar exercise, your first job in the Teach is to check the correct answers. So let's do that by going back to the task on articles.

Key to task

1 *The* actor, because there's only one and you know who is being referred to – it is definite.

2 *The* concert, for the same reason (compare this with *I'd love to go to a concert some time* – one concert, any concert).

3 *A* gift, because you don't know what gift, so it is any gift, but just one.

4 *The* unemployed (the jobless, the disadvantaged...) – referring to particular groups in society.

5 *A* book / *the* book – going from any book to the specific book that I bought.

6 No article (the bus can carry 45 passengers) – there is no article before a number except when referring to a particular group (e.g. the 45 passengers on the bus had a lucky escape when...).

7 *In* England, in *the* United States. No articles before most countries, except when the country includes a plural, e.g. *the* Netherlands.

8 No article before politicians because you are talking about a general group in society (compare with Question 4).

9 *A* bar (unless there's only one where you live, or you are referring to your 'usual' bar). No article before names of drinks when you

are talking generally. Compare this with *I'd like a beer* **(meaning a glass of beer), and** *the beer in this bar is particularly good.*

10 *The* **last evening (referring to a specific evening);** *the beach* **– only one;** *the moon* **– only one. No article before** *love* **– referring to a general and uncountable noun.**

As you go through the answers and reasons it is absolutely essential that you do not assume that because one student has given you the correct answer and reason, everybody else in the class agrees or has understood so you need to ask concept questions and elicit further examples as you go along. This is partly why this approach is harder for new teachers. Unlike previous approaches, and especially the situational presentation, where the teacher has more control over how the lesson flows, this approach may require you to deal with a lot more student questions.

However, if you have planned and researched your lesson, as you should have done, this should not be too much of an ordeal. Remember, students ask questions not to trap you, but because they are inquisitive about the language. You may not always have a grammatical answer to give, but more often than not you can answer based on what you instinctively know is correct.

New teachers might feel safer giving students a more communicative first task (such as the two examples above) because this way they won't have to cope with explaining why certain answers are right or wrong but, of course, they will still have to clarify meaning, form and pronunciation, as in any other kind of language lesson. In this Teach stage you are doing the essential tasks we mentioned earlier – you are clarifying meaning (concept questions, more examples etc.), form, and pronunciation. You may wonder about pronunciation of articles, but the weak pronunciation of *a* (/ə/) is important. Having said that, there will be much less pronunciation work on articles than on a grammatical structure.

You might possibly think that articles are quite straightforward – they are not, especially when you consider their different usage in other languages. The earlier task did not even get into areas such as those nouns which sometimes have an article and sometimes don't (*I'll see you at school* vs. *I'll see you at the school*). So, as with any piece of language – research it, anticipate problems, be prepared.

The final stage in this approach is the second **Test**. If the first Test is really *discovery*, then the second Test is really *practice*. And the example task earlier could also be used as 'practice'. You may, then, ask 'What's the difference?' The difference is the *aim*. With Test 1, the aim is to find out how much the students know about the language before the teacher focuses on it. The aim of Test 2 is to have practice of the language *after* the teacher has focused on it. So the nature of the activity may be very similar, but the aim – the reason for doing it – is quite different. Test 2 could involve one, or more than one, practice activity, perhaps one that is an 'exercise' and one that is communicative. See Unit 11 for more on practice activities.

It should be noted that all the approaches to teaching grammar that we have looked at can be used with teaching vocabulary as well, and you need to bear this in mind when you read the next unit (Lexis).

TIPS

1 **If the first Test is an accuracy-based exercise (like the one on articles here), make sure it only deals with those aspects of the target language that you want to focus on in your lesson.**

2 **Monitor carefully this first Test in order to assess how much or how little the students know, and what specific problems you might have to deal with later.**

3 **Help with individual problems as they come up at this stage.**

4 **Make sure that the task you choose for the first Test is appropriate for the level.**

5 **Have varied tasks for the respective Test stages of the lesson.**

6 **Make sure you know what the correct answers are and the reasons for them.**

If you are unsure, refer to the previous two units.

Advantages of this approach

As with the text/recording method described in the previous unit, Test Teach Test is more student-centred in its approach. Indeed, of the three approaches, this is the one which immediately has the students working together and not responding to the teacher. Even with the text/recording approach, the teacher still has to establish interest and maybe teach some vocabulary. This method, however, presents the task (Test 1) straight away and only requires instructions. For this reason it is particularly effective with higher levels, but it can be used with lower levels (for example, having students categorize nouns represented in pictures into 'countable' and 'uncountable'). Another positive point is that you are assuming some prior exposure to the language and are allowing the students the opportunity to show you, and remind themselves of, what they know. By getting students to work things out for themselves, you are encouraging learner autonomy and reducing over-reliance on the teacher. What's more, this can be a challenging approach – just how challenging will depend on the level and the class but, unlike the text/recording approach, the focus is very much on the language. Consequently it is clearer to the students what the point of the lesson is, and what the teacher's aims are. As mentioned before, another advantage is that the teacher can discover just how well the students know the language before focusing on it – thinking time.

Just as course books frequently introduce a language focus via a text or recording, so too they frequently introduce language via an activity ('Test'). This is a good way of having students think for themselves. It also helps the busy teacher as it is far easier to use an activity provided in the course book than to have to create one for yourself.

Possible dangers

Picking up on the last advantage, if you are relying on an activity in the book then you will be asking for trouble if you don't do the activity yourself beforehand. You need to check that it covers what you want to cover in the lesson and no more, and that you know what the answers are and why. It can be embarrassing if you confirm the answer given in the Teacher's Book but cannot give a reason for it if asked – or worse, if it is not the answer you would have given.

As mentioned before, the unpredictability of the approach can unnerve new and trainee teachers – you just can't be sure how well the students will do that first activity. However, if you have researched and planned properly, you'll be OK; and if you have monitored the students during the task, you will have an idea of what problems you will have to sort out in the Teach.

With high-level classes there is the possibility that they will complete the first activity successfully and with no difficulties, and they might wonder why they are doing something which is 'easy'. In truth, this might suggest that the teacher has simply chosen something at too low a level. Or maybe the students don't know as much as they think they do, so don't be afraid to challenge them with lots of questions. However, even if they do know it all, there's no harm in reviewing the language and giving them more practice of it. In fact, reviewing familiar language is a very important thing for them to do, so tell them so.

Summary

We have looked at three different approaches to the teaching of language – a situational presentation, via a text or recording, and now Test Teach Test. Let's again review the main points.

▶ The approach used should be varied and appropriate for the level, students and language being taught.

▶ The essential ingredients of language learning are **Meaning**, **Form** and **Pronunciation** with plenty of varied practice, and whatever the approach, **MFP** should be covered.

▶ Text/recording or **Test Teach Test** approaches are more initially student-centred and challenging – therefore more appropriate for higher levels.

▶ Teachers should always research carefully the language they are teaching and anticipate possible student problems.

▶ Students should always be kept fully involved in the learning process and be encouraged to tell you what they already know.

▶ Students should be allowed and encouraged to ask questions and raise issues for discussion in relation to what is being taught.

▶ 'Grammar' should include communicative practice, but the more conventional exercise is good for focusing on accuracy; such exercises are often popular with students who perceive this as 'real' learning!

▶ Language learning should be varied, interesting, and challenging.

All three of these approaches can be adapted for the teaching of vocabulary, and the next unit looks at other approaches used specifically for the teaching of new words or review of previously taught ones.

7 Focusing on language via Task Based Learning

Tasks are something we perform in our everyday lives all the time. We get our shopping done. We get the TV fixed. We plan our next holiday. We pull out the weeds in the garden. We arrange a birthday party. We get up to date with correspondence. We renew our passport. We get a job application sent. We send out our Christmas cards – you get the idea. Think about it for a moment and you'll realise that we complete tasks every day of our lives, however small they may be. So the idea of getting students to complete a task in class as part of their learning, and developing their language use at the same time, makes good sense. Thus we have '**Task Based Learning**' ('**TBL**') as another way to focus on language, and anyone using the *Cutting Edge* (Cunningham and Moor, Pearson Longman) series of course books will be familiar with this as each module builds towards students completing a task whilst building on their language knowledge and use along the way.

Doing Task Based Teaching, Willis D. and Willis J. (Oxford Handbooks, 2007) and *A Framework for Task Based Learning*, Willis, J. (Longman, 1996) are the ultimate guides to focusing on language this way, and they answer the basic question 'What is a "task"?' by saying that 'a task is an activity where the target language is used by the learner for a communicative purpose (goal) in order to achieve an outcome'. The task and the communication involved in completing that task needs to be meaningful, and both require use of target language as well as other emerging language. This freedom of language use is an important feature of TBL. The focus is more on the successful completion of the task rather than absolute accuracy of language use, so fluency is developed, and by completing a task successfully, so is learner confidence. An activity with no outcome cannot, therefore, be considered TBL.

Which of the following activities do you think would classify as suitable for TBL, and which would not?

1 **A discussion about possible holiday destinations.**

2 **Agreeing on a programme of events for a weekend trip.**

3 **Producing an action plan to improve your use of English.**

4 **Talking about food in different countries.**

5 **Negotiating and agreeing on which members of your group should perform the household tasks in your shared flat next weekend.**

6 **Acting out a role-play of two people complaining about local transport.**

1, **4** and **6** do not involve any kind of task completion as they stand, but **2**, **3** and **5** definitely do. Taking **2** as an example, there is a significant difference between talking about what to do on a weekend trip, and actually coming up with an agreed plan. The latter requires the completion of a meaningful task with all the required language use, including the language of suggestion, persuasion, agreement and disagreement, as well as the use of 'turn taking' (e.g. 'what about you?') and opinion-giving. All of this 'target language' is everyday language and that, coupled with the fact that the task itself is one we have probably all done for real at some point in our lives, makes the whole process meaningful and familiar, and is likely, therefore, to be memorable.

The task cycle

Willis, in her 1996 book, outlines the following shape for a TBL lesson:
▶ Pre-task activity as an introduction to the topic and the task.
▶ Task cycle: task, planning, report.
▶ Language focus and feedback.

Here, the task provides fluency and the language feedback focuses on accuracy. So, in the above model and following the pre-task activity, students perform a task, usually in small groups, and then prepare their report before giving it to the rest of the class. Following this, the teacher will focus on some language issues, grammatical and lexical, that arose from this stage. In addition, during each task cycle the teacher should be on hand to respond to students' questions or problems about language and to feed in language as appropriate.

Students may either do a very similar task or the same one again, but this time with modifications and improvements following that language focus.

So let's see how this works in classroom practice by looking at such a lesson from *Cutting Edge Advanced* (Cunningham and Moor, with Comyns Carr, first published by Pearson Longman in 2003).

One of the example tasks listed above was 'producing an action plan to improve your English', and this task is given in this edition of *Cutting Edge*. This is how the lesson is laid out by Cunningham and Moor.

PRE-TASK ACTIVITY

Students are asked to look at a Learner questionnaire and to discuss it and answer the questions together in pairs.

TASK CYCLE

Students underline useful advice in the questionnaire for both themselves and their partner before going on to think about how they can improve their English and then devise an action plan together (headings are given such as 'six targets for this year'). On completion, they are asked to present their targets to the rest of the class explaining why they have chosen the targets they have. As they prepare this, students can also refer to 'useful language' on the same page (e.g. 'one thing I'm good at is ...', 'my main aim is to ...' and 'I'd find it really useful to ...') and this useful language will be added to by both the students and the teacher during the planning stages as well as the language feedback stage.

LANGUAGE FOCUS AND FEEDBACK

Although this is not explicitly mentioned in the book, this is the stage that the teacher would automatically move on to following the student reports. During this stage the teacher may work with the students to do some correction, will acknowledge and praise examples of good language that she has heard, and suggest or elicit other language that could have been used, too. Following this, there is the option of doing a similar task but this time with the added language input from the previous cycle.

You have already read many references to meaning, form and pronunciation and in a lesson such as this the MFP would be focused on as needed both in the language feedback stage with the whole class, but also during the monitoring of the planning stage on a 1–1 or 1–2 basis.

So now it's your turn. Refer back to those task examples before and look at tasks **2** and **5**.

▶ Agreeing on a programme of events for a weekend trip (two of you are going together and you will be visiting London from Friday evening until Monday morning).

▶ Negotiating and agreeing on which members of your group should perform the household tasks in your shared house next weekend (three of you share a house and it's in a bit of a mess).

Here is your task. Imagine you are teaching a high level class of 12 students, let's say upper intermediate. For each of the above tasks you want to prepare a TBL lesson using the lesson shape and guided by the example lesson described before. So that's two lessons for different days. In simple and brief terms, make notes to describe what you and your learners would do at each stage. In addition, think of some examples of 'useful language' for each task that students could refer to during the planning stages. Try to come up with ten examples of language for each one.

STOP NOW AND DO THIS TASK BEFORE READING ON.

Before we look at this task let us do what all learners should do and that is to reflect on what we've covered so far, and particularly in this section on focusing on language. So far you have read about situational presentations, language from a text, Test Teach Test, and Task Based Learning. These are what are sometimes called 'lesson shapes' and each has its own particular character and approach. Ultimately, though, they are all about focusing on the meaning, form, pronunciation and use of language, both in terms of improved accuracy and more confident use and fluency. Each requires a clear and consistent **context**. Each involves student **communication** and **input**. Each requires the teacher to clarify and check the understanding of the **meaning** and **appropriate use** of language, that the students know how to **form** the language, and are confident with its natural **pronunciation**. As we will see in later units, the teacher also has to provide varied and appropriate **practice** of the target language and to give positive feedback on language use and correction of certain mistakes.

Everything you have read about regarding language goes against the idea of standing at the front and explaining grammar – doing a PowerPoint presentation on the future perfect tense may give you a chance to show off your PowerPoint skills, but all it would be is the equivalent of reading a grammar book and would be of very limited help to your students. They have to be involved in the learning for it to be both more interesting and also more memorable. If they have no or little context, and if they have few opportunities to think for themselves and to play an active part in the learning process, then the language will have little practical meaning for them and interest levels will be low. In everything we do in life, we all learn better by being interested in the process, and by being involved in that process, and learning a language is no different.

Back to the task ...

There are, of course, no 'right answers' to this but below is one sample type of lesson for each of the two tasks. Your plans may well be different, but equally appropriate to this type of lesson.

Weekend trip	Household tasks
Pre-task	**Pre-task**
▶ Students talk together about their upcoming weekend plans. ▶ Students brainstorm famous tourist attractions in London.	▶ Students discuss different types of household task and which they particularly dislike and why. ▶ Students tell each other where they live and who they live with.
Task cycle	**Task cycle**
▶ Establish what the task is (as above). ▶ Set up the pairs / groups. ▶ Students do the task maybe with some 'useful language' to refer to and try to use. ▶ Teacher monitors, guides, helps, corrects, feeds in more language, answers questions about language, makes notes for later language feedback. ▶ Students plan their report / presentation (NB: a language feedback stage could take place first to help with the learning stage). ▶ Each pair / group presents their report to the rest of the class.	▶ Establish what the task is (as above). ▶ Set up the pairs / groups. ▶ Students do the task maybe with some 'useful language' to refer to and try to use. ▶ Teacher monitors, guides, helps, corrects, feeds in more language, answers questions about language, makes notes for later language feedback. ▶ Students plan their report / presentation (NB: a language feedback stage could take place first to help with the learning stage). ▶ Each pair / group presents their report to the rest of the class.
Language focus and feedback	**Language focus and feedback**
This could happen more than once (see above). Teacher works with the students to: ▶ Correct language used. ▶ Praise language used.	This could happen more than once (see above). Teacher works with the students to: ▶ Correct language used. ▶ Praise language used.

Weekend trip	Household tasks
▶ Elicit better ways to say certain things. ▶ Elicit or suggest other language that could have been used. ▶ Possibly provides a similar task, or repeats the same one (different groups) to allow use of this language feedback.	▶ Elicit better ways to say certain things. ▶ Elicit or suggest other language that could have been used. ▶ Possibly provides a similar task, or repeats the same one (different groups) to allow use of this language feedback.
Examples of useful language	**Examples of useful language**
▶ Why don't we ...? ▶ How about ...? ▶ Let's ... ▶ I'd prefer ... ▶ We could ... ▶ Shall we ...? ▶ I'd rather not. ▶ That's a (great) idea. ▶ Do you know about ...? ▶ OK, we're agreed.	▶ I'll do ... ▶ Why don't I / you do ... ▶ I'd rather you did that. ▶ I'd prefer to do / not to do ... ▶ I really (hate) doing that. ▶ Do I have to? ▶ I could do ... ▶ (The washing) really needs to be done first. ▶ The priority is ... ▶ Let's do ... together

The useful language in each case is just a list of some possible ways students may wish to communicate during the task. For the report itself they would need to think about other types of language, too (e.g. *we agreed that ...*, *we decided that ...*, *we couldn't agree on ...*, *both of us thought ...*, etc). The important thing to remember here is that whatever ideas the teacher may have beforehand of useful target language for the students, those ideas will be added to by both the teacher and the students during the task cycle, and the higher the level, the more language will be used. It is also worth remembering that the precise staging of a TBL lesson may vary, as long as the basic principles of the lesson remain in terms of completing a task and building on language use.

Summary

▶ **Task Based Learning** requires students to complete a meaningful task – there needs to be an outcome.
▶ It involves students working in (usually) small groups to do the task and plan how they will report back to the rest of the class.

- There may be a language feedback stage after the task and prior to the report as well as after the report.
- Useful language may be given to them at the start, but language that emerges during the task and language feedback stages is of at least equal importance – the teacher is helping to add to the language possibilities whilst monitoring as well as in the feedback.
- The task focuses more on fluency and the language focus and feedback stage focuses more on accuracy.
- Students may repeat the task or do a similar one after in order to put what they have learnt into practice.
- The aim is for the successful completion of the task.

8 Focusing on language – lexis

We saw in earlier units that **context** is essential if language is to have real meaning that students can relate to. Students learning lexis sometimes make the mistake of relying too heavily on dictionaries which give no more than a definition – and this often contains words unknown to the student.

It is important, first, to distinguish between 'vocabulary' and 'lexis'. We normally think of **vocabulary** as individual words such as *exhausted, job* or *promotion*. **Lexis** is more how these words relate to and collocate with other language. So we can have *to feel / be / always be exhausted*, or *to get / leave / resign from, be fed up with a job*, or *to apply for / be given / get / receive / be turned down for a promotion* as just a few examples. In addition, we can talk about expressions such as *to have a go* (at something), and idiomatic language (e.g. *to feel under the weather*). So we need to think more of 'lexis' rather than 'vocabulary' as this gives students a fuller and more useful guide to the language they are learning.

TASK 1

What is wrong with the following approaches to dealing with meaning in the classroom? The students are pre-intermediate.

1 Teacher asks class 'What does *scared* mean?'

2 Teacher asks class 'Does anyone know what *scared* means?'

3 Teacher asks student 'Tell the rest of the class what *scared* means'.

4 Teacher asks class 'Do you all know what *scared* means?'

5 Teacher tells class '*Scared* means frightened'.

6 Teacher tells class 'Check the meaning of *scared* in your dictionary'.

7 Teacher tells class '*Scared* is when you are in a situation and you feel really worried and think there might be some danger'.

8 Teacher tells class 'For example, you get *scared* before an exam'.

New teachers, especially, often use the above approaches because they are easy and safe and don't require much thought or planning. But in terms of clarifying meaning, they are practically worthless. Here's why.

Key to task 1

1/2/3 Even if someone does know, they are unlikely to have enough language to clearly tell the rest of the class. And how do you know if the other students can understand?

4 They might think they do, but don't. Maybe they'll say 'yes' just to escape the teacher's attention. And if someone does say 'yes', will the teacher then assume that everybody else knows?

5 If they don't know what *scared* means, they are unlikely to know what *frightened* means.

6 Very lazy! And just how helpful will the definition be? One dictionary definition is *to be filled with fear or alarm*. Whereupon the students look up *fear* and *alarm*!

7 A wordy explanation – and misleading, as *worried* is not the same as *scared*.

8 *Scared* before an exam? Or *worried*? Or *nervous*? If you say that *scared* means *worried* then students will think a person is *scared* about a friend's health rather than *worried*.

We will look later at a variety of more effective ways of clarifying the meaning of lexis, but first, consider your own experiences of learning new words in a new language.

Problems when learning new lexis

MEANING

▶ A word may have more than one meaning (e.g. *odd, cut, patient*).

▶ First language (L1) interference such as 'false friends' – words with a similar appearance or sound to words in their L1 but with different meanings. For example, compare *sympathetic* with the French *sympathique*, meaning a 'nice' person. In German *bekommen* means 'to receive', sometimes resulting in a German speaker saying what sounds like *I'll become a glass of beer* when they mean to say *I'll have a glass of beer*.

▶ Words may have different connotations, i.e. the meaning can be interpreted in different ways (e.g. *slim / thin / skinny*).

- A student may understand the meaning of a word, but not the appropriate context in which to use it. This is particularly true of language which is especially formal or informal.

FORM
- The spelling may be very different from the sound (e.g. *cough*).
- Students may be competent speakers of the language but poor writers.
- A word may be more than one part of speech (e.g. it may be a verb and a noun).
- If you teach a word like *to rely*, you also need to teach that it is followed by *on*.
- Some words are irregular (e.g. the plural of *person* is *people*, the plural of *sheep* is *sheep*).
- Different varieties of English have different spellings (e.g. *color / colour*).
- Spelling patterns are not obvious (e.g. *happy / happier* ... *hit / hitting*).

PRONUNCIATION
- The sound may not correspond to the spelling (another example being *sign*).
- Students may have difficulty knowing how many syllables the word is broken up into (a typical mistake being *clothes* pronounced with two syllables).
- It is hard to know which syllable is stressed.
- Some words have shifting stress, e.g. *his conduct / to conduct*.
- A group of consonants together – a consonant cluster – can be difficult, e.g. *crisps*.
- A speaker of a particular language might have difficulty with certain sounds, e.g. the Japanese with / l / and the French with / h /.
- Some words with different spellings and meanings are pronounced the same, e.g. *bear/bare*.

Issues of pronunciation are looked at in Unit 10 but in this unit we will concentrate on how teachers can clarify meaning to a class. However, as with any language, and as with any lesson, teachers need to anticipate possible problems students might have and why they might have them. This way the teacher will be better equipped to help the students. With vocabulary, it is all too easy – as we saw at the start of this unit – to give a quick dictionary-type definition of a word rather than properly to illustrate meaning.

THE PROS AND CONS OF STUDENTS USING DICTIONARIES

We need first to distinguish between different types of dictionary. A Spanish student, for example, may want to use his English/Spanish dictionary. Or a standard English/English dictionary. Or an English/English dictionary produced for English students (and available at different levels). Of course, this student will need his Spanish/English dictionary out of class. However, in my view, teachers should greatly limit the use of the bilingual dictionary in the classroom, especially at higher levels, because literal translation is not always helpful or accurate. I believe it is unreasonable for students to be prevented from referring to dictionaries in the classroom. Why buy a dictionary and bring it to class only for a teacher to say 'No dictionaries'? Dictionaries, after all, have many advantages. They provide:

▶ meaning (but see disadvantages below!)
▶ spelling
▶ a pronunciation guide (syllables, stress, sounds)
▶ information about the part of speech (e.g. *v* for *verb*)
▶ and sometimes, example sentences

However, for students to benefit from all this, they have to know how to use a dictionary, what the symbols mean, how to locate an entry, etc. As teachers, we have to help them with this, maybe even spending a lesson or part of a lesson on dictionary training.

We also need to make students aware of the potential disadvantages of using dictionaries, including:

▶ All meanings will be given, not just the one your students need – so they can be confusing.
▶ In an ungraded dictionary, the definitions may be too complex (remember the example earlier with *scared*).
▶ Students may not know how to find the information they need (thus the need for dictionary training).
▶ If they are using a bilingual dictionary, the definition given may not be 'correct' (false friend).
▶ Students may become too reliant on dictionaries.

So the teacher needs to encourage use of English/English dictionaries in the classroom. She needs to provide some training on how to use them. She needs to allow use of the dictionaries, but not at any time. She needs to be realistic in allowing students occasional use of their own dictionary – sometimes it saves a bit of time. But she has to make sure that the student doesn't rely on the dictionary as a substitute teacher, or as a constant 'check' on what the teacher has said!

When do we teach lexis?

▶ You may be doing a lexis-based lesson (e.g. words associated with weather).

▶ You may need to teach lexis required for the reading or listening coming up later – but only the essential words that the students will need to complete the task(s).

▶ You may be asked a question about what a particular word means.

We saw in Unit 4 that language teaching should cover MFP (Meaning, Form, Pronunciation), as well as providing Use (practice). This applies to lexis as much as it does to grammar. However, if you are teaching a word that is only going to be read or heard and not spoken (i.e. vocabulary for passive use – recognition only), pronunciation is less important, whereas if you are teaching it for active use (it will be spoken), then pronunciation will be very important.

How can we illustrate meaning effectively?

If explanations are to be kept to a minimum, especially at lower levels, then teachers need to employ other more effective methods which serve to illustrate and clarify meaning.

TASK 2

Try to think of a way to illustrate the meanings of the following words, avoiding any wordy explanations. As with the grammar, we want to try and see if any students already know the word, so we try to elicit the word if we can. Therefore, do not write up or say the word and then ask 'What does this mean?' Start with meaning.

If no one knows the word, tell them, but by this time the meaning should be clear.

Elementary

1   to jump (e.g. *He was so happy he jumped up and down*)

2   to feel tired (e.g. *She was very tired because she had worked all day*)

3   credit card

4   to be rich (e.g. *Bill Gates is very rich*)

5   heavy (e.g. *The bag is very heavy*)

Intermediate

6 to be greedy (e.g. *Don't be greedy, you've eaten enough*)

7 to be a patient (e.g. *The hospital has 75 patients at the moment*)

8 similar (e.g. *These houses are very similar*)

Advanced

9 to take after someone (e.g. *She takes after her mother; they look so similar*)

10 to be hard up (e.g. *Teachers are usually hard up*)

TIPS

1 **Use pictures or drawings.** For example, rather than explaining what *lorry/truck* is, show them a picture of one.

2 **Use realia (the actual object).** For example, rather than explaining what a *credit card* is, show them one.

3 **Use mime.** For example, rather than explaining what *tired* or *jump* is, mime it. Also, with *heavy* ... try to pick up something in the class and exaggerate the fact that it is heavy to lift.

4 **Use contrasts.** For example, with *heavy* you could also pick up something which is not heavy to emphasize the point.

5 **Use synonyms of a lower level.** For example, for *exhausted* you could say 'a word meaning very tired'. If you are teaching them *exhausted*, then they should know tired but if the synonym is not of a lower level, you are wasting your time. The same approach can be used with antonyms.

6 **Use spoken gap-fill sentences.** For example: *I ate four pieces of cake ... I was very _____* . If the students know *greedy*, they will complete the sentence. If they don't, you tell them – they now know the meaning. Much better than 'What does *greedy* mean?' You could treat *patient* in a similar way – *Sick people in a hospital are called _____* . This combines the gap-fill with a simplified definition. With *similar* you could combine the gap-fill approach with two drawings on the board of, say, two houses which are similar, but not the same.

7 **With higher levels, try to use more student-centred approaches to increase learner independence.** This respects the fact that your students already have a good level of English. Higher levels need to be challenged more, and they quickly get bored

if there is too much coming directly from the teacher. One way is to provide contextualized sentences – a sentence containing the word and making the meaning clear. Rather like the gap-fill sentence, but with no gap! Students work together, and if they don't know the word, they can deduce it from the context. For example, 'I am so *hard up* I can't even afford a newspaper.' You could use a similar approach with *take after*, maybe combined with pictures. Obviously, you have to check afterwards that the students really have understood the meanings (refer again to Unit 9).

8 Matching exercises can combine some of the above approaches. For example, match words with pictures, words with synonyms, words with simplified definitions, words in sentences with simplified definitions.

9 Following a reading task, students can look at given words in the text and match them with, or deduce, their meaning.

10 Course books usually have an excellent and varied selection of vocabulary tasks including all of the above. In general, teachers should avoid too much of a teacher-centred approach and instead encourage students to work more independently.

This idea of *illustrating* meaning rather than explaining it, and of starting with meaning rather than the written or spoken word, makes the learning of meaning more effective. But the point made in Unit 4 remains valid here. If you successfully elicit a word or correct answer from one student, it does not mean that everyone else has understood. You need to check understanding (e.g. with concept questions).

TASK 3

How could you check understanding of the words in the previous task? When you're finished, check the suggestions in the Key at the end of the unit.

How will the students remember what they have learnt?

Students have different ways of remembering. Some prefer to write up their own personalized dictionary with translations into their language, for example. Some try to learn and remember a certain number of words a day/week. Others keep a record of what they have learnt, but in a disorganized, random way. So what can the teacher do to help the longer-term learning process?

TIPS

1 Show students how they might keep an organized record of their work (not just vocabulary) – there is no 'right way', but there are plenty of 'wrong ways'! One possibility is according to themes or topics.

2 The record should include a guide to meaning, form and pronunciation. The word should appear in a contextualized sentence.

3 Students should be encouraged to be selective in choosing the words they really feel are useful to them longer-term. They should disregard the others. They also need to know the difference between 'active' and 'passive' vocabulary.

4 Students need to be encouraged to personally review what they have learnt in whatever way they find helpful.

5 Teachers should do review activities in class from time to time – you can't just teach something in one lesson and never return to it.

Key to Tasks 2 and 3

1	*Jump*	You could do a mime contrast, e.g. hop and ask 'Is this the same as jump?'
2	*Tired*	'I work all day with no break. Am I tired?' 'I slept for twelve hours. Am I tired?'
3	*Credit card*	Show examples of credit cards/travel cards/ID cards and each time ask 'Is this a credit card?'
		'Can I buy something with a credit card? Do I need real money?'
4	*Rich*	'I have a million pounds/dollars – Am I rich?' 'I have ten dollars/pounds in the bank – Am I rich?'
5	*Heavy*	A series of contrasts with objects in the room.
6	*Greedy*	'I eat eight pieces of bread – Am I greedy?' 'I share my food with you – Am I greedy?' 'Is greedy positive or negative?'

7	*Patient*	'Is a patient usually sick?' 'Is everyone in a hospital a patient?' 'Do patients need to see a doctor?'
8	*Similar*	Use of pictures and realia would be effective (e.g. the clothes different students are wearing).
9	*Take after*	Again, pictures would be best. 'My brother and I look completely different. Do I take after him?'
10	*Hard up*	'I'm rich. Am I hard up?' 'I have very little money. Am I hard up?'

Notice with the last item that I did NOT say *If I'm rich, am I hard up?* This is a conditional sentence and may be too complex to understand. Keep your check questions simple!

Summary

- ▶ You should avoid the 'What does this mean?' approach.
- ▶ It is usually more effective to start with meaning and then elicit or give the word.
- ▶ Avoid giving non-simplified definitions or explanations of words.
- ▶ Train students how to use their dictionaries effectively. Limit, but do not put a ban on their use in the classroom.
- ▶ Be aware of some of the problems students have learning lexis as this will help you in your planning.
- ▶ Use a variety of ways to illustrate meaning depending upon the level of the class.
- ▶ With higher levels especially, but not exclusively, encourage learner independence – student-centred learning.
- ▶ Check that meaning really has been understood.
- ▶ If appropriate for the lesson, check pronunciation
- ▶ Check that students are clear about the form of the word and sentence-fit.
- ▶ Make sure the lexis is being taught for a reason
- ▶ Help students to keep effective records of what they have learnt.
- ▶ Review what has been learnt from time to time.

9 Checking understanding of meaning

We saw in earlier units the importance of illustrating / conveying meaning of language, rather than explaining it. By providing meaning in context, teachers are providing their students with real language rather than abstract rules. But this is not enough. We have to make sure they have understood. If, as in the example in Unit 4, the teacher has used a situational presentation to illustrate the meaning of *should* for giving advice (*You should wear a suit*), the meaning may have been clearly illustrated. However, this does not guarantee that it has been understood. Teachers, therefore, must employ effective and efficient methods for checking the students' understanding of the meaning which has been illustrated. So how can this be done? And how should it not be done?

- ✗ 'Do you understand?', 'OK?', 'All right?', etc.
- ✗ 'So, Gabriel, what does *should* mean?', 'Do you know what this means?'

It is easy to ask these obvious questions but when, as is usually the case, the students give the answer we are hoping for ('Yes'), it does not mean that we can safely move on to the next part of the lesson. 'Do you understand?' – 'Yes' proves absolutely nothing. Quite possibly, the student just wants to get the attention of the teacher placed elsewhere and saying 'Yes' is a quick way of doing this. Maybe the student thinks she does understand, but doesn't really – 'Yes' doesn't tell the teacher this. Maybe the student does indeed understand, but still the teacher has no evidence – and besides, what of the other students?

Asking a student to repeat or give the meaning is flawed for different reasons. Principally, does the student – even if he has understood – possess a sufficient range and level of language to express himself? Would other students understand him? Would the 'explanation' be correct? This approach can only really succeed with very high-level students, and when the teacher knows her class very well. In such circumstances, it is more effective with lexis than with grammar.

Concept questions

It is necessary, then, to use other methods of checking understanding, of which the most effective is concept questions. Let us consider again the model sentence featured in Unit 4 – You should wear a suit (advice to casually dressed friend about to go to a job interview). In order for the teacher to first illustrate the meaning of *should* in this context, and then check it has been understood, she needs to have recognized the essential meaning of the language in this context:

▶ we are talking about a possible future action (wearing the suit)
▶ the person we are talking to does not have to wear a suit (no obligation)
▶ it would be a good idea if he did – I want him to (friendly advice)

We can now turn these statements into simple questions:

1 **Are we talking about the past, the present, or the future? future**

2 **Does this person *have* to wear a suit? / *Must* he wear a suit? no**

3 **Do I think it would be good for him to wear a suit? yes**

If students give any answers different from the above, the assumption must be that they have not understood and some further clarification will be required.

✘ Should he wear a suit?	Avoid using the grammatical form being tested in the question. If they haven't understood it before, they won't understand it now!
✘ Will he wear a suit?	Irrelevant, and impossible to answer, anyway. Avoid questions which focus on the **context** rather than the **concept**.

Let's look at another example – She's been to Hungary – and consider the **essential information** of this present perfect simple statement:

▶ it happened in the past
▶ the listener doesn't know when, according to the sentence alone
▶ the listener doesn't know how many times the person went
▶ she's not there now (compare with She's gone to Hungary).

Again we can turn these into **concept questions** as follows:

1	Are we talking about the past, present, or future?	past
2	Do we know exactly when she went?	no
3	Do we know how many times she went?	no
4	Is she there now?	no

✗ *Has she been to Hungary? / Have you been to Hungary?* etc.

The second question is asking for information, not checking meaning. Both questions use the tense that is being tested – compare with Question 3 above, which uses a simple tense instead.

We can use the same method with lexis. The **essential meaning** of *library* is:

▶ we can borrow books from a library (we assume here that our students understand *borrow*)
▶ we cannot buy books from a library
▶ we can sit and read in a library

Increasingly, libraries also contain other facilities such as DVDs and music loans, but for the sake of this example we will focus on books.

The **concept questions**, therefore, become as follows:

1	Can you borrow books from a library?	yes
2	Can you buy books from a library?	no
3	Can you sit and read in a library?	yes

For *engaged* (as in *Steve and Jo have got engaged*) the essential meaning is:

▶ they are not married now
▶ they plan to marry
▶ they have promised each other / it is a definite plan.

1	Are they married now?	no
2	Will they marry in the future?	yes
3	Is this definite / sure?	yes
4	Have they made a promise to marry?	yes

TIPS TO FORMULATE CONCEPT QUESTIONS

1 First analyse the language and its meaning within the given context.

2 Define the essential meaning in simple statements.

3 Turn these statements into questions.

4 Keep the questions simple in terms of both language and length.

5 Avoid questions which are not relevant to the meaning of the language.

6 Avoid using the same grammatical forms in the questions that you are testing.

7 Ask questions which do not require a lot of language in the answer.

8 Make sure the answers are clear and unambiguous.

9 Plan them in advance – until you have more experience and confidence, they will not be easy to think of on the spot.

10 Avoid the 'absurd' (e.g. *honeymoon* – 'Can you find honey on the moon'?)

TASK 1

Now you try. For each of the following language items (underlined), think of a context, define the meaning, and devise concept questions and expected answers.

1 <u>I wish I had</u> a car. (subject + *wish* + subject + past simple form)

2 <u>You shouldn't have taken</u> that book. (subject + *should(n't) have* + past participle)

3 <u>I'm looking forward to</u> my holiday. (subject + *to be* + looking forward to something)

4 <u>I had</u> my suit cleaned. (subject + *had* + object + past participle)

5 They're going on their <u>honeymoon</u>.

6 That watch is really <u>expensive</u>.

When you have finished, look in the Key and see if you're on the right lines.

It is also good, when appropriate, to use examples, realia, mime, pictures, etc., to check understanding.

Examples	For *difficult* you could contrast 3 + 3 with 37 × 37 and for each sum ask if it is difficult.
Realia	For *mug* (mug of tea) you could show a plastic cup, and a cup and saucer and ask if they are mugs.
Mime	For *slowly* you could mime walking quickly and then slowly and check that students have understood which is which.
Pictures	For *lorry / truck* show pictures of other vehicles and ask for each 'Is this a lorry/truck?'

As we saw previously, any of these methods can also be used for the initial illustration of meaning. In other words, you could convey the meaning of *difficult* by using the sums above, then check understanding via a similar example.

Timelines

Time can be represented using many different verb forms. This can be confusing for a student when, for example, we use the present simple tense to refer to future time (e.g. *The train goes at 3.30 this afternoon*). Concept questions can be used to check understanding of tenses and time, but there is another way which is particularly effective and that is using **timelines**.

Looking at the sentence *I was watching TV at 10 p.m. last night* we can identify the **form** as past continuous (progressive) – subject + *was* or *were* + verb-*ing*. The **time** reference is an action which started before 10 p.m. and may have continued after 10 p.m., but the action was already in progress at 10 p.m. This can be represented on a timeline thus:

```
past              now          future
•      ~~~~~?      •                    •
   10 pm yesterday
```

The **x** here represents the moment of 10 p.m. The wavy line represents the ongoing action / state of watching TV. The wavy line begins before 10 p.m. and goes right up to the moment of 10 p.m. The subsequent question mark beyond 10 p.m. represents the fact that we do not know if the person continued to watch TV after 10 p.m., though they may have done. The wavy line is clearly set in past time only, consistent with this use of the past progressive.

Another example. *I had been waiting for the bus for 10 minutes before it came*. The first clause is in the past perfect progressive (subject + *had been* + verb-*ing*) and the second is in the past simple (*came* being the past simple form of *come*). This sentence is also set entirely in the past with one action going on for a period of time (*waiting*) before being stopped by an event (the arrival of the bus). In the timeline below, the wavy line again represents an ongoing action/state whilst the cross represents an event which effectively interrupts or ends the ongoing action.

Timelines can be used to help illustrate meaning, and they can be used to check students have understood what has gone before. And here's an important point. If the teacher is using a timeline to check her students have understood the concept, then she must involve the students in the process of drawing the timeline. Students, then, need to know what a timeline is, and what the symbols the teacher uses actually mean (e.g. the wavy line). The teacher needs to be consistent in the way she draws timelines. The students can then effectively tell the teacher how to construct the timeline, or even draw it themselves. Timelines can be used in conjunction with concept questions. For example, a teacher may ask 'Where do I put the cross? Here?

Or here?'

TIPS FOR USING TIMELINES

1 **Plan how to do them.**
2 **Practise drawing them.**
3 **Make sure the line can be clearly seen on the board.**
4 **Use different colours for effect and clarity.**
5 **Make sure students know what everything on the line represents.**
6 **Involve the students.**
7 **Use them in conjunction with concept questions.**
8 **Be consistent in how you draw them.**
9 **Make sure they accurately reflect the essential meaning.**
10 **Give the students the opportunity to copy the line, and check to see if they have copied it correctly.**

TASK 2

Now you try. Draw timelines for the following, then check the Key.

Start by analysing the language and defining the essential meaning, then draw the timelines.

1 I've lived here for 10 years.
2 This time next week I'll be on the plane.
3 I'll have finished by 3 p.m. tomorrow.
4 I've been to Ghana.
5 I saw Titanic yesterday, but I had seen it before.

Key to Tasks 1 and 2

Task 1: Concept questions

1 Do I have a car now? **no**

   Do I want a car? **yes**

   Is it likely I will get one soon? **no**

2 Did you take the book? **yes**

   Do I think you were right to take it? **no**

3 Are we talking about the past, the present, or the future? **future**

   Will I have a holiday? **yes**

   Am I excited about my holiday? **yes**

4 Was my suit dirty? **yes**

   Is it clean now? **yes**

   Did I clean it? **no**

   Did another person clean it? **yes**

5 Are we talking about the past, the present, or the future? **future**

   Is a honeymoon a kind of holiday? **yes**

   When you go on holiday with your friends, is that a honeymoon? **no**

   Do you go on honeymoon straight after getting married? **yes**

6 In my opinion does the watch cost a lot of money? **yes**

   This watch (pointing) cost me £10 ($15). Was it expensive? **no**

   That watch (pointing) cost my friend £300 ($450). Was it expensive? **yes**

Note: These are only sample questions. You may have written different ones which are still relevant.

Task 2: Timelines

Summary

In this unit we have established the following main points:

▶ Teachers have to check that students have understood what they have learnt.
▶ Questions such as 'Do you understand?' are ineffective.
▶ Asking a student to explain meaning is, with few exceptions, unrealistic and can do more harm than good.
▶ Concept questions are an effective and efficient way to genuinely check understanding. They should:
 ▷ focus on the essential meaning of the language in the context being provided
 ▷ be short and simple in nature
 ▷ avoid ambiguity
 ▷ require very short answers
 ▷ avoid the use of the grammatical form being tested
▶ Timelines provide a visual representation of time.
▶ Students need to be involved in the drawing of a timeline.

- Timelines need to be clear, simple, and accurate.
- The process of checking understanding may take up a tiny percentage of your lesson, but it is a crucial stage. If the students remain unsure of meaning now, then they will struggle for the rest of the lesson, and will be unable to use the language naturally or correctly after the lesson. Checking understanding effectively is a difficult teaching skill, but it becomes easier with practice. After a while, you will find that you can do this 'on the spot' because your own confidence with language and its meaning and use will have grown with experience. To begin with, though, analyse the language carefully and plan how you will check understanding.

10 Pronunciation

What is **phonology**? In general terms we can say that it includes:

sounds the individual sounds of the language

stress both word stress and sentence stress

intonation the rising and falling of our voice to convey different meaning

connected speech including how sounds and words relate to each other in natural speech; how sounds alter or disappear, how words link, etc.

Phonology is the subject of many books. This unit is more of a guide to how pronunciation can be incorporated into lessons rather than a unit about phonology.

Whether you are a Californian or a Texan, a Londoner or a Glaswegian, the Queen of England or a bus driver, there is no right and wrong way to speak, just different ways. People have different accents and maybe dialects. There are numerous varieties of English spoken around the world – and they are all English. Of course there are differences. Between American and British English, for example, there are many differences, not least in pronunciation. Sometimes it really does seem as if they are different languages, and one is sometimes referred to as 'correct' English, and the other not. But I disagree with this. Indeed, I believe strongly that students should be exposed to as many different accents, dialects and varieties of English as possible and that we are doing students a disservice if we expose them only to what in Britain is sometimes referred to as 'the Queen's English', or 'BBC English'. 'BBC English' refers to the days when all announcers and newsreaders seemed to possess standard south of England pronunciation. These days it is different.

As a teacher, I try to play recordings that represent different British accents, and different varieties of English. At first, students find these difficult to understand. And that's the point. A student studying in

London who visits Glasgow, or a student studying in San Francisco who visits Georgia, is going to find it difficult at first to understand what is the same language. I also strongly emphasize to my students that there is no right and wrong way to speak English (in terms of varieties of pronunciation), and that it is important for them not to be restricted to 'standard' English, whatever that is. And it is unhelpful, in my opinion, when TV programmes in either Britain or the United States feature a character from the other side of the Atlantic who speaks in an extremely unrealistic and exaggerated way, unrelated to any recognizable variety of English.

Spelling and pronunciation

There is no clear relationship between spelling and pronunciation in English. Look at the following words:

cough – tough – though – through – they all end *-ough* but the pronunciation is different each time.

How can a student seeing the word *laugh* for the first time have any chance of knowing that *ugh* is pronounced /f/?

heard and *beard* both end *-eard*, but the sound is quite different.

How about *both* and *brother*? Both contain the letters *oth*, but they are pronounced differently.

Wednesday – so is that 'wed – nes – day'? No, it's /wen/ – a silent *d*.

Convinced now? This is a very strange language.

The sounds of English

What students need, then, is some representation of the sounds of English so that when they look up a word in a dictionary and see its phonetic transcription, they can work out the standard pronunciation of that word. This is not to say that we are trying to make our students speak in a certain way, just that they need a guide. Such guides will have alternative versions depending on the variety of English, so please do not consider the following example to be representative of the only 'correct' way to say these sounds; many readers will have additional sounds in their own speech, and may not recognize some of these examples.

The underlined part of each word represents the given sound (phoneme).

VOWELS

b<u>ea</u>d	/ i: /
b<u>i</u>d	/ ɪ /
g<u>oo</u>d	/ ʊ /
f<u>oo</u>d	/ u: /
b<u>e</u>d	/ e /
th<u>e</u>*	/ ə /
b<u>ir</u>d	/ ɜ: /
d<u>oor</u>	/ ɔ: /
c<u>a</u>t	/ æ /
c<u>u</u>t	/ ʌ /
c<u>ar</u>d	/ ɑ: /
c<u>o</u>d	/ ɒ /

*known as the 'schwa' – the most common sound in English. In a word like *potato*, the first *o* is pronounced with a schwa (weak form); also the *e* in *terrific*.

CONSONANTS

<u>p</u>i<u>p</u>	/ p /
<u>b</u>ul<u>b</u>	/ b /
<u>t</u>ac<u>t</u>	/ t /
<u>d</u>are<u>d</u>	/ d /
<u>ch</u>ur<u>ch</u>	/ t ʃ /
<u>j</u>ud<u>ge</u>	/ dʒ /
<u>c</u>a<u>ke</u>	/ k /
<u>g</u>ar<u>g</u>le	/ g /
<u>f</u>ear<u>f</u>ul	/ f /
<u>v</u>i<u>v</u>id	/ v /
<u>th</u>irtie<u>th</u>	/ θ /
<u>th</u>is	/ ð /

cease	/ s /
zones	/ z /
sheepish	/ ʃ /
treasure	/ ʒ /
murmur	/ m /
nanny	/ n /
thing	/ ŋ /
hope	/ h /
lull	/ l /
red	/ r /
went	/ w /
yacht	/ j /

DIPHTHONGS

rear	/ ɪə /
may	/ eɪ /
pure	/ ʊə /
boy	/ ɔɪ /
go	/ əʊ /
rare	/ eə /
buy	/ aɪ /
now	/ aʊ /

Why use such a transcription? Well, it helps give students a record of pronunciation. It helps them to use a dictionary more effectively, and it can aid the teacher doing correction work. Students need to get the chance to hear a sound within a word before being expected to try and repeat it – in other words, teachers should raise students' awareness. How to do this we will look at later.

TASK 1

In Unit 20 you will see how important it is for teachers to anticipate problems students might have with the meaning, form, and pronunciation of any language being taught. With this in

mind, look at the following, and consider what peculiarities of pronunciation exist in terms of sounds and their relationship with one another.

Example: *a pint of beer* the *a* is a schwa, *of* is pronounced / əv / and *a pint of* sounds like one word.

1 **asked**

2 **Can you help me? Yes, I can.**

3 **Do you want some?**

4 **Do you have to go?**

5 **I used to drive ...**

6 **fish and chips**

7 **peas**

8 **goodbye**

9 **Shall we go?**

10 **I was working at home.**

Before checking your answers, let's consider one way of raising students' awareness and improving their own pronunciation skills, not just regarding sounds, but all aspects of pronunciation: **drilling / repetition drills.**

Repetition drills involve students repeating what they have heard. Consider the sentence *She's worked here for two years*. The teacher is covering the present perfect simple in her lesson for unfinished state and has illustrated meaning using the context of a teacher who ... *has worked here for two years*. The given sentence has been elicited by the teacher and it contains the target language. Students, however, need to keep the language in context – it's no good their repeating *has worked* in isolation; they need to say the whole sentence. A good approach to drilling is as follows:

1 **Having elicited the sentence *She's worked here for two years* the teacher repeats the sentence naturally, two or three times so the students can hear it.**

2 **Then, the teacher should 'break up' the sentence using her fingers as representations of each word:**

   She – has – worked – here – for – two – years

   and as she repeats *She – has* she joins her first and second fingers and say *She's*, and repeats the remainder of the sentence.

3 Finally, she repeats the whole sentence again naturally, perhaps demonstrating rhythm. This first stage is *giving a model pronunciation*.

4 Then, giving a clear direction to the students (spoken and gesture), the teacher tells the class to repeat what she has said. At this stage she says 'Repeat', and avoids vague instructions such as 'would you like to say that?' Students repeat the sentence together first (*choral repetition*) to give them confidence.

5 Then, the teacher gestures to some students in turn to say the sentence individually, eliciting correction / improvement as required.

   With this sentence, the teacher's model needs to include the /i:z/ in *she's*; the /t/ sound of *-ed*; and the weak form with schwa of *for*.

Drilling applies equally to lexis, and the aim is for students to hear and give the correct and natural pronunciation of a piece of language. There are teachers who don't like drilling, or don't believe in it, but in my experience students who are not confident about pronunciation welcome the controlled opportunity to have practice saying a new piece of language. They need to have confidence in their pronunciation, and this is one way to give it to them. Of course, you shouldn't overdo it at any stage, but done properly and appropriately, drilling is valuable and effective.

Key to Task 1

1 *a* is pronounced /ɑ:/ and d is pronounced /t/.

2 The first *can* is pronounced weakly /kən/, but the second is not – /kæn/.

3 *do you* is normally pronounced / djə / or /djʊ/.

4 *do you* as above. *v* in *have* is pronounced /f/; *to* has a schwa.

5 *d* is pronounced /t/ and the to is weak. The words used *and to* are linked as if they were one word.

6 *and* is reduced to /n/ and the whole phrase sounds like a single word.

7 /pi:z/ – the /z/ sound is especially strange for students who see the spelling.

8 Say the word quickly and you'll notice *d* disappears and the word sounds like /gʊbaɪ/.

9 Similar to above, the *ll* disappears and *shall we* sounds like /ʃwɪ/.

10 *s* sounds like /z/, and the word is pronounced weakly /wəz/.

So why is all this important? For a start, teachers need to be aware of how English sounds in order to help students produce the natural pronunciation themselves. It's not really a case of being 'correct', but of sounding 'natural'. However, students can't sound natural unless they have clear models to follow.

Teaching monolingual classes, you can focus on specific problems encountered by that nationality. For example, students who have difficulties distinguishing between two different but similar sounds (minimal pairs) such as /i:/ and /ɪ/ can be given tasks where they have to hear and recognize the two sounds in various words; or / and think of examples themselves. You do not need to 'teach' all the sounds, but focus on those which are relevant to your students and which they need help with.

Word stress

Word stress is another area which can cause difficulties. In the word *advertisement* the stress falls on the third syllable in American English (ad-ver-TISE-ment), but on the second in British English (ad-VER-tise-ment).

TASK 2

Where does the main stress fall on the following words? Be careful, there are some tricky ones included.

1 **telephone**

2 **cassette**

3 **surprising**

4 **conduct**

5 **notebook**

6 **address**

7 **worked**

8 **examination**

9 **photograph**

10 **photographer**

Before going through this task, why is it important to focus on word stress in the classroom? It is probably less important than other aspects of pronunciation because meaning is rarely affected by mis-stressing a word but if the pronunciation is so incorrect that it becomes almost unintelligible, then meaning would become affected.

Stress can be marked in different ways.

newspaper nĕwspaper 'newspaper Ooo NEWSpaper <u>news</u>paper

The third of these is how dictionaries normally mark stress, but most teachers, in my experience, prefer the second (with a small circle or square). The fourth example (stress bubbles) are a very visual way to represent stress, good with very low-level classes. Whatever mark you adopt, be consistent, and make sure your students know what it means. Make sure, too, that students know how to read a dictionary for word stress – this, accompanied by the phonetic transcription, gives the students a good guide to pronunciation.

Key to Task 2

1 **Ooo**

2 **oO**

3 **oOo**

4 **Oo (noun) oO (verb)**

5 **Oo**

6 **oO (British) Oo (American)**

7 **There is no stress because there is only one syllable, though many students will mistakenly say work-ed.**

8 **oooOo**

9 **Ooo**

10 **oOoo**

In the classroom there are many activities you can do with word stress.

If you have been teaching lexis, you could have words on one side of a sheet and stress patterns on the other, and students match them (or any variation thereof). Students can listen to words and decide for themselves what the stress pattern is.

You can give two columns (e.g. oO and Oo) and a series of words which students have to categorize. As mentioned before, drill new words which will be needed to be used actively.

Sentence stress

Sentence stress can certainly affect meaning. Consider this simple sentence:

> I gave Gaston a book.

So, which word is stressed most?

TASK 3

How does the meaning of this sentence change when the words are stressed as follows?

1 <u>I</u> gave Gaston a book.

2 I <u>gave</u> Gaston a book.

3 I gave <u>Gaston</u> a book.

4 I gave Gaston <u>a</u> book.

5 I gave Gaston a <u>book</u>.

Consider, too, the implied difference between *I'm going now* and *I am going now*. And what about *Today's Wednesday – No, it's **Thursday***?

*I **am** going now* is emphatic, almost a show of determination to leave, despite efforts to make you stay. This could be correct in the right context, but the more natural pronunciation will be the contracted form, and this is what you should drill. With the 'Thursday' example, the second speaker is correcting information given by the first speaker, the stress falling on the correction – a very useful aspect of sentence stress to focus on.

Key to Task 3

1 **It was I who gave him the book, not someone else.**

2 **I didn't lend him the book; I gave it to him.**

3 **I gave the book to Gaston, not another person.**

4 **I gave Gaston only one book, not more.**

5 **It was a book I gave him, not something else.**

Such a task raises students' awareness of the importance of sentence stress and how it affects meaning. What is stressed depends in part on the important information a student wishes to convey.

We can signify sentence stress by saying the sentence ourselves, 'beating' the sentence (e.g. knocking on a table), humming it (e.g. 'da da da DA da'), clapping it, etc. but context is essential if the task is to be meaningful.

Intonation

Sentence stress goes hand in hand with intonation. Very often, someone we are speaking to may appear rude because of their intonation patterns. It is quite easy to make *Thank you very much for your help* sound rude or sarcastic. But intonation is so hard to teach because students invariably end up exaggerating intonation patterns until they sound completely unnatural. A case in point is question tags, e.g. *Your name's Luc, isn't it?* A rising intonation on the tag *isn't it?* implies a real question requiring an answer. But a falling or flat intonation implies that nothing more than confirmation is required of a fact already known (*it's really cold today, isn't it?* – there is no disputing the temperature). But just try making students use tags naturally! They usually end up leaving what sounds like a huge space between the statement and the tag, and then really exaggerating the intonation of the tag.

What students can do is to listen and identify polite versus not so polite intonation patterns. The *Thank you very much for your help* example might be said once, naturally and politely, and again, sarcastically; students must identify the difference.

A variation of this is to do the same task with a single word (e.g. *Hello*) and students must interpret the speaker's feelings (pleased to see me, not pleased to see me, surprised to see me, etc.).

Students could also mark intonation patterns on sentences (which have context) with rising, falling, and level arrows.

Pronunciation is sometimes focused on as a lesson, or part of a lesson, but most of the time, the most valuable pronunciation work takes place spontaneously as problems arise. Drilling, too, is a common feature of many teachers' classes, especially with lower-level students. Pronunciation work is generally more effective with monolingual classes because you can deal with common problems.

You will find that some course books integrate pronunciation work into their units while others keep it quite separate. Some books feature pronunciation work a lot, others much less so, just as some teachers do more pronunciation work than others.

There are lots of good books available which contain various pronunciation tasks for different levels, often with a 'fun' approach (stress bingo, phonetic crosswords, picture 'spot the difference' containing minimal pairs, etc.), and you can provide whatever pronunciation work you feel is appropriate and useful for your students. But do not neglect this part of language learning.

Summary

▶ Meaning can be affected by unclear pronunciation, whether sounds, stress, intonation, or any other feature of it.
▶ As teachers, we should expose our students to the different varieties of pronunciation and not portray one as 'better' than another.
▶ We should not ignore pronunciation work – we can have specific parts of a lesson devoted to it or deal with issues as they arise.
▶ Drilling provides students with safe, controlled practice of new language but the activity needs to be executed efficiently.
▶ Course books provide ideas for pronunciation work, as do other specialized books, but the pronunciation areas to focus on should be determined by the needs of your particular students.
▶ With monolingual classes, focus on the common problems experienced by that nationality.
▶ With all classes, focus on any problems which are affecting meaning and intelligibility.

11 *Practice activities*

In earlier units, we looked at various ways of focusing on language. We established that a teacher needs to cover the meaning, form, and pronunciation of new language and to do so in a way which involves the students and which uses appropriate methodology for the level. But the missing element in this learning process is getting students to use the language they have learnt – to practise it. Without this, students are restricted to learning rules and patterns, albeit in context, without having the opportunity to operate the language they have learnt.

We saw that with Test Teach Test a task which could be described as 'practice' takes place right at the start, but with the purpose of being diagnostic. Normally, of course, practice tasks take place after the teacher has focused on the language itself.

We will look in this unit at some examples of practice tasks for both vocabulary and grammar, as well as looking at the teacher's role before, during and after the task.

Controlled and less controlled / freer practice

First, let's go back to Unit 4 when we had a context of an unemployed man, Jason, going for a job interview at a bank. Jason was very casual in his appearance, too casual for a bank employing a new person. This context led us towards the sentence *You should wear a suit* which contains the language *you should* + base verb with the function here of giving friendly advice. We saw in this unit how we could cover the meaning, form and pronunciation. Having done all this, the teacher now needs to provide one, and probably more practice tasks so the students can gain confidence using this language.

TASK 1

Here are two possible activities, but very different in nature. Look at how each is described and consider what the main difference is in the nature of the tasks.

Activity 1

The teacher elicits from the students ideas of what a good café is like. She asks for examples of local ones and what students think of them. She also elicits examples of what would be considered unacceptable in a café. Throughout, the teacher is eliciting and personalizing, and at the same time establishing interest in the topic.

At this point, the teacher says she has a friend called Erik who owns a café. She shows them a picture of Erik in his café. The picture shows a café that is dirty, with three cats inside, and an owner who is smoking and unclean in appearance. The teacher elicits opinions from the students, as well as other ideas of what this café might be like.

All of this will take no more than three or four minutes. The teacher reminds the class that Erik is a friend of hers whose business is doing badly and she wants to advise him on how to improve his position. She elicits an example from the class in which they have to use either *should* or *shouldn't* – for example, *You shouldn't smoke*. Students then work together to say / write more examples using *should / shouldn't* based on the examples of problems given by the students earlier. They might come up with something like this:

You shouldn't have cats in the café.

You should wear clean clothes.

You should cook good food.

You should clean the café.

You shouldn't make your food and drink so expensive.

The teacher then gets back from the class what they have come up with and writes sentences on the board as confirmation of correct usage.

Activity 2

The teacher says she has another friend, Javier, who is Spanish. Javier is studying English in Miami but he has a problem. There is a large Spanish-speaking community in Miami and Javier finds himself speaking Spanish most of the time he is not in class. Consequently he is making very slow progress with his English. He calls you and asks for advice. The students imagine Javier is their friend and have to suggest ways in which he can improve his English and give reasons why. The teacher elicits an example – *Try to meet some American friends because they will speak English with you*. The students work together and think of more examples and then the teacher asks the class for their suggestions.

So what's the difference in the nature of these practice activities? The first requires the use of the target language because the teacher has set it up that way and told the class to use *you should / you shouldn't*. The second does not require this language to be used, but the opportunity is there for the students to use it because strong friendly advice is being given but this time the teacher did not say 'use should', she just said 'give suggestions' and reasons. By asking for reasons, the teacher is getting the students to use other language, and by not insisting on *should* and *shouldn't* the teacher is allowing students to use other appropriate language in a more natural way. So, this task is much less controlled in terms of the language being used by the students.

We have, then, a task where the language being used is controlled, and a task where the language being used is guided, but not controlled. By doing the controlled task first, the teacher is giving students confidence in using the language, before asking them to be a little more varied in what they say. Remember that this class is around elementary level, perhaps pre-intermediate.

What the activities have in common, apart from the function and the related language being used, is the teacher's role. In each case she set the context, established interest, gave instructions with an example, and checked answers afterwards. More of this later.

Forms of practice activities

Practice can be spoken or written, controlled or less controlled (to varying degrees). It can also be in the form of an 'exercise' (e.g. gap-fill), or something more communicative.

TASK 2
Prepositions

If we take another piece of language – prepositions of place – we can look at various types of practice. Prepositions of place include *in* the corner, *on* the table, and *under* the bed.

Try to think of five different ways in which students at pre-intermediate level could practise this language.

Prepositions are difficult for students because there are no nice, easy rules to follow, or even much logic to them. You can have prepositions of time (*at* 3 o'clock), prepositions of movement (go *down* the street), and prepositions of place (*under* the bed)...and that's just for starters. Students of all levels generally find prepositions very difficult and confusing.

Here are five possible activities:

1 **Students see a picture of a room and have to complete five sentences with the appropriate preposition from a given list.**

   Example: *The newspaper is _____ the table.* – students look at picture and select *on* to complete the sentence.

2 **Students are given two very similar pictures of a room and in pairs they have to find differences. They cannot show each other their pictures, but they can ask questions, and describe their own pictures.**

   Example: *How many people are sitting on the sofa?*
                I have a cat sleeping under the bed.

3 **Students have a picture of a room with completed sentences. But each sentence has the wrong preposition which students must correct. A variation of this is: students listen to a recording of someone describing their room and look at the accompanying picture to discover which sentences on the recording fail to match the details in the picture.**

4 **Students tell each other about a room in their house / apartment and what is there. Afterwards, the teacher asks one student to tell the class about her partner's room.**

5 **The teacher provides various objects and students tell each other where in the room to place each object.**

Activities **1** and **3** are what one might describe as 'traditional exercises'. Students usually like these more than teachers, and they definitely have value, as long as students are doing other types of activity as well.

Activities **2** and **4** are more communicative. **4** in particular is much less controlled in terms of the language being used.

3RD CONDITIONAL

Let us now look at the 3rd conditional (e.g. *If I had forgotten your birthday, you would have been angry with me*) and at typical types of practice activity, both controlled and freer.

1 **Complete the sentence with the words (in brackets) in the correct form:**

   If I (win) the competition, I (be happy).

   If I had won the competition, I would have been happy.

2 **Find the mistake in this sentence:**

If she hadn't of seen me, she would never have known.

✗ *'of'* If she hadn't seen me ...

3 **Rewrite this sentence in the 3rd conditional:**

I didn't study hard and I failed my exam.

If I had studied (more/harder), I would have passed/wouldn't have failed...

4 **Chain sentences ... one student gives the first half of the sentence for another student to complete.**

5 **The teacher provides the ending of a story (e.g. a man gets dismissed from his job). Students have to write a sentence which explains this ending and which climaxes with a 3rd-conditional.**

Example: *If he hadn't slept late, he wouldn't have lost his job.*

6 **Students have to think of a conversation between two people. They decide on the context and the relationship between the characters. Somewhere in the conversation a 3rd conditional sentence must appear in a natural and appropriate way.**

7 **'Noughts and Crosses' ('Tick-Tack-Toe') – half the class are the 'noughts' and the other half are the 'crosses'. Each team selects two verbs from a given list and thinks of a 3rd conditional sentence that uses these verbs. If they produce a correct sentence, they choose in which box to place their 0 or X. A team wins when they form three noughts or crosses in a row, in the usual way. This is an example of using a classic game for language purposes. Most such games can be adapted in some way.**

8 **Matching sentence halves. In column A you have the if-clauses, and in column B the main clauses. Students have to match correct halves. A more interesting variation of this is to have the sentence halves on separate pieces of paper, face down on the table. One student picks up an if-clause, the other student picks up a main clause. If they match, put them to one side; if they don't, put them back face down in the same position. This activity is sometimes called 'Pairs', or 'Pelmanism' and can be used to practise many different language items.**

9 Jumbled sentences.

Example: *wouldn't – I – eaten – have – if – sick – less – had – I – felt*

If I had eaten less, I wouldn't have felt sick.

10 Students talk about their lives so far and include information about the consequences of what they did or didn't do.

Example: *If I had worked harder, I would have gone to university.*

TASK 3

Think of one practice activity of any type for the following which is different from the ones given below.

1 Giving directions (elementary)

2 Comparatives (intermediate)

3 Question forms (intermediate)

For each of the above, there are numerous possible activities, and of various types. Normally, you would want your students to do a couple of quite different activities, as explained above (*should*). Of the many possibilities for these three language items, here is one example for each.

Directions

Students work in pairs and each has a diagram of a street, but each diagram has different places shown (e.g. post office). Each student has to ask directions to find the places not listed on her diagram. They listen to the directions and write in the location of the place. Afterwards, students look at each other's pictures to check.

Comparatives

Students compare their country with the country they are now in, if applicable. Alternatively, use pictures to make comparisons of people and places.

Question forms

Each student in a pair is given an incomplete text about a person. The missing information is different in each text. One student has to ask relevant questions of the other in order to complete their text.

Example: Student A: *His name is Marco and he is _____ years old.*

Student B: *His name is _____ and he is 19 years old.*

Student A asks B *How old is Marco?* and B asks A *What is his name?*

Many of the activities described so far can be used with lexis as well. Let's look at some possibilities.

Imagine you have 'taught' your students lexis related to the following topics:

weather (elementary)

sport (intermediate)

music (upper intermediate)

Certain types of activity could be used with all of these. Examples of these are **matching** (e.g. word to definition/picture) and **gap-fill** (putting the correct word into the sentence gap). But more communicative activities are also needed; some ideas for **speaking** in Unit 14 are appropriate for language practice, too. A good example is **ranking**. This is when students put items in a particular order. With 'sport', this could be according to which they like watching most, or which are considered healthiest. With 'music', it could be according to their favourite type of music, or which instrument is the hardest to learn. With 'weather', it could be according to the most common type of weather in respective seasons, or favourite weather types and why. The point about ranking is that there are no right and wrong answers. It is designed to promote speaking which allows use of the vocabulary items.

For the weather lexis, students could have pictures of different weather types, and then write in the description. For the sport lexis, students could mime a sport for the others to guess. For the music lexis, students could discuss examples of musicians who are associated with different kinds of music, and whether they like them or not.

For review purposes, students could be given **anagrams** (words with letters jumbled up) of words previously learnt and from which they can make sentences. Or, they could be asked to find words in a **word puzzle**.

Example:	frtg**football**kdrwqy	Your actual puzzle
	sinnetbjeutifcheux	would be bigger than
	gnixobjuytedfghytg	this!

So where do you get ideas for practice activities from?

▶ Course books and accompanying workbooks are usually excellent sources. You should adapt and supplement in the way described in Unit 22.

- Other resource books which give various ideas of practice activities for different language points. Make sure the activity is suitable for the level and students you are teaching.
- You can find a wide variety of online resources, from simple ideas or classroom tips to colour worksheets with teaching notes that you can download.
- Your own ideas and creativity. If you come up with a successful activity, keep it for future use.

The role of the teacher

I have already mentioned the teacher's role in the practice stages of a lesson; that role comes in four parts.

1 BEFORE THE LESSON

The teacher needs to find an activity (activities) appropriate in terms of the class level, age group, composition and nature of the class, time available, and language focus (does it really provide practice of the specific language point you will have focused on earlier in the lesson?). Creating your own activity sounds a good thing to do, but don't spend two hours preparing an activity that will last five minutes!

2 BEFORE THE ACTIVITY

Prepare students linguistically – are there any words you need to check they know before they begin the practice? Set the context and establish interest. Give / Elicit an example of what they have to do. Arrange the class in the way you want them to work and with whom.

3 DURING THE ACTIVITY

Do not participate. Monitor to check they have understood, to give help, to keep things moving, to respond to difficulties or to quick finishers. If they are doing a speaking activity, listen and note down mistakes with the target language as well as general good use of language for delayed language feedback later (see Unit 17).

4 AFTER THE ACTIVITY

Go through correct answers with reasons, if applicable, or get feedback on what has been discussed. Do correction of mistakes noted, if applicable.

If you fulfil your role for these four stages, you will surely achieve your aims for this part of the lesson.

TIPS FOR PRACTICE ACTIVITIES

1 Be varied in your choice of activities from lesson to lesson.

2 Do not consider 'traditional exercises' to be boring for the student – they will be only if you do nothing else; otherwise, they tend to be very popular.

3 Do not spend too much of your time preparing original material, especially if you are only going to use it one time.

4 If you are using an activity from a book, check carefully for yourself how it is going to work, what instructions you will need to give, etc.

5 If it is an activity with right and wrong answers, make sure you know what the answers are and the reasons for them.

6 Leave sufficient time for the activity to be done properly.

7 Leave sufficient time to go through answers / get feedback.

8 Do further practice another day as review – you must recycle your input and not treat pieces of language as something you 'do' in a single lesson.

Summary

▶ Covering meaning, form and pronunciation is not enough if students do not get any opportunity to use the language and practise it.

▶ Practice activities need to be carefully selected, and properly set up with instructions and examples.

▶ Ideally, practice will involve more than one type and include something which is communicative.

▶ Teachers should familiarize themselves with the activity first, and with why the answers are what they are.

▶ They should monitor the practice carefully and leave time to get feedback.

▶ They should not participate in the activity.

▶ Correction of mistakes and looking at emerging language is essential.

▶ The language being used in the practice may be controlled, or freer allowing for other language to be used.

▶ Practice activities should be as relevant and interesting as possible.

12 Receptive skills 1: reading

The receptive skills of reading and listening (compare with the productive skills of speaking and writing) require an understanding of the text (*text* here referring to both reading text and recording) but also some related language work or other productive tasks before or after the text. Therefore, there will be a great deal of overlap when discussing the four skills for the very reason that they are very rarely focused on in isolation in the classroom. However, each of these four units will have a primary focus, and this one is reading.

TASK

Here are some questions for you to think about before you read any further. Make some notes.

Why do I ask you to do this? You may think it is easier just to skip the questions and read the rest of the unit. Well, the analogy with the classroom is that as teachers we don't just 'give a lecture' but we try to involve our students in the learning process; to make them work. In any learning process, a student is more likely to remember something in the future if they have had an active part in the learning process. That is why this book includes some tasks for you to do, just as, when you teach, you will ask your students to do a task before you go through it with them.

So, look at these ten questions:

1 **Think about your own schooldays – How much did you enjoy or not enjoy reading lessons (in any subject)? Why? What was the role of the teacher in these lessons?**

2 **Is reading aloud a reading lesson?**

3 **Is a reading lesson going to be boring? What can prevent potential boredom?**

4 **What different types of reading skill can you think of? What should we focus on in the classroom?**

5 **In an ESL class, what do you think a reading lesson might consist of?**

6 **Should students be given tasks before or after they read the text? Why?**

7 Do you think it is necessary or desirable for your students to understand all the vocabulary in a text? If not, how do you decide what they need to know?

8 Is a reading lesson always going to have a grammar focus (refer to Unit 5)?

9 How will you find texts to use in your lessons? What factors affect the selection of texts?

10 Could one text be used at two quite different levels? If so, how?

One other task. Please go and find a reading text – maybe something from a newspaper or magazine, or a brochure, or a TV guide ... anything at all as long as it is not too lengthy, and I will use the text below.

Schooldays

They say that schooldays are the happiest days of your life. Well, they weren't for me! I enjoyed very little of my time at school and was glad to leave. My college days, however, were much more fun and the subjects I was studying were the ones I wanted to study!

At school, I used to have a one-hour bus ride each day there and back. We started school at 9 o'clock and finished at 3.45. There were some lessons that I really hated – mostly the 'practical' classes like Woodwork because I am hopeless at that sort of thing. I was useless at Art, too. Other kids used to have fun trying to guess what it was I had drawn. No, I was good at sitting behind my desk and listening to the teacher and making notes – English, History, Geography, etc. Days when I had Woodwork, or Art, or Physical Education – those were the days I hated, the days that most other kids loved!

My teachers were a mixed bunch as well. Those that were good were very good, and those that were bad were very bad. Then there were the student teachers! The kids always gave them a really rough ride and it made you wonder why anyone would want to go into a class of 40 loud and misbehaving kids and try and teach them!

Thinking back, I'm not sure I learnt too much that was to be useful in my life. Some of it was interesting for sure, but I wish I had been taught more about the practical things in life – how to deal with interviews, filling in application forms, finance management – rather than trying to figure out what x equalled in some fancy equation.

The strange thing is, I always wanted to be a teacher myself. I had the ambition of starting off in the classroom and ending up as a school principal – of being a popular, successful, respected teacher. Well, it never happened and I don't regret it. Teachers nowadays have too much paper work to do, too many discipline issues to deal with. That's not for me. These days my ambitions are different and more realistic.

Back to the task ...

1 THE ROLE OF THE TEACHER

I can only remember one approach to reading lessons, whether in French or in English. The teacher would ask us to read a set number of pages either in silence, or taking it in turns to read aloud. This would be followed by questions, done individually, and checking of answers. The teacher's role was minimal, and more often than not he would use the time to mark homework, etc.! I did not enjoy these lessons. In particular I remember one English Literature teacher whose sole approach throughout the school year was to set us pages to read in the lesson – there weren't even any tasks to focus on, and certainly no communication between students or between students and teacher. It was thoroughly demoralizing. Talking to many trainees over the years, I discovered that a large majority have had similar experiences. Those few that had had positive experiences invariably referred to the role of the teacher in making the lesson interesting, even fun.

2 IS READING ALOUD A LESSON?

It may be in part, but the actual reading aloud focuses on pronunciation and not on comprehension. Unless your students are advanced, they are going to struggle with such a task, and other students may have trouble understanding. There is the possibility of some students feeling pressured – either as they are reading or as they await 'their turn'. So please don't ask students to do this if your aim concerns reading comprehension. They may (if you are very lucky) read well, but are they 'listening' to what they are saying?

3 IS A READING LESSON BORING?

Of course, there is real potential for boredom. Maybe the topic is dull, irrelevant, or too difficult. Maybe there seems no point to the lesson. Maybe there is no communication, no interest. So, yes, such a lesson could well be very boring but it shouldn't be, not if the teacher stages the lesson appropriately. It is the teacher's responsibility to keep interest high.

4 DIFFERENT TYPES OF READING SKILL

You may be rushing out of your home one day and there's a newspaper on the table and you see a headline which attracts your interest ... but you must hurry to catch your train, you have just 30 seconds. So you quickly look at the story to see what it's about, to get the gist. You are not concerned at this stage with detail, and you are not looking for particular information. You just want to know what the story is about. This is **skim** reading, or reading for gist. It implies reading quickly. It is something we do a lot.

Maybe you are looking at a train timetable. You need to know what time your train departs and where from. Or maybe you are searching for ticket prices and journey length. You have a timetable and information booklet, but it contains a huge amount of information which is of no use to you whatsoever. So, when you are reading you can – and should – disregard this information and look for what you need as quickly as possible. This is **scan** reading, or reading for particular information. This also is something we do a lot.

As you settle down to read a good book, or to study a contract you must sign, or maybe an article about a film star you like, you will not be in a hurry. Far from it, you need, or want to, read carefully ... detail is important. You need to understand what you are reading. This is **intensive** reading, or reading for detail. And yes, we do this a lot, too!

We should, therefore, provide tasks which require a combination of all these different skills, not necessarily in a single lesson, but over a period. How this can be done, we shall see next.

5 AN APPROACH TO A READING LESSON

There are many different approaches to a reading lesson, or part of a lesson. Here we will look at just one – a fairly standard approach, commonly used by teachers and in course books. Have the text you selected earlier handy for this, and also refer to the one above ('Schooldays'). What we will concentrate on here are **stages** and **aims of stages**, and this will further prepare us for Unit 18.

Here, then, is a possible approach:

Stage 1

Check understanding of 'essential' vocabulary (see Question 7 for more on this). Don't spend too long on this.

Aim: For students to understand the meaning of words essential to the completion of set tasks.

Stage 2

Establish interest in the topic. In any lesson, but especially a skills-based lesson, this is an absolutely crucial stage. This is where the skills of the teacher are contributing to stopping this from becoming a boring 'read this' lesson. What you need to do here is to get the students interested in the topic, to make them want to read the text. This shouldn't take up too much of your lesson, but nor should it be a 10-second effort along the lines of 'Did you like school?' 'Yes / No' and on to the text! Looking at the text above on Schooldays, and a lesson for intermediate students, you might have your students discussing their likes and dislikes from their time at school; or describing their typical day; or remembering different subjects studied; or teachers they remember and why.

With other text types this stage might involve **prediction** (e.g. from a newspaper headline, or from words in the text, or from a picture accompanying the text); **contextualization** (e.g. using pictures to set the scene of the topic); or **building interest** (e.g. describing an almost impossible scenario and then say 'Well, it really happened and we're going to read about it'; or sound effects from a story – this can be combined with prediction).

More often than not, this stage involves either some personalized discussion based on the topic, or prediction, but it depends on the text and the level of the class you are teaching. Using a basic text on holidays for a low-level class, you might just ask them to list as many names of countries as they can think of. But whatever you do, you are working to create interest in the text that is to follow.

Look at the text you chose. How would you create interest for whatever level you think you might use it with?

Aim: To generate students' interest in the topic of the text.

The two stages so far have merely prepared your students for the reading task. What follows will depend on a number of factors, but usually a combination of two (maybe three) different tasks based on the text will provide the main focus of the lesson.

Stage 3

If you set two different reading tasks then you should give the easier task first, to build confidence. This would be a task which requires either skim or scan reading. A task to encourage skim reading would be any that focuses on the gist, the overall theme, of the text. A task to encourage scan reading would be one that requires the students to find specific information in the text (names, numbers, places, prices, etc.) without having to read carefully or understand in detail. So, with 'Schooldays' a scan reading task might include questions such as:

Did he start school before or after 8.30 a.m.?

Did he love or hate Woodwork, Art, and Physical Education?

When he was younger, what job did he hope to have?

None of these questions requires anything more than 'pulling out information' from the text, just as you have to 'pull out' the time of your train from a timetable. Consequently, the teacher should impose a fairly strict time limit for the completion of the task to encourage 'quick reading' (which is what scan reading involves). If the teacher allows five minutes to find the answers to those questions, then the students will read slowly and carefully, and be concerned about understanding everything they read.

Scan reading tasks could include multiple choice / true or false / matching pictures with sentences. Revising the first question above, you could ask 'He started school at (a) 8.00 (b) 8.30 (c) 9.00 (d) 9.30'. Or 'He started school at 9.00 – true or false?' Or, use four clocks showing different times – a visual multiple choice.

What scan reading tasks could you use for your selected text? Try to think of three or four different questions, and at least two different question types.

Aim: For students to have practice in scan reading skills.

Stage 4

Now you can move on to providing a task(s) that require more detailed reading. Any of the question types mentioned already could also be used here, but this time requiring understanding – and this could be linked to the vocabulary covered in Stage 1. To clarify this, look at these questions for 'Schooldays'.

Was he good at Art? (No, he was *useless* at it.)

Were all his teachers of the same standard? (No, they were a *mixed bunch*.)

Did student teachers have an easy time in class? (No, they were given a *rough ride*.)

Does he still want to be a teacher? (No, interpretation of final paragraph.)

These are just some possible questions. The first three demand understanding of essential vocabulary: *useless, mixed bunch,* to be given a *rough ride.* To answer the questions the students must understand the meanings – so these would be words to check in Stage 1. The final question requires more of a general understanding of the final paragraph. 'Why?' questions are also good for this kind of reading. And another possible interpretation question could be 'Do you think he liked Metalwork at school?' No, because he didn't like practical subjects – the answer is implied but not stated.

This kind of task, then, needs careful reading and greater understanding – but not of everything (see Question 7).

It is important, though, not to just give a series of questions every time – you should vary the types of questions that you ask. The nature of the text may suggest a certain type of task. For example, matching headlines from newspapers with stories would be intensive reading. One possibility with much lower levels is matching meaning with pictures.

This stage obviously needs more time, and students should be allowed to work together and help each other – the task should be communicative, not a test.

In terms of true / false or multiple-choice type questions, however, it is very important that the teacher does not just give / elicit the answers, but asks for reasons why. Otherwise, an answer could be a guess with no understanding.

What intensive reading task could you set for your chosen text?

Aim: For students to have practice in intensive reading.

Stage 5

This is very much an optional stage, but it is nice to finish such a lesson with something communicative. So, any of the suggestions made for Stage 2 could be expanded and used here as a class speaking activity. Anything relating to education, schooling, teaching, or even ambitions would be an appropriate topic for a speaking activity (see Unit 14 for more on speaking). If you were continuing with the same class in the next lesson you might use this reading text as a springboard for some language work (e.g. *I wish* + past perfect from the text), or for further skills work (e.g. some listening on the same topic, or writing). What you do will depend on time, but try to have something as a follow-up to your reading activity.

What speaking activity could you provide for your students based on the text you have selected?

Aim (for example):	For students to describe and discuss their own schooldays in a free-speaking activity.

You now have a 'sandwich effect' – the main part of the lesson (reading skills) is sandwiched between other activities (generating interest / vocabulary and speaking). This makes the 'heavy' part of the lesson more digestible and far less boring than the 'read this' approach which so many of us experienced at school.

Main lesson aim:	For students to have practice in scan and intensive reading skills.
Secondary aim:	For students to have practice describing and discussing school experiences in a free-speaking activity.

So, what would you do if you only had this class for one lesson and the reading was taking longer than anticipated. Would you (a) skip the last part of the reading and go on to the Speaking, or (b) continue and finish the reading and drop the speaking?

Faced with that choice, go for (b). The reading is the main part of the lesson and teachers should try to achieve their main aims. If there is no time for the speaking in this lesson, it doesn't matter. Failure to complete all you planned is not a sign of a failed lesson if you have still achieved your main aims.

Once again it needs to be stressed that this is only one of many ways to approach a reading lesson – it is an effective and popular approach, but do not feel this is the only way!

6 Give task before or after text?

Give the tasks **before** handing out the texts. This gives the students a reason for reading – an aim. If you let them read it, before handing out the task, they will just have to read it all over again. And the first time, they will read carefully and try (and want) to understand every single word! This would not be skim or scan reading, and it would be pointless anyway with no task.

7 Which lexis?

We have already established the need to deal only with those words which will be needed for the completion of the tasks. In the 'Schooldays' text, three words were selected, but words such as *misbehaving*, *fancy* (equation), and *ambition* did not have to be understood in order to complete the tasks. If you check too many words, you won't have enough time for the reading part of your lesson, and your main aims will be affected. Having said that, your Stage 5 could be lexis-based, maybe guessing meaning from context, possibly using multiple choice. It is good to focus on lexis after as well as before a reading / listening task.

8 Reading and grammar

Reading texts may or may not lead in to 'grammar', as we saw in Unit 5 but there is nothing wrong in focusing primarily on skills work along with vocabulary.

9/10 Selection of texts

If you are using a course book, this will have a rich supply of texts and tasks, though you may need or want to adapt the tasks to make them appropriate for whom you are teaching. Otherwise, use authentic texts (see Unit 22) and create appropriate tasks. One text could be used for different levels – the degree of difficulty will depend on what you ask your students to do with the text. Of course, this is not to say that any text can be used with any level but there is an element of adaptability possible to allow one text to be used with, say, two different levels. Apart from the level, your choice should be influenced by suitability (choice of topic, consideration of cultural issues, etc.), and interest (is this something which will be useful? or interesting? or maybe both?).

TIPS

1 **Select texts which will be interesting, relevant and suitable.**

2 **Provide tasks which will be appropriate for the level and the students.**

3 **Stage the lesson so that you establish interest and give a variety of tasks.**

4 **If possible, conclude with a follow-up activity based on the text.**

5 **Remember that the main aims relate to the reading task(s).**

6 **Give the tasks before the text.**

7 **Give an approximate time limit which is appropriate for the task / reading skill.**

8 **Check answers / reasons for answers.**

9 **Go on to some language work from the text (optional).**

10 Don't ask students to read the text aloud when the aim is comprehension.

11 Be encouraging and supportive – try to stop students worrying about what every single word means! At the start, only check the meaning of those words they really need to know.

12 Make sure your tasks match the type of Reading skill that you are focusing on.

Summary

All of this is very different from the experience I had of 'Read pages 22–42 and then I'll give you some questions to answer individually'. The approach described above is more communicative, more meaningful, more interesting, more useful. It is important to 'package' a receptive skills lesson this way in order for this to be so. We will continue to focus on receptive skills in the next unit.

13 Receptive skills 2: listening

Listening (by which I mean students listening to a recording – usually a CD, but perhaps a DVD – not listening to the teacher or each other talking) is one of the hardest activities for most students. Like reading, it is a receptive skill, but it is usually much more difficult than reading. Why is this? We'll come back to this question later.

TASK 1

In the previous unit I described a possible approach to a reading lesson, and we also looked at different reading skills. Can you remember now, without looking back, what skim and scan reading skills are, and what intensive reading skills are? And can you remember the stages described?

The stages were, in broad terms, as follows:

1 **Check the meaning of any vocabulary essential to the completion of the tasks. Don't spend too long on this.**

2 **Create interest in the topic of the text so that students actually want to read the text.**

3 **Set two or three different tasks which give practice of different reading skills.**

4 **If possible, have some follow-up activity based on the topic. Or, go on to some language work from the text.**

The skills described were:

▶ **skim** – quick reading for gist
▶ **scan** – quick reading to pick out certain information
▶ **intensive** – careful reading for detail/understanding

TASK 2

1 **How might you stage a listening skills lesson?**

2 **What different listening skills can you think of?**

Why listening is difficult

First, let us go back to the question of why listening is difficult for most students.

Within the classroom environment, students become used to the voice, accent, or dialect of their regular teacher(s). Furthermore, the teacher grades her language and perhaps speaks just a little slower than is usual. The teacher constantly uses gestures, and will check understanding. A student can interrupt and ask for repetition or clarification but with a recording, none of these factors are present.

A natural-sounding recording will usually consist of two or more speakers using ungraded language. Their voices, accents, and maybe dialects will be new to your students. These 'new' voices often come as a shock first time round. Often, too, the conversation is, or seems, fast. There is no body language and there are no gestures to help understanding. Students cannot ask the voices to slow down, or clarify ... the recording starts and continues. There is no control – at least, not on the students' part in a lesson. Compare this with a reading. Students have some control over how fast or slowly they read (though they may have been given a time limit). They have to contend with new language, as they do with a recording, but they don't have the problem of accents and speed. They can quickly re-read a line that they have not understood, but they cannot rewind the recording. With a reading, then, students have some control. With a listening they have none. Add to this the fact that they will be trying to answer questions as they listen and the obvious result is pressure.

STAGING A LISTENING SKILLS LESSON

As teachers, of course, we must be aware of these difficulties and try to help our students in every way we can. Just as with a reading, we shouldn't just go in and say 'Read pages 20–5 then I'll give you some questions', so we shouldn't just go in, play a recording, and hand out questions. We have to stage the lesson. The first part of Task 2 asked you to consider how this might be done. Well, the simple answer is that a listening lesson could be (but doesn't have to be) staged in a similar way to the reading stages described in Unit 12. If we take an example of a recording about two people discussing a film they saw on TV, the lesson could go as follows:

Stages 1–5

1 Pre-teach lexis essential for the completion of tasks (as per reading).

2 Establish interest in the topic (as per reading) – maybe talking about films recently seen, stars they particularly like, identifying actors in photos, etc. Another possibility is **prediction**. You might, for example, show some pictures in the book from the listening and ask students to predict what they think the recording will be about.

3 A **listening for gist** task (e.g. 'What are they talking about?' or 'Did they like the film they saw?');

    or

    Listening for **specific information** (e.g. 'How many people are talking?' / 'Where did they see the film?' / 'Which actors were in it?').

    Either of these tasks would provide a gentler introduction to the recording, with relatively easy questions to build confidence and get students used to the voices and speed, etc. Of course, the precise type of questions will depend on the recording and the level of your class.

4 **Listening for detail** (as reading for detail) – maybe asking how you know they liked or didn't like the film (requiring identification and understanding of adjectives).

5 A follow-up activity based on the topic. This could include listing and talking about the types of film that they like, favourite actors, writing a review of a recently seen film, etc. With a low-level class this could be adapted so that students give a mark out of ten for different types of film (e.g. Western) identified in photos;

    or

    using the recording to focus on a specific language point in the recording (as for a Reading text).

By staging the lesson in this way we are 'sandwiching' the listening as we did with the reading. In other words, we prepare the students for what is to come, and we try and create interest so that they end up wanting to listen.

PROBLEMS OF 'REAL-LIFE' LISTENING

In order to genuinely improve our students' listening ability we need to focus on specific skills, and for the majority of teachers around the world who are teaching in countries where English is not the first language spoken, students' exposure to listening in English outside the classroom will be very limited.

So let's consider some examples of 'real-life' listening:

▶ listening to announcements at a bus station / airport, etc. (in an English-speaking country)
▶ face-to-face conversation
▶ speaking on the telephone
▶ watching TV (perhaps with subtitles)

For someone standing at a station wanting to catch a train to Edinburgh, there are different ways to seek the required information (time of train, platform number, etc.). One is to read the monitors that display the information. Another is to listen for **announcements**. Now, you don't have to be a visitor from another country to find it very difficult to understand announcements at public places. The sound is often distorted, the accent or dialect may be difficult to understand, the delivery may be fast, there is a lot of background noise, and you can't stop and ask for the person to repeat any information. On the other hand, you do usually have the visual back-up. Announcements are often repeated, and you can always ask someone for assistance.

In order to help our students improve their listening skills, we need to be aware of, and to acknowledge, the specific difficulties they might have with a certain type of listening; but we also need to direct students to the type of help they can get.

With this kind of listening the most important skill is 'listening for and extracting specific information' (times, numbers, etc.) – the equivalent of scan reading. Therefore, if we can provide an authentic-sounding recording of a station announcement, then we can provide a task which replicates real life, even if we can't replicate the exact conditions.

Face-to-face conversation has many difficulties in common with the announcements – fast delivery, different accents or dialects, background noise, having to participate in the conversation rather than 'just' listening. However, the other person's gestures and body language will help; you can ask for repetition, clarification and for the person to speak more slowly; and the context of the conversation will be established (whereas on a recording you may not have any idea what the conversation will be about until the CD is played!).

The skills are likely to be different from those needed for announcements, though. Normally, in face-to-face conversation, you are focusing on gist, or detail. Maybe the person is giving directions, or telling you what you could do over the weekend, or maybe they are telling you their impressions of a film they saw. You can have 'face-to-face' listening in the classroom – role plays. And you can provide appropriate tasks as well.

Speaking on the telephone is really difficult and stressful for most students. For a start there are no gestures to help. There is the possibility of distorted sound as well as different accents and dialects. There is specific telephone language ('Please hold the line', etc.) to deal with. The problem of 'turn taking' can be difficult (when is it your 'turn' to speak?). Dealing with 'menus' can frustrate anyone ('if you want X press 4, if you want Y press 5', etc.). Also, a student may have difficulty making himself understood. If the student is making the call, he might be able to prepare questions or check what information he needs to find, in advance. In any case, he can ask for repetition – unless he's listening to a machine. If he is, there is nothing he can do but repeat the process and listen all over again (something I have had to do more than once myself). As teachers, we can help by teaching students' telephone language and procedure, and by giving them a variety of tasks – including listening for gist, specific information, and detailed understanding; taking a message; making notes; and leaving a message on an answering machine. Best of all, maybe, is to give them a real task to do which involves them calling someone, maybe to get information.

Watching TV is much less pressurized, but the language tends to be fast and often colloquial. It is obviously not graded in any way, and as such can be very difficult to understand, but the visuals are a huge help. If the programme has been recorded, then students can rewind and listen again, and having subtitles can help a lot. All kinds of listening skills are required, but detail is particularly important. Thus, getting students to watch and listen to a news broadcast is very valuable, and you can provide varied tasks to help improve the students' listening ability.

These examples show the importance of recognizing the factors that help and hinder students in different kinds of listening, and some of the various skills that they need to improve. Therefore, we need to select types of recordings and types of tasks which will be relevant and useful as well as interesting. These recordings will normally come from the course book you will be using, but you can add authentic ones as well. As we have already seen, texts and recordings can also be used as a springboard for language focus work.

As for the issue of different dialects (e.g. south of England vs. north of England) or different varieties (e.g. American vs. British), it is a good thing for students to be exposed to as many types as possible – though it is often very difficult for them!

By breaking the lesson into stages, choosing appropriate material and tasks, you will be decreasing the stress levels of the students. There are other things you can do as well.

TIPS (TO HELP THE STUDENTS)

1 **Try to place the machine (i.e. CD player) as close as you can to your students (or have them move close to it). If you have a form of audio streaming in your class, then the sound quality will usually be much better.**

2 **Maybe play a few seconds first, to check they can hear the recording.**

3 **Give out the task before they listen and give them time to read it.**

4 **Make the first task relatively straightforward to give them confidence.**

5 **Reassure the students – tell them not to worry if they find it difficult at first, that you'll play it again; that they don't need to understand everything, etc.**

6 **Let them discuss their answers after the first play. Communication is important – it's not a test.**

7 **Nearly always you should play the recording a second time (occasionally three times if it is not too long).**

8 **Sometimes, it is appropriate to play the recording and 'pause' at crucial moments, isolating the answers. This usually helps a lot.**

9 **Go through the reasons for the answers.**

10 **Have a copy of the audio script to hand so you can clarify important dialogue in case students are unclear about something.**

It is not only students that can find listening lessons stressful, so can teachers. As with any kind of lesson using technology, things can go wrong – and they do!

TIPS (TO HELP THE TEACHER)

1 Check there is an appropriate machine (i.e. CD player) in your room. If not, find out where you can get one.

2 Check you know how to use it.

3 Get the audio material you need well in advance of the lesson – if you leave it to the last moment and you can't find it, you will have a problem.

4 Check the correct CD is in the box – sometimes teachers put the wrong one back.

5 Listen to the recording before the lesson – check it is there and that it is audible.

6 Make sure you know which recording you are going to listen to. Check the recording number and check that you can find it. Don't leave this until the lesson has started. It adds to your stress and it gives a poor impression to the students.

7 Have a copy of the audio script just in case you need it.

8 Know what you will do if something goes wrong.

9 Never trust any technology!

If you have access to a DVD player or are able to show a YouTube clip, then you have the possibility of extending your listening into listening and watching. There are many specially made DVDs on the market which you can use. This does not mean a 'watching TV' lesson, it means staging the lesson as you would any other, having clear aims, appropriate tasks, etc. But with DVDs and YouTube you have something different.

Integrating the skills

So far, we have looked at reading and listening as almost separate entities but we have seen that there are considerable similarities in terms of types of task, types of skill, and typical lesson staging. If you look at typical course books, you will find that more often than not, reading and listening feature in a single lesson presentation. A reading activity about someone shopping for food might be followed by a listening activity on the same subject (or vice versa). A listening activity about a tourist visiting New York could be followed by a reading passage about life in this city. And so on.

We can go further than that. In the next two units we will look at the productive skills of speaking and writing. A truly integrated skills lesson (or, more likely, back-to-back lessons) might feature all four skills. Let's consider an elementary class doing a fully integrated skills lesson on the theme of holidays.

A possible lesson frame could be:

1 **Check essential lexis.**

2 **Establish interest in the topic (e.g. postcards from around the world).**

3 **Reading about a holiday in Australia (with a couple of tasks, maybe).**

4 **Listening with two people discussing a trip to Australia (again, a couple of tasks).**

5 **Writing – students write a postcard from one of the characters in the listening based on the information on the recording.**

6 **A speaking activity – maybe students rank favourite holiday destinations from 1 to 10.**

Obviously, each of these stages needs detail – and for stages **1** to **4** you can refer back to the relevant units. For stages **5** and **6** you should refer to the next two units. The principal point is that you shouldn't always treat these skills in isolation – in fact, you should rarely do so, for the simple reason that we don't in real life. We might watch something on TV and then talk about it. We might listen to a news story and then read about it in the next day's newspaper. We might write a letter or email to a friend and then read their reply. So, integrating skills work is important.

In addition, as mentioned in Unit 5, skills work can lead on to (or follow on from) language focus work (other than the checking of essential vocabulary). To focus on a particular piece of language from a text or recording is useful and relevant.

What must be stressed, then, is that there are no prescriptive lesson types. Of course, trainers, and books such as this one, and also all course books, will suggest approaches based on experience and research. New teachers usually appreciate such guidance early on, to have lesson 'patterns' to follow but as long as you have achievable and appropriate aims for your lesson, any lesson frame is possible. We have already seen in an earlier unit how a 'grammar' lesson might begin with free speaking. It may not fit the traditional image of a grammar lesson, but that does not matter. So, as your experience increases, have the confidence to vary your lesson patterns and approaches, to integrate more. Don't do it a particular way because 'that's how the book does it' if you do not think the 'book' way is appropriate for your class. Don't follow a suggested approach given in this book if you can think of a more suitable approach for your class. You know your students, I don't.

Summary

▶ Listening is a difficult skill for students, more so than reading.

▶ Teachers need to stage listening lessons in such a way as to reduce the difficulty.

▶ We should be aware of the specific problems that students might have with different types of listening – but also of the factors that help understanding.

▶ We should provide tasks which are relevant and interesting (though their relevance will be less in a non English-speaking country).

▶ Listening can, and should, be integrated with other skills and language work.

▶ Teachers should check the audio material and hardware well in advance.

▶ It is important for students to work together on tasks in order to make the activity less pressured. Don't play the recording and then immediately ask for answers to the task!

▶ Play the recording more than once and pause it, if appropriate.

▶ Use of DVD / YouTube, if available, also provides good practice of listening skills.

14 Productive skills 1: speaking

A school I worked at used to ask students on their first day to put in order what they most wanted to 'do' on their course, from a list including grammar, vocabulary, reading, listening, speaking, writing, and pronunciation. I would estimate that 90% put speaking as their number one choice. But what is speaking? Is it talking to the teacher? Is it talking to each other about a grammar task? Is it reading aloud? Is it spoken practice of language learnt? Or is it chatting? I wonder how many of the students completing that first day questionnaire knew what was meant by speaking. And is a speaking lesson / stage of a lesson one of the easiest for a teacher to set up? Or one of the hardest? In short, speaking as an activity in the classroom is much more complex than one might at first think.

TASK

Think about the following questions and make some notes before reading on.

1 **What's the difference between fluency and accuracy and which is more important?**

2 **What do you understand by 'speaking' in a lesson?**

3 **Do you think it is relatively easy for a teacher to set up a speaking activity? Why? Why not?**

4 **What's the point of doing speaking? It's not 'learning', so isn't it a waste of time?**

5 **What problems might occur in the execution of a student-speaking activity?**

6 **What do you think is the teacher's role before, during and after a speaking activity?**

7 **If the students are speaking, should the teacher correct their mistakes sometimes? Never? Always?**

8 **What kinds of speaking activity could you do in a lesson?**

1 Fluency vs. accuracy

In simple terms, **fluency** is the ability to talk fairly freely, without too much stopping or hesitating – to 'keep going'. More than that, it also requires that the listener understands what is being said, so there must be intelligibility and meaning. With **accuracy** the emphasis is on 'correct English' – the right grammar, the right vocabulary.

Can you have one without the other? Yes, definitely. I have taught many students who were very fluent but not very accurate. They could talk a lot and I could understand them but their speech was littered with errors. On the other hand, some students focus their minds so much on being accurate that they lose their fluency. Just a few weeks before writing this, I taught a student who was obsessed by accuracy. He was of an intermediate level and had a pretty good range of language, but he was simply unable – or maybe unwilling – to just talk. He would begin a sentence and ask me or himself grammatical questions about how to continue the sentence. Time and time again I said that I could not answer him because I did not know what he was trying to say. For example, he might say 'Yesterday I ... what's the word?' Well, how could I know? He was so determined to construct his sentences bit by bit that the listener could rarely understand what he was trying to say.

So, is one more important than the other? The easy answer is that they are equally important but to be honest, I don't think they are. It also depends on who you are teaching. If you are teaching a high-level student who is about to take an exam to enter college, accuracy is very important indeed. However, in most ESL exams the accuracy is tested most in a 'grammar' part of the test with gap-fills, multiple choice, etc. In the speaking part of the exam the emphasis is as much on fluency as it is on accuracy but accuracy is important.

If you are teaching beginners, or other very low levels, you cannot possibly expect fluency. Here, you really do have to help them build their language accuracy bit by bit until they reach the stage when they can speak more fluently.

With a reasonably high-level student who does not need to prepare for an exam, and especially if they are living in or are going to visit an English-speaking country, then I would argue that fluency is much more important. Does it really matter if they make the odd mistake when asking someone in the street for directions? Does it really matter if they use the past simple instead of the present perfect when telling an English-speaking friend about their last vacation? No, it does not – though some students think it does, as I said earlier. What is far more important is that they can make themselves understood, and can talk relatively fluently but even if their level is not high, the ability to be understood is greater than the need for accuracy in the situations just described. For this to be possible, we as teachers need to give our students confidence when speaking and not to be obsessed with constant correction (see Unit 16 for more on correction). We need to make it clear to our students exactly why we want them to just speak for 20 minutes in a lesson. The accuracy-fixated student I described earlier thought speaking was 'boring' – 'I want to do grammar'. Unfortunately, as accurate as his English sometimes was, he had no fluency and he drove everyone crazy as we waited for him to finish a sentence. Fluency is very important.

2 What is speaking in a lesson?

First, let me say what speaking is not. It is not reading aloud (**pronunciation**). It is not reading the answer to a grammar question (**accuracy**). It is not reading the answer to a reading / listening question (**comprehension**). In each of these cases the aims are not speaking-related.

In a lesson, speaking is one of two things. It could be a speaking activity designed to give practice of language just learnt or reviewed. Here the emphasis is as much on accuracy as it is on fluency and correction at some stage will be important. This type of speaking was covered in Unit 11. In this unit we are looking at the other type of activity – speaking designed to promote fluency. That said, if you are teaching a low-level class then fluency is not a realistic aim, so we will look later at how you can still give low-level classes speaking activities.

3 / 4 / 5 Practical difficulties

It sounds straightforward – just give them something to talk about. Unfortunately, at least with some classes, speaking stages can be the most difficult to execute successfully. There are many reasons for this:
▶ Teachers might get complacent and not plan this stage properly.
▶ Students may not see it as 'real learning' (as with the student I described before).

- The class may be very small.
- The class may be very big (making 'control' a problem).
- The class may (and probably will be) all from the same country – so they will end up speaking in their own language.
- They might perceive it as an 'exercise' that has to be finished as quickly as possible.
- They might not have sufficient language to do what you have asked them to do.

Let's look at each of these problems in turn:

NEED FOR PLANNING

We all do it. It's been a long day; we're tired; we don't have anything planned for the final 30 minutes, so we say 'OK, I want you to talk about food for the rest of the lesson'. If you'll pardon the pun, that's a recipe for disaster. Speaking must be planned properly and with clear aims. See Question 6 for much more on this.

'SPEAKING IS NOT REAL LEARNING'

No, they might not see it as 'real learning'. And, in fact, it's not learning; this is an important point. Learning a new language must include a high proportion of practice, of using the language. Students should not always be **learning** and teachers should not always be **teaching**. We saw in Unit 2 that the teacher has many roles to perform, and the teaching of language is only one of these. Another is to set up opportunities for students to use the language they are learning, and fluency activities are one example. New and training students often complain after such an activity 'but I didn't teach them anything', to which I would reply 'No, exactly'. You must not feel that you are not doing your job if you are not constantly teaching them. If you do, there will be severe overload.

As for the reluctant students, the school questionnaire I referred to at the start of this unit (and supported by my own experience over the last 30 plus years) confirmed that speaking for fluency is a very high priority for most students, so convincing them of its worth is rarely a problem – unless you do too much of it. However, when you do have a student or class that needs convincing, tell them why you're asking them to do it. Tell them about accuracy vs. fluency. Tell them about the importance of using the language confidently. In other words, involve them in the teaching rationale.

PROBLEMS OF LARGE AND SMALL CLASSES

If you teach in the UK in winter you could well find yourself with a class of two, three or four students. This does not mean that you cannot do a speaking task. It does mean that it will be harder work for you setting it up and keeping it going, and harder work for them. It may also mean that the activity may be over quicker but this is all OK. You must not deny them the opportunity to speak because you don't think you have enough students. Similarly, if you have a very quiet class, don't give up.

In many contexts you might have classes of 20, 30 or 40 students, most likely monolingual. This is a much greater problem than the class of three. It is unrealistic to expect such a class not to use their own language for at least part of the time, and if it is a big class, you cannot properly monitor. You may even have a situation where the class becomes excessively noisy. So be realistic. If you have 30 Spanish-speaking students, they are certain to use Spanish as well as English at times. Remind them of the importance of using only English and encourage them to do so. Set up an activity with a clear purpose and a time limit. However, if you have your 30 Spanish students, and you are in Madrid and when class is over they have no need to speak English, the value of speaking activities is lessened. Motivation is lower compared with students who need to use their English outside school. You may, though, find that some of your 30 Spanish students (to continue with that example) need to speak English in their jobs, or they are going to do an exam. So do not abandon the idea of doing speaking activities, because if you do, you will not be providing the complete learning package.

STUDENTS' ATTITUDES

Students who do not understand, or who are not convinced by, doing speaking for fluency in the classroom, sometimes view such activities as they do a 'grammar exercise' – as a task to be finished as soon as possible. This can be frustrating for the teacher. You set up an interesting speaking activity designed for 20 minutes of conversation, and after two minutes one group proudly says 'We've finished'. It's this kind of student who will treat a 'Where did you last go on holiday?' question, with a one word answer 'Brazil', and not follow it up as anyone would in 'real' conversation with questions about Brazil. This is in sharp contrast with the class who will happily chat for half an hour and very reluctantly stop when the teacher says time is up. This is one of the big problems with this kind of lesson, it is so unpredictable. You just don't know how a class is going to respond to your speaking activity. If you want it to last 20 minutes, and it lasts two, you have a problem. For possible solutions – see Question 6.

If the teacher sets up a speaking activity which is beyond the students' language ability, then the teacher has either misjudged the level of the class, or she has failed to ensure that the students have the necessary language to complete the activity. It is a planning issue. This, too, relates to Question 6.

6 The teacher's role

Speaking is no different from any other kind of classroom activity – it needs planning and it needs proper execution. The role of the teacher is as important with speaking as it is with teaching grammar, but the role is very different. Remember what we said before – this type of activity is not 'teaching' or 'learning'. We are focusing here on speaking for fluency, rather than practice of specific language. With this in mind, we can consider the role of the teacher in three stages: before, during and after.

STAGE 1: BEFORE

In the previous two units we looked at listening and reading skills, and described typical lesson 'patterns'. In each, it was suggested that such a lesson could finish up with what was described as a 'follow-up activity based on the topic'. For example, a lesson where the main focus was a reading about Culture could end with a speaking activity on the same topic. A listening activity about Education could finish with students talking about the educational system in their countries (or, for a much lower level, ranking favourite subjects at school from 'favourite' to 'least favourite'), and so on. Typically, then, your speaking activity will fit in to a lesson structure naturally rather than just be 'thrown in' for no apparent reason – it will be part of the lesson package. Sometimes, however, teachers will give a speaking lesson (the entire lesson will be speaking). Such lessons might have a less obvious aim, and be harder to sustain, but all teachers do them from time to time. Sometimes, for example, you have a class that is tired and is in the mood for just 'chatting', or it is your perception that they would benefit from a 'relaxed' lesson with no pressures of language learning or practice. This is not uncommon, but you shouldn't over-do such lessons.

Before the lesson, then, know why you want your students to speak – what your aim is. In all likelihood, it will be part of a lesson containing other skills and/or language work and so the 'lesson fit' will be obvious not only to you but also to your students. Choose an activity (possibly from the course book) that is suitable for their level and interests, and that is appropriate in terms of the lesson fit and aims. Plan your instructions and class management. Anticipate any possible problems you might have, and that the students might have. If, for example, you would like pair work, what will you do if you get an odd number (usually two students can work as 'one')? How do you want the students sitting (if you have a choice)? Opposite each other? In a circle? Semicircle? In other words, plan how you will set up the activity.

That is before the lesson, but you also have a role before the activity itself. You should give very clear instructions, with an example of the activity if possible. The task should be clear (the students need to know exactly what you want them to talk about and why). You need to arrange the class how you want. If the activity involves role playing, the roles should be clear as should the purpose for speaking. And give an approximate time limit. If you emphasize that you want the students talking for ten minutes then they are more likely to speak at greater length. With much lower-level classes, give a specific task – in other words, avoid 'Talk about ...' instructions which require a lot of language. Instead, give them an achievable goal (e.g. ten jobs to rank according to which they would most like to do, and with a very brief reason why). If you say 'talk about jobs you would like to do' they won't have enough language to do so.

STAGE 2: DURING

You should remove yourself from the central position of the room because as long as you are there, the students will feel you are part of the activity and will try to keep you involved in it. By getting out of the way you are effectively saying 'get on with it'. With very small classes, turning on suitable background instrumental music can have a similar effect. With very small classes, the music can make it less intimidating for the students to speak. That's up to you. Some teachers like using music; others don't.

Once the activity is under way, monitor it as best you can (but it won't be easy if you have a very big class) to ensure everyone has understood, is speaking, is using mostly English, and doesn't have any problems. Also, you are there to ensure one or two students in a group don't dominate the activity, and that a group doesn't finish far too quickly. You are not monitoring in order to join in, and you are not monitoring to interrupt with error correction. If you do there will not be any fluency and you will not have achieved your aim. If you have planned and set up the activity properly, it should work well, but you always face the danger of accuracy-obsessed students who don't want to speak without constant correction, and of the very shy students who are not used to such activities in the classroom but these are problems for you to anticipate and be ready to deal with if they occur. We have discussed already the accuracy-obsessed student, but for the very shy one you could gently interrupt the group briefly and gesture for that student to say something (e.g. 'Sonoko, what do you think?'), and then walk away so as not to intimidate her. You can't, and shouldn't, do any more than this. It's all down to confidence. I remember teaching three Korean female students once who were out of their country for the first time ever. I was their teacher in a communication class – which was quite a challenge because they simply would not speak. They were shy and lacking in confidence. When learning English in Korea they just listened to the teacher giving explanations, and then did exercises. As a result, their accuracy was very good, but their fluency was non-existent. Three months later, after much gentle encouragement from the several teachers they had, you couldn't keep them quiet. Their confidence had grown, they had observed the communicative approach, and slowly had come out of their shells. So, never be discouraged by quiet students – help them, guide them, but don't put pressure on them.

STAGE 3: AFTER

Try to allow enough time to get some feedback from the class. For example, one group could tell another group what they decided / discovered / discussed, and vice versa. Or you could select certain students to give some feedback. It is nice to get some kind of feedback so that you can show your interest, as well as for the students to share some of what they have talked about. This needs only to be a few minutes.

7 When to correct?

Don't interrupt the speaking activity with correction because you will stop the flow and the students will not be able to improve their fluency. But some correction and other language work (e.g. praise of good language that you have heard) should take place after the activity has finished. See Unit 17 for details on this.

8 Types of speaking activities

Of course, it depends on the level and who is in your class. Avoid culturally-sensitive topics, and avoid politics and religion at all times! As you will see more, when you read Unit 22, you should not assume an activity is 'OK' just because it is in your course book. You have the responsibility to decide what is appropriate in every sense. Having said that, course books do provide a multitude of ideas for speaking, nearly always as part of a lesson 'package'. What you must do, as we saw earlier, is to set it up and make it work.

Beyond your course book, there are many speaking resource books on the market. Again, be confident to reject a suggestion if you feel it would be unsuitable for your class for any reason and be prepared to adapt ideas to make them more suitable, but do explore whatever resources are available in your place of work. Quite often, I come up with my own, very simple, ideas. That's the beauty of speaking stages; you don't actually need materials every time, and you can sometimes verbalize the task.

There are certain types of activity that tend to be very popular. Ranking has been mentioned before (putting items in a particular order). If Sport is your topic, students could rank sports from those they like most to those they like least; or from the most beneficial for the body to the least beneficial. If Food is your topic, you could again do favourite to least favourite; or most healthy to least healthy. If Travel is your topic, it could be most comfortable to least comfortable, and so on. The point of ranking is that there are no 'correct' answers, because it is designed to promote discussion. Higher levels can add reasons for their choices.

Sometimes, such activities may appear unrealistic or contrived, but the speaking skill involved is very real. Take the old favourite, the 'Balloon debate'. This is where students take on the identities of famous people travelling together in a hot air balloon which is overloaded. One person has to go over the side to lighten the load. The students, in their roles, argue who it should be and why. Hardly a realistic activity, but the skill of giving opinions and justifying them is very real indeed.

Debates can be organized, though only for high-level classes. Make sure the topic has obvious points on both sides and is not too controversial.

Students can prepare and carry out surveys / questionnaires. This involves finding out information and reporting back. If possible, let your students go beyond your own classroom, maybe to interview other students or staff or people on the street!

Describing visuals is another good area to explore, and can be a good way to allow students with imagination and sufficient language to extend their normal classroom speaking.

Role-plays can work with any levels. With lower levels, give them a realistic context (especially if in an English-speaking country) like shopping, and a realistic role (i.e. the customer, not the shop assistant).

Student talks are good for more advanced levels. Maybe, each day, one student could give a talk for about five to ten minutes on a subject of interest to them, and the other students can then ask questions. Make sure the students have had notice of this so they can prepare some notes.

Discussion on topics of interest, or maybe in the news, is a relaxed way to promote fluency, but make sure the students have something specific to talk about, and that you don't end up doing more speaking than them.

These are just a few ideas. Remember, use your course book for initial ideas, then supplementary materials. Don't expect fluency from very low-level classes – give them something much more controlled.

TIPS

1 **Plan the activity properly.**
2 **Know what you'll do if not everyone turns up and your hoped-for even numbers don't materialize.**
3 **Think in advance about issues of classroom management, especially if you have a very large class, rows of tables, etc.**
4 **You may have to 'justify' the activity to the class if you are teaching a monolingual class in a non English-speaking country.**
5 **Plan your instructions carefully so it is clear what the activity is, what students' 'roles' are, etc.**
6 **Give an idea of time so as to increase the likelihood of the activity lasting as long as you want it to! (e.g. 'You have ten minutes, so keep talking for that time.')**
7 **Get out of the way. If you remain the focal point in the class, they are likely to be more inhibited. With small classes, light background music can help, too. With very large classes, however, you might need to remain at the front in order to keep everything under control.**
8 **Make sure the activity is appropriate in terms of language required and topic choice.**

9 With much lower-level classes, do not expect fluency – provide a clear task.

10 Monitor the activity as best you can, but do not interrupt. Encourage quieter individuals or groups, though.

11 Try to allow enough time afterwards for some feedback to the activity.

12 Do some delayed language feedback (see Unit 17).

Remember that whereas some students want to do as much speaking as possible, others can be resistant to the idea of 'just chatting' and may need convincing of the worth of doing such an activity. Don't be afraid to do this. If you are teaching adults, as this book pre-supposes, then they should be treated as adults, and that includes explaining the rationale of what you are asking them to do if they seem sceptical.

Summary

▶ Fluency and accuracy are both important, but with speaking there is generally more emphasis on fluency – the ability to talk fairly freely without stopping or hesitating too much.

▶ The types of activities you carry out will depend on the size of the group and the level.

▶ Speaking activities need to be properly planned. Be aware of the size of your group and how this might affect your classroom management. Motivation for speaking may be higher for students in an English-speaking country because they need to use their English outside the classroom.

▶ Speaking activities often fit naturally into the structure of a lesson, as a follow-up activity to a reading task, for example. You might occasionally have a lesson that is exclusively speaking, but that is harder to sustain.

▶ During a speaking activity you should observe and monitor, and give gentle encouragement where necessary. The key is not to join in and not to correct during the activity.

▶ Always allow time after the activity for feedback and for some language feedback.

15 Productive skills 2: writing

Maybe this unit should be subtitled 'The forgotten skill' since less time appears to be spent on this lesson type than any other, except in exam or literacy classes.

With the receptive skills of reading and listening it was apparent that there were more similarities than differences. Most things we said about reading also applied to listening, and vice versa but the same is not true of the productive skills.

TASK 1

Answer these questions before reading on.

1 **How does writing differ from speaking as a productive skill?**
2 **What makes writing difficult for students? And what makes it easier than speaking?**
3 **Why teach writing?**

MOTIVATION FOR WRITING

For a start, many students need the writing skill much less than they need any of the others, and if they are studying General English in their own country then their interest in writing lessons may be minimal. Even if they are studying in an English-speaking country there is often limited value for them in doing writing unless they need it for their job, for an exam or their studies

If they write a postcard home, they will not be using English, for example. On the other hand, they might have to complete an application form in English. If they are working in an English-speaking country then they might need to do some kind of writing as part of their work. And in this age of social media, they are likely to be texting, tweeting, blogging and Facebooking on a regular basis.

If students are preparing for an exam, then writing is much more important because they will be tested in some way. Exams usually require students to write at least two different types of answer, e.g. discursive, descriptive, analytical, letters, etc.

You might be teaching students who have no writing skills at all, not even an awareness of the script and how to form it.

So with writing lessons more than most, the motivation is very varied. Some students will need, or will want, to do it, but for others, writing will be seen as a waste of time.

However, writing should never be totally neglected, and if it is an important part of the course you are teaching, it should be focused on extensively. It can be difficult to get students to write in class (or at home for homework), but as with any other kind of activity, the teacher can 'sell' it. The lesson staging can be such that the students are more inclined to write with at least some enthusiasm.

Written language is often more formal than spoken language. Of course, this is not always the case. Email style tends to be very informal, even more so than conversation at times.

A student studying in an English-speaking country might have to do many different types of writing including forms, phone messages, formal letters and CVs. In addition, students preparing for an exam will need to write compositions, including formal and informal letters, descriptions, discursive essays, graph interpretation, narratives, etc. These different types vary in their degree of formality, and each requires specific skills and language. It is this variety which makes writing much more difficult than speaking.

DIFFERENCES BETWEEN WRITING AND SPEAKING

With writing, the emphasis on **accuracy** is much greater than with speaking. For a start, the written form is visible and mistakes are seen. With speaking, students often make 'slips of the tongue' – they have said something wrong, but if they could hear a recording of what they said, they could correct the 'mistake' themselves. As we saw in the last unit, 'mistakes' when speaking are often not that important. Written tasks on the other hand often require accuracy (e.g. completing an application form) and formal language. Because they recognize this, many students feel under pressure when writing. However, when writing, students can proofread and self-correct and they can go more slowly and carefully than when they are speaking. It is an important skill we must teach our students – read what you have written.

Punctuation is another factor absent from speaking. Increasingly these days, one might question the importance of correct punctuation, but whereas one can accept that the correct use of colons or semicolons is not really so important, surely the correct use of capitalization and question marks, for example, does matter. It certainly does matter in an exam.

Spelling may also cause problems, something which mother-tongue speakers have difficulty with, never mind learners from another country. Again, people differ in their views of the importance of correct spelling, but the fact remains that, as teachers, we have to recognize what is 'correct' writing, and what is 'incorrect'. If we cannot recognize a mistake, then we cannot correct it.

With writing, students do not have to concern themselves with aspects of pronunciation, or being fluent. Those students I mentioned in the last unit who are much more interested in accuracy than fluency, are often very good when writing. It is very common to find students who have had accuracy-based language learning, writing extremely well and accurately, but struggling to speak more than a sentence or two.

Writing tends to be more economical in its use of the language. There are no 'hesitators' ('mmm', 'er', 'well', etc.) that litter our conversation. Written language is direct and efficient.

Another difference between writing and speaking is that, when writing, students cannot express themselves visually. There is no 'body language' or gestures to aid understanding. With writing, students rely exclusively on the language itself.

Speaking is naturally acquired and students in an English-speaking country are immersed in the language all the time but writing is something which has to be taught. What's more, writing can be a lonely skill – we speak to other people but we write individually. All of this makes writing harder than speaking.

Writing skills

What students need is to have specific writing skills developed. It's not enough for the teacher to say 'OK, write about a country you like'. This is writing for the sake of writing, but the teacher isn't 'doing anything'. For the students' writing to improve, they need to have help in particular areas. So let's consider three different types of writing that a student might do in the classroom – a postcard, a letter, and a discursive essay. We have already said that it is rare for a student to write a postcard in English if they are sending it to their own country, but once they return home they might send postcards back to friends met when they were learning English. We will take a letter of application for a job as an example of letter writing. As for the discursive essay, (one which argues for and against a particular topic) we will assume this is for an exam class who will need to write this kind of essay.

Writing a postcard (elementary level) requires the writer to use an informal writing style, use simple linkers (e.g. but rather than on the other hand), know how to begin and end a postcard, and, arguably, to spell correctly. The writer also needs to know the type of subjects covered in a postcard (e.g. weather) and the layout including which side the name and address are written.

TASK 2

What different skills are required to successfully complete a letter of application (intermediate)?

Before looking at this task, let's consider some of the general skills required when writing. We have already mentioned **punctuation**, **spelling**, and **style of language**. To these we can add correct **structure**, correct **layout** (on a letter), **linking expressions** (*on the other hand*, *nevertheless*, *firstly*, etc.), **paragraphing**, **organizing**, **appropriate vocabulary**, language of **comparison** and **contrast** (e.g. *similarly*, *conversely*, *in conclusion*), **precis writing** (taking messages on the phone we need to summarize the main points), and **presentation** (e.g. presenting a neatly and correctly filled-in form). Obviously, the skills required will vary according to the task being set and the level being taught. We saw with the postcard writing at elementary level that the skills required are fairly basic. This is not the case with the other types of writing mentioned.

Key to Task 2

For the letter of application, students will need to know how to correctly lay out the letter – where to put their address, their name, the recipient's address, etc. Layout conventions vary and change from time to time, but there are basic layouts which can be taught. Students also need to know about punctuation and capitalization. They need to know how to organize the letter, and that each paragraph should have a specific purpose. They need to know how to be economical with their language so as to keep the letter to a reasonable length. They need to know about the style of language to use (formal), and about how to use linking words and deconstructed forms (not *I'm* but *I am*).

One way of helping students to recognize an appropriate style of language for letters is to present a selection of language from two different letters – one formal and one informal. So, phrases like 'Dear Sir', 'Dear Marc', 'I'd like to have this job', 'I would like to apply for the position ...' are all mixed together, and students have to separate the formal from the informal. Maybe the different examples could be from one complete letter so students can then put the letter together and have a model of a complete letter.

For the discursive essay, students will need to know spelling, punctuation, language of contrast and comparison, language of summing up, vocabulary related to the topic, how to organize, how to develop and support ideas, and how to be concise.

If we take, for example, the language of contrast and comparison (including *while*, *whereas*, *despite*, etc.), the teacher could present these expressions in sentences that are incorrect in some way, and the students try to correct them.

To practise the skill of organization, the teacher could present a complete, but jumbled up, letter and ask the students to put the paragraphs in the correct order.

By knowing which skills different writing tasks require, the teacher will be better able to help her students with their writing.

One way to stage a writing lesson

As with speaking, we can distinguish between a lesson that includes writing, and one which is exclusively writing.

We saw in previous units that skills work is not usually dealt with in isolation, and when this is the case it is the role of the teacher to 'package' the lesson in a way which is appropriate for the level, the students, and the aims of the lesson. As an example of this, we shall go back to the earlier examples of writing a postcard (elementary class), and writing a letter of application for a job (intermediate level). We shall assume a lesson of about 60 minutes and look at possible lesson packages to include these writing activities.

For the 'postcard lesson' we could follow this procedure – one of many variations possible.

1 Show real postcards from different countries and students try to guess the countries.

    Aim: For students to become interested in theme of lesson.   5 mins

2 **Stick six completed postcards around the room (writing side on display) and give students a reading task (e.g. they have a form to fill in showing the countries each writer is in, who they are writing to, and if they seem happy or unhappy in this place). Teacher then gets feedback.**

   Aim: For students to have practice in scan and gist reading skills.
            10 mins

3 **Students are given extracts of language from a letter and from a postcard (formal vs. informal) and they have to distinguish which is which. Teacher then checks.**

   Aim: For students to recognize appropriate style of language.
            10 mins

4 **Teacher elicits what types of topic are usually written about in postcards.**

   Aim: For students to be able to identify appropriate postcard topics. 5 mins

5 **Students are each given one of the completed postcards from Stage 2 as a model of postcard writing. They also get a blank postcard. They have to write a real postcard to someone they know who speaks English (it could be you) and to whom they will send this postcard. This adds authenticity to the task (compare this with them writing an imaginary postcard on a piece of paper).**

   Aim: For students to have practice in postcard writing skills.
            15 mins

6 **Once the postcards have been written, and later sent, you could have a follow-up speaking activity – maybe ranking the six countries featured in the model postcards in order of which place they would most like to visit.**

   Aim: For students to have practice in speaking (putting items in order and giving reasons). 10 mins

In a lesson package such as this, writing is just part of the lesson, but it fits in with all the other parts. The teacher has established interest, provided a model of the writing task, prepared students with the style and type of language required, established what needs to be included, and also included reading and speaking. All of this is suitable for an elementary class, but it remains a full lesson of language and skills. The writing task is real life.

TASK 3

Now try and think of a lesson package for an intermediate class doing a letter of application.

Before going on, let's consider further examples of the types of writing that can be done at these three broad levels.

At elementary level, in addition to postcards, students could do gap-fills, dialogues, informal letters, simple forms, and guided writing. By 'guided' writing I mean that students are, for example, given part of a written text already completed, and students complete the rest. 'Parallel texts' can also provide lower-level guidance – as, with the example above, students see a complete model of the type of task that they will have to do. At this level, though, the amount of writing required will be much less than at higher levels.

At intermediate level, in addition to formal letters, students could do simple report writing, simple discursive essays, guided narratives, and complex form filling.

At higher levels, in addition to discursive writing, students could do unguided narratives, note taking, précis writing, statistical interpretation, report writing, and speculative writing.

Key to Task 3

Going back to the last task, one possible lesson package for a lesson including writing a letter of application could be as follows:

1 Class discussion on types of jobs.

> Aim: For students to start thinking about basic theme of lesson.
> 2 mins

2 Reading 1 – students sequence the process of getting a job (sentences on seeing a job advertisement, completing an application form, etc.)

> Aim: For students to have practice in reading for detail.
> 8 mins

3 Teacher shows an advert for a job for which the students will apply. Discussion as to why they want to apply for the job and why they would be suitable.

> Aim: For students to start thinking about reasons for applying for the job. 5 mins

4   **Reading 2 – students read a completed letter of application and look at a list of paragraph functions. They match paragraphs with functions.**

Aim: For students to identify the purpose of paragraphs in such a letter. 5 / 10 mins

or

Students are given a completed letter of application which contains some inappropriately informal language. They have to identify and improve the inappropriate language.

Aim: For students to focus on appropriateness of language. 5 / 10 mins (if time allows, you might include both of these stages)

5   **Writing – students write a letter of application for the job featured in Stage 3. This could be a letter already partly written (perhaps with letter layout completed).**

Aim: For students to have practice in writing a letter of application. 15 / 20 mins

6   **Students read (or are read) all the letters and choose the best applicant.**

Aim: For students to have practice in evaluating qualities of job applicants. 10 mins

As with the 'postcard lesson', the above staging is only an example; there are many possible variations but what the two examples given show is how a writing activity can be integrated into a lesson which focuses on other areas, too. Of course, and especially with an exam class, you might instead have a lesson which is exclusively concentrated on writing. In such a case you will almost certainly be using a course book designed for the preparation of this exam, and it will guide you as to how to approach such lessons. When teaching General English, as we said before, you will probably be using a course book as well, and this book, too, will give you ideas of how to do writing in the classroom. Most of the time it will suggest an integrated approach, as I have in this unit. Sometimes, you might find it more appropriate to set the actual writing task for homework – that depends on your context with your students.

One very important aspect of the teacher's role has not been mentioned yet. Given the emphasis on accuracy in writing, the need for **correction** and other language feedback is important. We will be looking at correction of both oral and written work, in the next unit. For now, it is enough to say that correction of written work does need to occur, and that there are various ways of approaching it.

TIPS

1 **Do not ignore the writing skills.**

2 **Integrate writing with other activities, linking and staging the different parts of the lesson.**

3 **Be prepared to have lessons which focus entirely on writing when appropriate.**

4 **Be aware of which writing skills are required for a particular task and help develop your students' ability to use these skills.**

5 **Be aware of which style of writing is required for a particular activity and help develop your students' ability to write in this way.**

6 **With low levels especially, provide models of the activity.**

7 **With low levels especially, provide guided writing activities.**

8 **In all cases, provide writing activities which are relevant to your students' needs both inside and outside the classroom.**

9 **Use ideas given in course books and specialist resource books.**

10 **When appropriate, let students work together in the preparation of a writing activity. This will reduce the pressure and feeling of isolation.**

11 **Work with the students when they are writing, help and support them, for the same reason as '10'.**

12 **Use varied techniques for correction and other language feedback (see Unit 17).**

Summary

We have seen in this unit that writing is a skill that is often neglected, partly because its relevance is not always clear, and partly because teachers don't always know the best way to approach it. The potential for boredom is great but we have also seen that for many students, writing is very important, either for their own lives if in an English-speaking country, or in their jobs. It can also be very important for those students preparing for an exam of which writing will be one part. So teachers need to work on developing their students' writing skills.

▶ Teachers have to develop the specific skills required for a particular task, and make sure the students know what type of language to use.
▶ Teachers should also know how to integrate writing into a lesson.
▶ Correction is very important because the focus on accuracy is much greater than it is with speaking.
▶ Teachers should work on ways to reduce the pressure that students feel when doing a writing activity:
  ▷ **by properly staging the lesson**
  ▷ **by supporting students during the activity**
  ▷ **by allowing students to help each other**

So writing should not be ignored. However, the amount of time you spend on it compared with the other skills will be less, and will vary a lot according to who you are teaching and in which country you are teaching.

16 *Spoken and written mistakes*

If you are trying to use a language which you are learning, you will make mistakes. It is inevitable. Some of these mistakes are 'slips of the tongue or pen' which you can correct yourself without prompting; others are what one might call 'real' mistakes, where you do not know what the problem is and need someone to tell you. Mistakes can be spoken, or written. This unit will cover both types, and will not differentiate between **mistakes** and **errors**. As for the role of the teacher, when it comes to correction and other language feedback, this is by no means as straightforward as you might think, or as the student who says 'I want all my mistakes corrected' might think. **Correction**, in short, is a complex part of the teacher's role.

We will look at the following areas in this unit and the next one:
▶ Why students make mistakes.
▶ Types of mistake.
▶ When the correction should take place.
▶ Different ways of correction.
▶ Techniques of correction.
▶ Why students make mistakes.

First, consider this. A child of five utters the sentence *Yesterday I went to school*. Two years later that same child says *Yesterday I goed to school*. What is your conclusion regarding this child's learning progress?

The obvious, easy answer is that the child has regressed. He has gone from correct use of language to incorrect use, but, in fact, the opposite is true. The initial correct utterance was probably imitation of a parent using *went* with *yesterday*. However, the second utterance suggests that the child has learnt the rule that verbs in the past end with *-ed*. What that child hasn't yet learnt is that English has many irregular verbs where this rule does not apply but the child is trying to apply a rule he has learnt, albeit incorrectly, and this is a good thing. This is the first point that needs to be made – 'mistakes' are part of any learning process (including teaching) and as such should be treated positively, assuming the student can learn from his mistakes. Students need to realize that they will make mistakes because it is impossible not to if you are learning a language. What they must do is know why it is a mistake so as not to repeat it. Teachers have the responsibility of making the whole process of mistakes and correction a positive one that all students can benefit from. Teachers also have to acknowledge effort, praise good use of language, and help reformulate students' use of language into something even better.

TASK 1

1 **Why do students make mistakes (written and spoken)?**

2 **Think of as many examples of types of mistake as you can.**

Stop now and do the task.

As I have said before, some students are obsessed with accuracy and want every mistake corrected. When a teacher does correction work, out come their pens and they write everything down as if this is the part of the lesson when they are truly learning. You get the students who want to know which mistakes were theirs. And you get the students who insist on correcting other students' mistakes whenever they hear them. In other words, it is easy for some students to start seeing language learning as essentially learning rules and correcting errors. Fortunately, such students are in the minority because neither students nor teachers should view constant correction as desirable; indeed, it can be counter-productive and become a negative experience when, as I said at the start, mistakes should be seen as a positive part of the learning process.

Key to Task 1

Students, as you might expect, make mistakes for many reasons. Some of these reasons are common to speaking and writing; others are not.

1 *First language (L1) interference.* **An example of this is 'false friends' (see Unit 8) but it is any case where a student's first language may 'get in the way'. Another example is different nationalities experiencing particular problems. Japanese learners, for example, have difficulties with using articles.**

2 *Forgetfulness.* **Students learn. Students forget. We cannot expect a language learner to remember everything we teach them.**

3 *Lack of understanding.* **Maybe the student simply hasn't understood what you have taught them. They are still trying to correctly apply a rule or form.**

4 *Slip of the tongue.* As mentioned before, in an attempt to achieve fluency a student will 'trip over' and make mistakes which are not genuine ones.

5 *Unclear teaching.* Yes, for whatever reason, maybe the teacher has not taught a language point or checked it sufficiently clearly.

6 *Incorrect application of rules.* A student may try very hard to use what they have learnt, but is as yet unaware of 'exceptions' or development of this language point. For example, you cannot cover all ways of talking about the future at once, so students will only use what they have learnt. Refer, too, to the example earlier (*went* and '*goed*').

7 *Incorrect model.* Students will hear 'incorrect' English all the time – from each other, from speakers outside the school, from TV and they will copy what they hear.

8 *Habitual.* Some students continue to make the same mistakes time after time however often they are corrected.

9 *Unawareness.* If students don't know (haven't learnt) something, they cannot be expected to get it right. Most of the above can apply, too, to writing (with 'slip of the tongue' becoming 'slip of the pen'). In addition we can add the following:

10 *Alternative script.* Consider, for example, the Japanese or Arabic scripts – they are completely different from the English script and this makes writing in English especially difficult.

11 *Pressure.* As we saw in the last unit, writing is a pressurized activity and there is a strong focus on accuracy. Such pressure can induce mistakes.

12 *Style of language.* The specific styles of written language, the discourse, etc., provide specific problems and the likelihood of mistakes.

13 *Lack of practice.* Students generally get much less practice, and even less 'teaching' of writing than practically any other classroom activity.

Types of mistake

By recognizing why students make mistakes with the language, teachers are in a better position to anticipate problems and to help. It also helps to be able to recognize different types of mistake. These can be very broadly categorized as follows:

▶ **Grammar**. Any mistake of structure or form.
▶ **Lexis**. Any vocabulary mistake, which may or may not affect meaning.
▶ **Pronunciation**. We looked at this area in Unit 10.
▶ **Appropriateness**. The utterance is technically correct, but not appropriate in the context.

Apart from pronunciation, all of these can apply equally to writing. To this list we can add:

▶ layout
▶ spelling
▶ punctuation
▶ organization and general cohesion.

TASK 2

Look at the following examples of students' spoken mistakes. What do you think was the cause, and what type of mistake is it?

1 **He writed me a letter.**
2 **I am seeing the television.**
3 **When I will see you again?**
4 **We need airballs for the party.**
5 **Will you borrow me your dictionary?**
6 **Teacher: 'Ask her what her name is.'**
  Student: 'What your name is?'
7 **He drive very slow.**
8 **I've watched television last night.**
9 **Student in pub: 'Give me a beer.'**
10 **She go home later.**

Key to Task 2

1 **This is a further example of a student trying to apply a rule she has learnt (add -ed to a verb to put it in the past) without knowing that many verbs have irregular past forms. So it is a grammar mistake, but a very understandable one.**

2 **The student has learnt to use the present progressive to describe an action in progress at the time of speaking (e.g. It is raining). What she does not yet know is that some verbs are**

not formed with *-ing* in this way, and *see* is one such verb. In this case *watching* is the verb we would use. Another grammar mistake.

3 The student has learnt the typical sentence structure in English (subject + verb + object – *I will see you again*) but has not yet learnt the correct question form, and is unaware that we invert the auxiliary verb and subject (*When will I see you again?*). It is another example of a student making a mistake because she does not know the rule.

4 A vocabulary mistake. This student wanted to use the word *balloon* but just didn't know the word. So he invented the word *airball*, a much more descriptive word than *balloon* in fact.

5 Some languages do not make the distinction between *borrow* and *lend*, but even after students learn the difference, they invariably have great difficulty remembering the distinction. It is a vocabulary mistake, and one I have been asked about more times than just about any other vocabulary item.

6 Here's a mistake for which the teacher must take some responsibility, and it relates to the example in 3 above as well. *What* is a question word, and the teacher has said 'Ask her what ... and the student has listened very carefully to the rest of the sentence – ' ... what her name is' – and has repeated this as a direct question, which it isn't.

I once observed a lesson given by a trainee teacher. He was setting up a speaking activity based on questions. He gave examples of the 'questions to ask' by saying something like 'Ask your partner where they come from', and as he spoke he wrote on the board what he was saying. So on the board we had 'Where they come from', 'Where they are living now', 'What food they like', etc. As the speaking activity began, sure enough, the teacher to his horror heard student A asking student B 'Where you come from?', etc. An easy mistake for the teacher to have made, but with serious consequences.

7 The student either has not learnt the distinction between an adjective and an adverb (*slowly*), or has simply forgotten to use it, as often happens. Another problem students sometimes have with adverbs is they think that they all end *-ly*, which they don't (e.g. *She drove fast, He worked hard*).

8 The present perfect tense is a complex one, and is used differently in British and American English but one aspect is the same, you do not use a definite time reference (*last night*) with the present perfect. In this case you would use the past simple – *I watched television last night.*

9 *Give me a beer* is correct English, but if you go into a bar and use the words it might be considered rude (though this depends partly on your intonation). At the very least it would be considered unusually direct. So this is inappropriate language.

10 *I go, you go, he/she goes* – the verb adds -s / -es in the third person singular. However, whatever their level, students continually forget this. Forgetfulness is another consideration for the teacher. As well as treating mistakes as a positive part of the learning process, teachers should remember that students are trying to absorb so much new language and so many rules that they cannot possibly be expected to remember everything. If you are currently doing a teacher-training course, you will appreciate how hard it is to remember and put into practice everything your tutors have been telling you. And if you do anything 'wrong', it's all part of your learning experience as a new teacher.

'POSITIVE' MISTAKES

Let's look now at an authentic piece of written work done together by a group of elementary students. They wrote a letter of appreciation to a departing teacher. This is what they wrote. What is your overall impression?

> Dear Matt,
> we want to say good buy and hand over you a little present.
> We are most grateful to you for your help. You are a very good teacher.
> You've got empathy and you shaped the lessons very interesting.
> We think, do you like teaching.
> We hope we'll meet again on the occasion of the term of autumn.
> Today, we wish you many beautiful journey trought the German country.
> We wish you good luck and all the best!

This is a fascinating piece of work because it illustrates so well the idea of 'positive' mistakes. At first glance you might think there are lots of mistakes and it is a poor piece of work but consider two points. First, the meaning is clear throughout. Second, notice how well the students are trying to use the language. For example, *you've got empathy and shaped the lessons very well. Empathy* may not be the right word here, but it is a word they have acquired and are trying to use, and the meaning behind the sentiment is clear. As for *you shaped the lessons very well*, it may be a clumsy phrase, but it is a tremendous effort and clearly means the teacher staged the lessons well. *On the occasion of the term of autumn* may be technically correct, but is inappropriate and unnatural.

Of course, there are examples of good and appropriate language. *We are most grateful to you for your help* may be a little formal, but no sensitive teacher is going to do anything other than praise the sentence.

Overall, if I had been the teacher, I would have been delighted with this attempt from elementary-level students.

So what ways are there for a teacher to give useful feedback on language, including correction? That will be the focus of the next unit.

Summary

▶ Whether we are talking about spoken or written mistakes, teachers must recognize why mistakes might have happened (this, as we will see, can help with correction), and should treat them as a positive part of the learning process.

▶ If we perceive mistakes as a sign of poor teaching or lazy learning, we will not be helping ourselves or our students.

▶ If students are hard on themselves because their English is less than perfect – we must help them to understand they are being unrealistic and ultimately hindering their own progress. This applies equally to trainee teachers who say their lesson was a 'disaster' because a couple of parts did not go quite according to plan.

▶ We should focus as much on the 'correct' as the 'incorrect'.

▶ As teachers we must adjust our focus on accurate English according to who we are teaching.

▶ Mistakes are far more of an issue for students preparing for an exam than for those who are seeking only to improve their English. For the latter, it is more important to speak fluently and make themselves understood.

17 Language correction and feedback

In the last unit we looked at some examples of spoken and written mistakes and some reasons for them. We also discussed what the teacher's – and student's – attitude to spoken and written mistakes should be. In this unit we will look at when correction should take place, different ways of correction, and correction techniques as well as other forms of language feedback.

TASK 1

What are your views on the following questions about correction of spoken mistakes?

1   Should all mistakes be corrected? Should any mistakes be corrected?
2   If you answered 'no' to the first question, which mistakes should be corrected?
3   Should correction take place immediately, or later?
4   Who should do the correction – the teacher, the same student or another student in the class?
5   How should the correction take place?

Stop now and do this task!

The role of correction in the classroom is far from clear-cut. However, all teachers do need to know the skills of correction work, and trainee teachers on courses are assessed on their ability to recognize and correct both spoken and written mistakes.

1 Should all mistakes be corrected?

The first question is easy to answer – 'no', all mistakes should not be corrected. What's more, even if you thought they should be (as some students do), it would be impossible. Imagine a class of 20 students, all talking at different points, all making mistakes, and you trying to correct every single mistake. Impossible. Should any mistakes be corrected? Again, an easy question – 'yes', of course. How can any person learn any new skill without having important mistakes corrected? How can a person learn to be a teacher without knowing or being told when something has gone wrong?

As we have already seen, some students will say 'I want all my mistakes corrected'. Such a student is being unrealistic, but as a teacher you might have to tell that student, or the class, why it is unrealistic as well as undesirable. I have done so many times. With a class of the right level it is no bad thing to have a discussion about learning strategies, and the rationale of what the teacher does or does not do in lessons.

2 WHICH MISTAKES SHOULD BE CORRECTED?

Now it gets more difficult. Having established that some, but not all, mistakes should be corrected, we are faced with the question of which mistakes should be corrected. Ultimately, of course, this is for the individual teacher to decide, based on the context of the lesson and the nature of the class. However, I think we can make some general points about what mistakes should be corrected. If students are doing a practice activity, using specific language previously 'presented', as well as other language, then mistakes involving the 'target language' should be focused on for correction (when and how will be discussed later). In this type of activity, the focus is more on accuracy, and therefore, at least some of the inaccuracies with the target language need to be corrected. Common mistakes are also suitable for correction. If you are teaching a monolingual class, then you are more likely to get similar mistakes being repeated, and everyone will benefit from the correction. What a teacher might determine to be a 'significant' mistake, for whatever reason, can be corrected – for example, a mistake which results in unclear meaning, or a mistake which results in the wrong meaning. If a student, for example, says 'Can I lend your dictionary', then this is a significant mistake.

If some mistakes should be corrected, then others should not – or do not have to be. For example, if your students have done a reading comprehension and, in answering a question about the text, a student gives the right answer, but uses incorrect grammar, then the teacher can ignore the mistake because the aim of the task was comprehension, not accuracy. For example, if a question asks 'what time does Dave go to work?' and the answer is 8 a.m., and your student says 'he go work 8 a.m.' then he has given the correct answer. You could then say 'good, he goes to work at 8 a.m.' so you are giving the correct model but without focusing on it as a correction.

If you are chatting with students before or after the lesson, and they make mistakes when talking, ignore the mistakes as long as meaning is clear. If the students have done a practice activity and made mistakes with the target language, focus on those mistakes and worry less about any others, unless they are significant in some other way, or are very common. To correct or not, then, depends on the aim of the lesson or activity. A mistake that occurs in a controlled-practice activity might not be corrected if it occurs in a fluency activity, or a comprehension exercise.

In other words, be selective in deciding which mistakes need to be corrected, and which don't. Some teachers, myself included, might argue that from time to time higher-level students should be allowed to do a speaking activity where the sole focus is fluency and the teacher should ignore most mistakes.

3 When to correct mistakes?

Sometimes, you might feel that a mistake should be corrected immediately. For example, pronunciation mistakes would normally be corrected straight away. If a student was answering a question concerning target language and a mistake with the target language was made in the answer, again the mistake would be corrected immediately. Sometimes, in the normal flow of a lesson, if a student is talking and a mistake or mistakes in his speech impede your understanding, you might feel that you need to correct.

Besides the many mistakes that would go uncorrected, there are also those that you would not want to correct straight away. If your students are doing any kind of speaking activity, and especially if you want them to achieve some fluency, then to interrupt with corrections would stop the flow and possibly intimidate them.

One advantage of delayed language feedback is that the correction becomes less 'personal' – students will not necessarily remember whose mistake it was. You may wonder, though, if you do not correct straightaway, how you will remember what you hear – see Question 5.

In conclusion, some mistakes will be corrected straightaway, some later, and some not at all.

4 Who should do the correction?

There are three possibilities – teacher correction, self-correction, and student-to-student correction.

TASK 2

What do you think are the advantages and disadvantages of each type of correction?

Stop now and do this task!

In any class, there will be a combination of all three types. In the next question we will consider techniques of correction, and also how correction can become a lesson in itself. But now let us go back to the Task.

TEACHER CORRECTION

Advantages

▶ The correction will, or should be, quicker, more efficient, and 'accurate'.
▶ Student confidence – 'It is the teacher's job', 'The teacher is always right!'
▶ The teacher can ensure correction is handled sensitively and fairly.
▶ The teacher can use proper and varied techniques of correction.

Disadvantages

▶ It fails to encourage learner independence.
▶ It can be intimidating for students to have 'the teacher' correcting their mistakes.
▶ Students might feel embarrassed, however sensitive the teacher might be.
▶ Too much teacher correction might be demoralizing for students
▶ Other students might feel 'left out' of the lesson while a mistake is being corrected.

Despite the disadvantages expressed, the teacher should do some correction work, but must ensure it is done properly. As to how much of the correction should come from the teacher, there is no answer to that. It depends on a multitude of factors and opinions.

SELF-CORRECTION

Advantages

- Students are involved in the process – this renews confidence if they can correct themselves.
- Self-corrected mistakes are more memorable and less likely to be repeated.
- It encourages learner independence.
- It gives the teacher feedback on the student's knowledge, ability and awareness.

Disadvantages

- Students may not be able to self-correct and consequently become demotivated.
- Students may feel pressured or embarrassed.
- Students may 'correct' what was already correct and do more harm than good.
- It is potentially more time consuming.

On balance, self-correction is definitely more positive than negative. The first three advantages listed above are really important points.

STUDENT-TO-STUDENT CORRECTION

Advantages

- Some students might find it easier being corrected by a peer (but many won't).
- It involves other students ... gives them self-confidence.
- It encourages other students to stay involved in the lesson.
- It encourages an atmosphere of cooperation.
- It helps the teacher 'assess' awareness of other student.

Disadvantages

- The student doing the correction may get it wrong.
- It can be slower and less effective (if student does not have correction skills).
- The student being corrected may not understand the other student (pronunciation).
- The student being corrected may not know if the correction is accurate.
- Some students may feel it is the job of the teacher to correct.

Some student-to-student correction takes place naturally, and within reason, it should be encouraged. But beware the student who constantly tries to correct other students as if they were the teacher. This can be counter-productive and irritate almost everyone in the class.

Overall, the ideal is for there to be a mixture of all three 'correctors', but the precise balance will vary according to many factors. But avoid over using teacher correction because that produces a total reliance on the teacher and no encouragement of learner independence.

5 How to correct?

Obviously, you want to avoid 'No, that's wrong', or anything like it as this becomes negative and critical and goes against the idea of correction being part of the learning process. How you correct depends partly on who is doing the correction, the type of mistake, the context of the lesson, and the nature of the mistake. However, we can make some very general points.

TIPS FOR IMMEDIATE CORRECTION

1 **Indicate that a mistake has been made. How? Maybe facial gesture, verbal remark ('Again'/'Sorry?') or just a gesture for the student to stop their sentence, thus indicating a problem.**

2 **Locate where the mistake is in the sentence. How? A verbal gap-fill, perhaps. For example, if the student has said 'Everyday she go to the shops', the teacher might say 'everyday she _____ to the shops'. Use your fingers, too. With each finger representing one word, when you get to word 3 in this sentence indicate with your finger that this is the problem word. It might sound an odd thing to do, but it works. By locating the mistake the student will be able to focus on the correct part of the sentence, and not end up 'correcting' what doesn't need to be corrected.**

3 **Categorize the type of mistake. How? In this case you might say '3rd person singular?', if the students know the rule of adding -s or -es in these cases, or say 'I go, you go, she ...' This will show if the mistake was no more than a slip of the tongue and it will be possible to elicit self-correction, or student-to-student correction.**

   By indicating that a mistake has been made, where, and what type, the teacher is using her correction skills to make the correction efficient and successful, and is involving the students.

4 **At this point, either the student or another student is likely to correct. If they can't, you do it.**

5 Maybe get the student to repeat the whole sentence for reinforcement.

6 You could repeat the entire sentence, with mistake, with rising (questioning) intonation to make it obvious that the sentence is incorrect. Or just repeat the incorrect part in the same way.

7 Similar to Point 2, repeat the sentence only up to where the mistake occurred.

8 As mentioned before, use your fingers (clearly) to indicate, for example, that two words are the wrong way round in a sentence (e.g. 'Where you will go?'). You can use your fingers to indicate a 'swap over' of words.

9 Use word prompts to categorize, e.g. 'Tense?' 'Preposition?', etc.

10 If a student has incorrectly repeated what a previous student said, go back to the other student and ask her to repeat what she said before.

All of this might sound like a lengthy process. Normally it takes a matter of seconds for the simple reason that the student, or another, can correct easily. The process only slows down if the mistake was a real one and no one in the class knows the problem.

DELAYED LANGUAGE FEEDBACK

We saw in Unit 14 that if students are doing a fluency activity, or a speaking activity where they are getting practice of language previously presented, then to interrupt with corrections would spoil the fluency and potentially intimidate the students. In addition, assuming they are working in groups, other students would not benefit from the correction. So how can a teacher do correction and other language feedback later in the lesson?

The usefulness of the 'Tips' below depends on the size of the class and the ability of the teacher to monitor. They are most valuable with a class of no more than, say, 20, in a room where the teacher can walk around fairly freely.

TIPS FOR DELAYED LANGUAGE FEEDBACK

1 If possible, arrange the class so that it is possible for you to walk around the room, e.g. they work in groups of four in a circular-type formation.

2 Get a pen and a piece of paper.

3 Keep a 'low profile', listen to each group in turn and try to pick out mistakes.

4 Concentrate on mistakes in the target language, if appropriate, or common mistakes, or mistakes you view as important or useful to focus on.

5 Make a note, too, of particularly good language, or language which is OK but could be made better.

6 If you have real trouble hearing (it can be difficult), note down mistakes which could easily be made in such an activity – a language feedback phase does not have to consist of genuine language by students in your class.

7 At the end of the activity, or just before, write up all your sentences on the board. Tell the students that some sentences are correct and others are not. They have to decide and correct as necessary. If there's time, let them work on this in groups. If not, go through it together. This way, everyone benefits from the correction and it is 'depersonalized'. You will almost always have someone who wants to know 'Was that my mistake?' Tell them it does not matter!

8 When going through the mistakes, locate and categorize as indicated above, and write in the correction on the board. Don't only focus on mistakes. Give examples of good language you heard, and praise it. And give examples of language that is correct but could be better (compare 'the food was nice' with 'the food was delicious'). And include language that has naturally emerged during the lesson which you would like to focus on.

9 Another possibility, especially if time is short and you have lots of sentences, is to do the language feedback in the next lesson.

10 Linked to the previous point, you might 'collect' language from the week and have a language feedback lesson or part of a lesson as a kind of review at the end of the week. At least this way you won't have students trying to work out whose mistakes they were, because they won't remember!

My experience of working on teacher-training courses, where the new teacher's skills of correction are part of their assessment, is that there is often considerable reluctance to correct. There seems to be a number of reasons for this. One is the teacher's own lack of confidence in grammar and fear of being asked questions. Trust your instincts – you know what is right and what is wrong. Others feel that it is too negative to correct, to which I ask, how can someone learn any new skill (including teaching), if you are not made aware of what you are doing wrong? What you have to do is be sensitive and use your skills. As long as you deal with emerging language sensitively, It is something students like, want and need.

CORRECTING WRITTEN WORK

So far we have looked primarily at spoken language but much of what has already been said can apply equally to the correction of written mistakes. However, there are other factors, too, that need to be considered.

Most people's memories of written work at school being returned by the teacher probably include a long wait, the sight of red ink, lots of corrections and little praise. Or, they may remember pages of written work being returned with a single comment (e.g. 'Good'), or a mark (3/10) making you wonder just how carefully the teacher read your work.

1 When do we correct written work?

2 How do we correct written work?

As with spoken language, so with written language, there is an argument for leaving some mistakes uncorrected. Look again at Unit 15 and the example of written work given and the points made about 'praiseworthy mistakes'. Consider, too, the demoralizing effect of a student getting work back which is filled with corrections.

Yes, you might argue that to leave a mistake uncorrected implies that it is not a mistake – and you would be right, but it is a question of balance and personal judgement in the context of the teaching.

If students are writing in class, you might go round during the activity giving one-to-one help and corrections. Or, you might collect in their work, correct at home, and return it – preferably – the next lesson. In other words, you again have the choice between 'immediate' or 'delayed' feedback.

SYMBOLS

Just as with spoken language, teachers should try to involve the students in the correction process of written work and one way of doing this is to employ correction symbols. The teacher might underline or circle the mistake (locate it), then indicate the type of mistake (categorize) by putting in the margin the appropriate symbol (e.g. 'G' for grammar). The students have a copy of all the symbols and what they mean. They then go away and try to correct the work for themselves – though this still requires the teacher to check again afterwards, so it is a lengthier process. Symbols might include 'V' (vocabulary), 'WO' (word order), 'P' (punctuation), etc. You must be consistent in your use of symbols, and still include praise for good work and suggestions for improvement, as described before.

If you use the more traditional approach to correction (and, as ever, you should aim for variety), then do not litter the work with corrections. It is important to praise when you can, encourage, and be supportive. And sometimes it is clear that a student has really tried to use what they have learnt, even if they have done so incorrectly. An example of this might be 'I'm really look forward to hearing from you' at the end of a letter. It is wrong, but at the same time it's a really good effort.

CLASS CORRECTION

Another principle of correction of spoken mistakes which can apply to written correction is the one of class correction. Take the work away and make a note of common or significant mistakes as well as good language. Make a copy of this list (or write it directly on the board) for the next lesson, then have time where everybody looks at all the language from the different pieces of work. This de-personalizes the correction and everybody benefits from it.

With higher levels, students can exchange their work with a partner and look for mistakes in each other's work (student-to-student correction).

GRADING

As for 'grading' the work, this is up to you. Personally, I do not, unless the students are preparing for an exam, in which case I would grade according to exam standards for students to have an idea of their level in relation to the exam. Otherwise, I would always write a summary comment, as positive as possible, but no 'grade'. However, it's up to you, and also what your school policy might be about this.

Summary

▶ Correction should be part of the learning process and treated positively.
▶ It should include a variety of teacher correction, self-correction, and student-to-student correction (spoken and written).

- The teacher should indicate where the mistake is and categorize it.
- The teacher should employ facial gestures, finger work, verbal prompts, etc., to help with correction.
- With written work, the teacher should use a variety of approaches as well
- Use of symbols for written correction should be clear and consistent.
- Not all mistakes should be corrected – focus on target language mistakes, common mistakes, or mistakes which you feel are significant for some other reason
- If the aim is comprehension (the correct answer to a question), focus on the correct answer, not the correct = grammar.
- Don't interrupt fluency work – make a note of mistakes.
- Be positive, give examples of and praise good work as well as showing how language could be improved.
- Do correct – don't avoid it because it Is a vital part of learning.

18 Lesson planning: aims

If you are or are about to be a trainee teacher on a training course you will be required to submit a detailed lesson plan each time you teach. If you are a relatively new teacher, you may still be preparing less-detailed plans for your lessons. Once you have more experience, you will rarely produce an actual plan (unless you are being observed perhaps), but you will still plan what you are going to do. So in the following units we are looking at both planning in general, and producing actual lesson plans. This unit focuses on aims.

I have heard some experienced people in the profession argue against the notion of planning, suggesting that teaching and learning should be spontaneous according to the wishes and reactions of the students on a particular day. For some teachers this might work and be successful. I would argue, though, that there are very few teachers, however experienced, who would be comfortable just walking into a class with no idea of what will be done in the lesson. Further, I do not believe that most students in my experience would be satisfied with such an approach to learning, but whatever the arguments, such an approach is definitely not acceptable for new or training teachers. What is true, however, is that teaching should be flexible; students must have an influence on what you teach and how you teach it, and this has an important influence on the teacher's planning.

A good lesson plan will be one which is a clear working document. In other words, another teacher would be able to teach your lesson for you by using your plan as a guide. In my experience as a trainer, I can normally predict the quality of the lesson I am about to observe from the quality of the plan which has been handed in. Obviously, the length and precise contents of your plan will depend on the length of your lesson, the type of lesson, and also the stage of the course but all plans are likely to include at least the following:

> level of class, length of lesson, aims(s) of lesson, target language (if appropriate), personal aims, anticipated problems (for the students) and possible solutions, stages, aim of each stage, estimated timings, interaction, procedure, board layout.

We will look at most of these points in the next unit, but for now we will concentrate on aims.

Lesson aims

The aim of your lesson, or the aim of the stage of the lesson, is what you hope to achieve, or what you hope your students will achieve. It answers the question 'Why am I doing this?' / 'Why am I asking my students to do this?'. Clear and realistic aims are essential if a lesson is going to be successful.

Some teachers phrase the aims from the teacher's perspective, others from the students' perspective. Compare these examples:

'to provide practice in scan reading skills'

'for students to have practice in scan reading skills'

Personally, I much prefer the latter. As teachers, it is more beneficial if we think of what we are doing from the learners' perspective whenever possible. New teachers can get too involved in the teaching process (quite understandably) and neglect to give sufficient importance to the students' learning. As a teacher, of any length of experience, you should think about the students as much as, and probably more than, your own teaching. When observing classes, it is good to focus on one or two students, or the class as a whole, and observe their involvement and progress in the lesson – how has their learning been affected by the teaching?

Formulating clear aims is not easy for the new teacher and the result is often inappropriate or aims that are far too general. You don't always need the rest of a plan to recognize poor aims, as the following task will show.

TASK 1

Which of the following lesson aims seem inadequate? Can you improve them?

1 **'to teach the present perfect'**
2 **'for students to have practice in listening for gist'**
3 **'for students to learn new vocabulary'**
4 **'for students to have reading practice'**
5 **'to teach the positive and negative forms of the present progressive and to give written and spoken practice'**

6 'for students to improve their pronunciation'

7 'to set up a speaking activity clearly and efficiently'

8 'reading and speaking'

9 'for students to learn the correct usage of selected conjunctions in written English and to have practice in a letter-writing task'

10 'to teach writing'

Before looking at this task, I must emphasize the importance of a teacher having clear aims. I said before, I can usually predict the quality of the lesson I am about to see according to the quality of the plan. The first section I always look at is the one marked 'Aims'. If the stated aims are clear, appropriate, and achievable (according to the rest of the plan), then I would expect to see an effective and successful lesson but a plan with vague aims, or inappropriate aims (for whatever reason) is almost certainly going to result in an ineffective lesson.

Let's look now at the aims above.

Key to task 1

1 It is not uncommon in the early stages of training courses to see an aim such as this one. Personally, I am not keen on the focus on the teacher (the aim says what the teacher will do rather than what the students will achieve), but the real problem is that the aim is vague and unachievable. The present perfect tense is a complex one in any case, but all tenses (verb forms) have a variety of forms. You have the positive (affirmative), negative, question (interrogative), and answer forms. Is this teacher going to 'teach' all four forms in one lesson? Then you have to consider the different uses of this tense (bearing in mind that the tense is used differently in British and American English). Thus, *I've been to France* refers to a past experience, whereas *I've worked here for ten years* refers to something started in the past and continuing to now. Again, it would be unrealistic to include more than one usage with, say, a pre-intermediate class. The importance, therefore, of pre-lesson **language analysis** by the teacher is essential. Equally important is the teacher's own **language awareness** – actually knowing and understanding the language that she is to teach. We will look at this in Unit 20.

So, this teacher probably has little understanding of what the present perfect is and what is involved in teaching it. I would expect to see a lesson which covers far too much, and done via explanations and lots of exercises.

A better aim would be 'for students to learn and have spoken practice in the positive and negative forms of the present perfect simple (indefinite past event)'. Seeing such an aim would lead me to expect a focused lesson.

2   This is a good aim. It sees the lesson from the point of view of the students, but more than that, it provides a clear and specific objective. It's not 'to have practice in listening' (too vague), but listening 'for gist'. So the teacher is aware of different types of listening skills, and has prepared a lesson which focuses on one particular skill.

3   This aim is written from the students' perspective, which is good. However, like number 1, it is far too vague. What vocabulary? How much? For what purpose? Will there be any practice? If so, what type? There's nothing wrong in having a vocabulary lesson (rather than teaching vocabulary which will be needed, say, for a later reading task), but it needs to have focus.

An improvement would be 'for students to learn the meaning, form and pronunciation of ten words about television and to have practice using them in a written gap-fill and a free-speaking activity'. Better than '... to learn vocabulary'.

4   Again, it is good that it is written from the students' perspective. However, unlike Number 2, it is too general. Which reading skills will be used?

Compare this with 'for students to have practice in gist reading (scanning), and reading for detail'. A teacher who plans according to the original aim is one who will probably have given little thought to the tasks being given, and is unaware of what type of reading is required of the students. This teacher might, for example, give three gist questions and allow ten minutes for the task. As we saw in an earlier unit, gist reading should be relatively quick. If it takes ten minutes it is no longer gist reading.

5   A good, clear aim – albeit written from the teacher's perspective – and a big improvement on number 1. If this aim came from the lesson plan of a trainee at the end of a course, and the first aim in the task had come from the same trainee early in the course, it would demonstrate real progress.

6　I would be pleased to see a teacher doing a lesson focusing on pronunciation, and I would be very glad not to be reading 'to teach pronunciation'. However, the aim remains far too vague. Which aspect(s) of pronunciation?

An improvement would be 'for students to have practice in recognizing and using rising and falling intonation in question tags and to recognize the different meanings implied'.

7　This aim is what the teacher personally wants to achieve; it has nothing to do with the reason for doing the activity. It is a personal aim, not a lesson aim. There is nothing wrong in having personal aims (in fact, they are very important), but they should not be confused with teaching and learning aims.

8　There is a very common confusion for new teachers on training courses – the difference between the 'What?' and the 'Why'? **Aims** are the 'Why?' ('Why am I asking my students to do this?'), **stages** are the 'What?' ('What will the students do?'). Both 'reading' and 'speaking' are 'What?'s. Refer back to number four for a possible improvement.

9　This is fine.

10 This is not fine. Which aspects of writing? The aim as written suggests that the teacher is going to teach the class how to write – and all in one lesson.

An improvement would be 'for the students to have practice in writing a letter of application, using appropriate layout, language and paragraphing'.

Sometimes a lesson may have 'main' and 'secondary' aims. For example:

▶ Main (primary) aim: 'for students to have practice in reading for gist and for detail'.

▶ Secondary aim: 'for students to have practice in free-speaking on topic of text'.

We saw in Unit 12 that a teacher needs to be flexible according to various factors, including her aims. We concluded that a teacher should not 'rush through' the reading part of this lesson (or skip part of it) in order to do a speaking activity. It is important to achieve the main aim properly even if the secondary aim is not achieved. Teachers, then, need to be aware themselves of what 'must be done and done properly' in a lesson, and what can be adapted or even dropped (or kept for the next lesson). We will look at this 'flexibility' issue in the next unit.

If you are observing a lesson, try to see if you can write down what you thought the aims of the lesson were and then compare your aims with the actual ones written by the teacher. If the lesson was effective and successful, the task should be easy.

Stage aims

Everything a teacher does, and everything a teacher says, should have a purpose. Well, almost everything. Aims, therefore, are not only for the lesson itself but also for each part of it. A trainee on a teaching course, submitting lesson plans, should always indicate the aim of every stage. An experienced teacher knows instinctively why they are doing or saying what they are. The word 'stage' refers to what the students will be doing – it's a kind of 'title' for the part of the lesson. Examples would be 'reading', 'practice', 'boardwork'. The aim would then clarify the reason for this.

TASK 2

For each of the following stages, try to give a possible aim.

Example: Reading: 'for students to have practice in reading for gist'.

1 **Writing**

2 **Boardwork**

3 **Practice**

4 **Context**

5 **Language focus**

6 **Drilling**

7 **Checking answers**

8 **Speaking**

9 **Feedback**

10 **Correction**

Key to task 2

Of course, there are no single 'correct' answers because there are many possibilities according to the lesson being taught, but here are some suggested answers. Yours may be different but still 'correct'.

1 **'for students to have practice in using narrative tenses'**

2 **'for students to have a record of the target language'**

3 'for students to have controlled practice of the 2nd Conditional via a gap-fill'

4 'to establish student interest in the topic of the lesson (food)'

5 'to clarify the meaning, form and pronunciation of '*wish* + past perfect' (NB: each of the three points here would have separate sub-stages and sub-aims)

6 'for students to have controlled practice in repeating the new words correctly and naturally'

7 'for students to see if they have the right answers and to understand the reasons for the answers'

8 'for students to have practice in speaking fluently on the lesson topic (food), and ranking food from favourite to least favourite'

9 'for students to tell the rest of the class what they learnt from the pair work questionnaire'

10 'for students' significant mistakes with the target language to be corrected in groups and then clarified by teacher'

TIPS

1 Think of the lesson and its stages from the students' perspective – what they will do or achieve, rather than what you will do.

2 Keep the aim as precise and clear as possible.

3 Make sure the aim is realistic (in terms of the level, the students, the time).

4 If appropriate, distinguish between main/primary and secondary aims.

5 Give priority to the achievement of the main aim.

6 Ensure that every stage of your lesson also has an aim – these aims will usually also be from the students' perspective.

7 Make sure you are clear about what the aims are as well.

Having looked at aims of the lesson and aims of each stage of the lesson, we can go one step further. An experienced teacher always knows why she is doing or saying something. What might appear to an observer to be an aimless chat could in reality be the teacher guiding the students towards thinking about a particular question. A teacher showing a class a picture of a famous star, or a hot sunny country, might be going on to a lesson on

'I wish'. A teacher briefly telling the class what she likes and dislikes about a place might just be giving an example of what she wants her students to talk about together. Such a teacher won't have to write out a plan in advance to know why she is doing what she's doing, or saying what she's saying but until you have that experience, almost everything has to be planned in one form or another. Trainee teachers on courses will teach in one month what some teachers do in just one day, so they have the time to write a proper plan, and of course, this is expected of them. We will look in the next unit at what else, apart from aims, needs to be included in a plan, and how to approach it.

Summary

▶ Aims need to be clear, precise, achievable, and preferably stated from the point of view of students learning rather than of the teacher teaching.

▶ Teachers with vague aims in language lessons have probably not understood, or given sufficient thought to, the language being taught.

▶ The main aim of a lesson needs to be achieved, to some extent at least, even if this means being less effective in achieving the secondary aim.

▶ Every action, every word of the teacher, should have a purpose – whether this has been planned, or is instinctive.

▶ You should review the success of your lesson and to what extent you have achieved your aims.

▶ Resist the temptation to dismiss a lesson as a 'disaster'.

▶ You should think more about the students' learning than about the teaching process in isolation.

▶ Ask yourself 'what did the students do / learn / practise in my lesson?' – you might be pleasantly surprised!

▶ However, such a review might be misleading in one respect. It might give the impression that a teacher should stick, inflexibly, to her plan. Not only is this not true, but also it is a dangerous conclusion. As we will see in the next unit, a teacher must always teach with the students' needs in mind, even if this means departing from a carefully prepared plan.

19 Lesson planning: writing a lesson plan

This unit is specifically for those who are on training courses and who have to submit formal lesson plans for each lesson that they teach. We looked in the last unit at aims and how to formulate them, and aims are one of the items on any lesson plan. Indeed, they are the key item, since the aims say why the lesson is happening and what the students will get out of it. The aims of stages state the reason for each part of the lesson.

As a trainee on a course you will find lesson plans something of a chore in the sense that they take time and have to be done properly. However, they are an essential part of any training course. So, apart from the fact that you have to submit plans on such courses, what are the benefits of writing plans for teachers and students?

Most trainees on courses have never taught before and everything they are doing and hearing on the course is new. There is a lot of information, a lot of jargon, a lot of theories and techniques to digest. On many such courses the trainees have to start teaching practice right away ... a kind of 'learning by doing'. It is easy, then, to get confused and frustrated and to lose sight of the main focus of a lesson and how to teach it. Preparing a lesson plan will greatly help the teacher to think more clearly about **what** she is going to do, **why** she is doing it, and **how** she will do it. The result should be a more confident teacher, a more focused and effective lesson, and happy students. Students benefit most because they will be getting a well-thought-out lesson with clear learning objectives.

A good lesson plan ...

▶ is a clear working document for the teacher and should be a document that a teacher can work from in the lesson, so it should be neat, clear, well-organized
▶ has clear and appropriate and achievable aims
▶ should include assumptions of what will help the students achieve the aims – their existing skills and knowledge as known or assumed by the teacher
▶ should anticipate problems of any kind in the lesson and possible solutions (see next unit)

- should have clear and logical stages which link naturally. Ideally, the students as well as the teacher should see where the lesson is going and how the stages link
- should include a variety of activities and interaction
- should reflect how that lesson fits in with others being taught before or/and after
- should be realistic in terms of what can be achieved in the time available.
- should not be too long and detailed (see Point 1)
- should be flexible – a really important point which we'll come back to later

Lesson plan contents (1)

Typical features of lesson plans were listed in the last unit. Here we will look at each of these features and see an example of an authentic plan written by a trainee on a training course. The example is not presented as a perfect model but as a typical plan produced by a successful candidate on a course. Aspects of the plan are unclear, but overall it is a satisfactory plan from a Pass-standard trainee.

The central feature of any plan will be the lesson aim(s). This was looked at in detail in the previous unit. In our example plan the aims were stated as:

> For students to review and have practice using *like* and *don't like* for students to learn the use of *would like* and have practice using it.

(This was a 40-minute lesson given to an elementary group of learners.)

This teacher had covered *like* and *don't like* in the previous lesson. This, then, is indicated in the section **timetable fit** and **presumed student knowledge**.

> Follows on from previous lesson (*like / don't like*).
>
> Will continue tommorrow.

This emphasizes the point that lessons should be part of an overall syllabus or structure, with links not just within a single lesson, but between different lessons. In other words, aims should apply to a series of lessons / a course, as well as to a single lesson.

Plans normally also indicate the **materials** and **resources** to be used:

> *Headway Elementary* (Soars – OUP) Pages 62/63
>
> My own visuals and word/sentence cards.

Note here, in reference to Unit 22, how this trainee did not rely exclusively on the course book being used, but supplemented this with her own materials and ideas.

Good teachers – experienced as well as new – should always be working on improving their own skills and focusing on areas in which they have a weakness. On training courses, especially, there is an emphasis on assessment of **progress**; how trainees improve in areas where they have previously had problems. You should limit yourself to two or three areas in an individual lesson. The trainee in this lesson wrote ...

> To encourage students more to use the new / revised language in a communicative way.

A major part of planning is **anticipating problems** with accompanying possible solutions. This is something the next unit will focus on in more detail, but in the example plan the trainee wrote:

> Students might be confused by use of *like* and *would like* solution: ask concept questions.

It should be said here that this part of the plan needed to be much more detailed!

Boardwork needs to be neat, organized, and a clear 'takeaway' record for students who copy from it. Particularly if a teacher is going to use the board to write up target language covered in a lesson, she should plan how to lay out her boardwork. The teacher in the example here planned two phases of boardwork. The first part was planned as follows:

like			
subject	*like*	verb + *-ing*	
I	*like*	*flying*	
she / he	*likes*	*flying*	= enjoyment
we	*like*	*flying*	
Negative:			
subject	*do not like*	verb + *-ing*	
I	*don't like*	*flying*	
she / he	*doesn't like*	*flying*	
we	*don't like*	*flying*	

For the second part of the lesson the boardwork plan was as follows:

would like			
subject	*would like*	infinitive	
I	*would like*	*to play tennis*	
short form:	*I'd like*	*to play tennis*	= polite way of saying *I want*
Negative:			
I would not (wouldn't) like to play tennis			

Note that there is no reference here to question forms and answers. It would have been unrealistic to cover that as well at this level in just 40 minutes, so it was covered in a lesson the next day. The boardwork is not perfect – there is no sentence stress marked, for example, but it does provide clear examples and highlighting of the form.

The remainder of the plan refers to the actual stages and procedure employed to achieve the stated aims. The five sections of the lesson itself are **stage / aim / procedure / interaction / time**.

The **stage** is effectively a title for a part of a lesson – it states **what** you will do. The aim refers to the **aim** of that specific part (stage) of the lesson; virtually everything that a teacher says or does in a lesson is said or done for a reason. It states why you are doing something, or why the students are doing something. The **procedure** is a description of **how** something will be done. The **interaction** concerns **who** is working with whom – individual work / pair work / group work / whole class. The time is the very approximate estimate of how long something is likely to take. As we shall see later, this is very flexible according to various factors.

Going back to the example plan, this is how the remainder of the plan looked:

Stage:	**introduction**
Aim:	to get students interested in the subject
Procedure:	introduce imaginary friend, Eric, and ask students what they think Eric does and doesn't like
Interaction:	teacher to class
Time:	3 mins

Stage:	**focus on form (1)**
Aim:	clarify form of like (revision)
Procedure:	elicit when we use *I like* meaning something we enjoy doing. Give examples and elicit more examples, including the negative.
Interaction:	teacher to class
Time:	5 mins
Stage:	**practice**
Aim:	students have practice of *like* (questions and answers)
Procedure:	divide class into two groups, give each group a set of questions and answers, students match them up / one monitor
Interaction:	groups
Time:	5 mins
Stage:	**check answers**
Aim:	clarification of answers
Procedure:	get students to give correct answers / I will confirm or correct
Interaction:	teacher to class
Time:	2 mins
Stage:	**practice 2**
Aim:	students have spoken practice of like
Procedure:	divide students into pairs, give each student a picture and they have to tell their partner whether they like or don't like the items. Then get each student to tell the class about their partner's likes and dislikes
Interaction:	pairs
Time:	7 mins
Stage:	**focus on language**
Aim:	clarify meaning / form / pronunciation of *would like*

Procedure:	elicit when we use *would like* as a polite way of saying *I want*. Show form on board, including negatives. Check meaning via concept questions, and pronunciation via drilling
Interaction:	teacher to class
Time:	5 mins
Stage:	**practice 3**
Aim:	students have practice using *would like*
Procedure:	in pairs students get worksheet with sentences containing *like* and *would like* and students have to choose which to use
Interaction:	pairs
Time:	8 mins
Stage:	**check answers**
Aim:	clarification of answers
Procedure:	elicit answers from students, get others to say if they are right or wrong
Interaction:	teacher to class
Time:	5 mins

The resulting lesson, though not strong, did provide a clear focus on the target language, and practice – although this was not very varied.

NEED FOR FLEXIBILITY OF TIMING

However important a lesson plan is for trainee teachers, and however important lesson planning is for any teacher, the key word must always be **flexibility**. A successful lesson is not defined as 'finishing the plan'; teachers have to make changes to their plan as they teach, in response to how the lesson is going and how the students are reacting to, and dealing with, what you are giving them to do. Consequently, the timings for each stage are estimated and are very approximate guidelines for the teacher of how long each stage might take. If one stage is down as five minutes, and it takes six, seven, eight … OK. But if it takes 15, then the teacher either has misjudged the amount of time likely to be needed, or has allowed the activity to continue for too long. On a training course, teachers usually have very fixed time slots for their lessons, e.g. 40 minutes; they do not have the luxury of being able to carry on with their plan in another lesson, as working teachers do. So time becomes an issue, and rightly so because it forces the trainee to think about achievement of aims and the allocation of time to different stages in order to achieve the aims.

Look at this example of time allocation for stages in a 40-minute reading lesson:

		minutes
1	Establish interest in topic	5
2	Pre-teach necessary lexis	10
3	Reading task 1	5
4	Reading task 2	10
5	Speaking follow-up	10

Stages 1 and 2 prepare the students to complete the reading tasks. Stages 3 and 4 are the actual reading parts of the lesson. Stage 5 is a speaking activity related to the topic of the text. Let's imagine the main aim of the lesson is 'for students to have practice in scan reading and intensive reading skills'. As it stands, 15 minutes of the lesson is devoted to reading, but with the necessary vocabulary input this is effectively 25 minutes. But, what if the vocabulary takes 20 minutes, and establishing interest takes 10? Suddenly, most of the lesson has gone without any reading and it has become more of a vocabulary lesson. On a training course this is important because assessment is based in large part on achievement of aims. In a 'real' teaching situation it would not matter if the teacher was able to continue the same lesson after the break, for example but trainee teachers need to show they can achieve aims in a given space of time. In the example above, this means making sure the students get their 15 (or 12, or 18 ...) minutes of reading.

So, what if the teacher has taken longer than planned to get to the reading stages? The students are nearing the end of the first reading task, but there is only ten minutes left. What do you do – continue with the second reading task and forget the speaking task, or go on to the speaking task and leave out the second reading task? Or do you do both and finish your lesson ten minutes late? Well, if it's a training course you definitely don't do both and go over time because you are expected to finish your lesson more or less on time. And in a 'real' teaching situation you probably wouldn't be able to over-run by so much either.

The answer is, scrap the speaking and do the second reading task because if you don't, then half of your reading aims will not have been achieved. The speaking is a 'bonus', but does not relate to your main aims.

NEED FOR ON-THE-SPOT DECISIONS

So, the teacher has to make on-the-spot decisions all the time if, as usually happens, activities take longer, or less time, than anticipated. Sometimes you will need to 'stretch' an activity because something before took less time than expected. Sometimes, you will need to add something to your lesson for the same reason but whatever you do, the main requirement for you on a training course is to achieve your aims in the time given. I once observed a lesson where the teacher spent 20 minutes 'establishing interest' but only two minutes on the main focus of the lesson – therefore, the aims were not achieved. This is why trainees need to estimate the timings of each stage, and know what part(s) of the lesson need the main focus. Experienced teachers can do this instinctively, but if you are on a training course, or if you are a very new teacher, you must estimate times according to your aims.

It is very important in any lesson to respond to what is happening in your class. If you are teaching new language and some students are finding it very difficult, you should not move on just because you have more to 'get through'. You must spend more time on this piece of language and clarify it further. You must know when to 'slow down' or 'speed up', when to quieten things down or liven them up, when to stop students working on a task even if they haven't all finished, when to abandon an activity because it is far too difficult. These are very difficult decisions for new teachers who feel safer following a plan but as your experience and confidence grow, you will make all these on-the-spot decisions instinctively. You will 'read' your students' faces and know how to change your lesson as you teach it. Sometimes, the time of day, or week, will affect how a lesson goes. Or the weather. Or what the students did the previous night. Or something in the news. So many factors can affect the mood and performance of a class, and the teacher has to know how to respond to these factors. If you don't, you are not responding to your students and their needs. All of this relates to being flexible with your plan.

TIPS

NB: These tips are mostly for trainee teachers doing courses where lesson plans have to be submitted.

1 Don't leave the writing up of the plan to the last minute – this will result in greater stress and less confidence. The earlier you complete it, the better for you.

2 When writing it, make sure it is neat, organized and easy to follow.

3 Always think of your lesson and your aims from the point of view of your students.

4 Plan the lesson not just according to the level of the class, but also the composition of the class.

5 When teaching language, analyse that language beforehand and consider the most appropriate way to teach it.

6 Anticipate any problems students might have with the language you are teaching and with any other aspect of the lesson – and think of possible solutions.

7 Be flexible with your plan according to the reactions of your students.

8 Highlight stages that could be shortened if necessary, or dropped, and stages that must have a significant focus in relation to the achievement of stated aims.

9 In relation to Point 8, be flexible with your estimated timings.

10 After the lesson, ask yourself to what extent you achieved your aims; what worked and what didn't work (and why). In other words, review your plan and the lesson in order to continue developing your skills and awareness as a teacher.

We will look now at another authentic lesson plan written by a trainee teacher.

Lesson plan contents (2)

This was a 60-minute lesson given to intermediate students.

Aim(s):	for students to learn and practise modal verbs of deduction; for students to have practice in gist and intensive reading skills
Target language:	3rd person singular affirmative and negative (*must, could, might, may*) e.g. *He must be rich / He can't be* rich for making deductions

Anticipated problems:	students will be aware of *must* for obligation and might find this use of the word confusing; opposite of *must* for deduction is *can't*, not *mustn't*; students might produce the *-ing* form (not focus of my lesson); *must* is pronounced weakly with a silent *t* (*I must go*)
Personal aims:	not to rush instructions; clear concept checking
Boardwork:	

Modal verbs of deduction			
expressing degree of certainty about the present e.g. *He must be in love*		expressing degrees of certainty about the past e.g. *He could have been in love*	
certainty	possibility	certainty	possibility
must/can't	*might/may/could*	*must have* *can't have*	*might* *may have* *could*

(NB: boardwork fails to indicate what kind of verb follows the modal in each case.)

Stage:	context
Aim:	to generate student interest in topic
Procedure:	introduce topic of family relationships, elicit types of relationship; individual students read and think about questions (1 min), then discuss in pairs and report back three pieces of information
Interaction:	teacher to class / individual / students to class
Time:	5 mins
Stage:	reading
Aim:	for students to practise gist and intensive reading skills and locate target language
Procedure:	tell students topic of text / give out worksheet / 30 secs. for gist task / 5 mins for intensive task / students compare answers / teacher checks answers / ask concept questions relating to the modal verbs in the answers
Interaction:	individual, pairs, whole class
Time:	15 mins

Stage:	board stage
Aim:	to provide a written record of the target language (as above)
Procedure:	elicit sentences and structures from students / further concept checking as required
Interaction:	teacher to students
Time:	10 mins
Stage:	practice
Aim:	grammar reinforcement / check understanding
Procedure:	worksheet – 'What can you deduce from the following situations?'
	give example / students work in pairs
Interaction:	pairs
Time:	10 mins
Stage:	**follow-up activity (speaking)**
Aim:	authentic practice of modals of deduction
Procedure:	set the scene / students read task and I check they understand / give out clue cards / give instructions and check / students do task and guess the murderer
Interaction:	teacher to class / then groups
Time:	20 mins

What the procedure does not refer to is any reference to pronunciation work, even though the teacher referred to potential problems of pronunciation earlier in the plan. However, the resulting lesson did have a pronunciation focus, and it was a very successful lesson.

Summary

▶ Having established aims which are both achievable in the time available and appropriate for the particular group of students being taught, teachers must prepare stages that link naturally and lead towards these aims.

▶ Teachers need to be flexible with all aspects of their plan and should at all times teach according to the needs and reactions of the students.

▶ Plans focus the teacher's mind on what needs to be achieved and the best way of achieving it – students benefit from this planned approach.

▶ Experienced teachers can be more 'spontaneous' in their teaching, but until you reach that stage always plan carefully, not just a particular lesson, but a series of lessons – you must consider the 'timetable fit' and so avoid producing a series of 'one-off' lessons.

20 Lesson planning: anticipating problems

In the previous units we have looked at writing lesson plans, and formulating clear and appropriate aims but teachers must never assume that a lesson will always, or even sometimes, go exactly as planned. They should anticipate problems, and be ready with solutions – this is an essential aspect of planning. This unit will focus on language analysis, and anticipating problems with language; the next will look at more general problems that can occur when we are teaching. Before reading further, then, do the following task.

Language analysis

TASK 1

For each of the following sentences, decide what the form of the highlighted part of the sentence is; and what the meaning is in the sentence given. You need to be clear about this before we anticipate problems. Bear in mind that for these sentences there is no context, so more than one meaning might be possible.

Example: ***I've been** working here for two years.* (intermediate)

Form: subject + *has/have* + verb-*ing* (= present perfect continuous / progressive)

Meaning: something you started doing in the past, are still doing now, and might continue doing in the future.

1 She's **gone** to France. (pre-intermediate)
2 I'll **have finished** by lunchtime. (intermediate)
3 It **must have been** a mistake. (intermediate)
4 You **have to pay** taxes. (elementary)
5 Can you **put me up** for the night? (pre-intermediate)
6 I'm **meeting** Zsigi for lunch tomorrow. (elementary)
7 **Could you help me** with my bags, please? (low elementary)
8 She **goes** to the gym every day. (low elementary)

9 **This time next week I'll be lying** on the beach. (high intermediate)

10 **I used to believe** in Santa Claus. (pre-intermediate)

The form, as referred to in Unit 4, is the fixed part of the sentence, the part that does not change. Look at this simple example:

I'm going to leave / work / eat

She's going to drive / sing

Here we see that the fixed part is 'subject (*I*, *She*, etc.) + *going to* + base verb'. If we said *I'm going to leave tomorrow*, then *tomorrow* is not part of the 'grammar' of the sentence.

If we have the verb *to depend*, the form includes the spelling, the fact that *to depend* is followed by '*on* + object', and that it is a regular verb.

The meaning is what this particular bit of language means in the context given. The sentence *You've lost weight* could be an expression of concern, or congratulating someone who has been on a diet and successfully lost weight.

With these points in mind, let's go back to the earlier task.

Key to task 1

1 **This is the present perfect simple. She is the subject and is followed by *has* or *have*, and the past participle. The past participle is the third form of the verb – *go, went, gone*; *eat, ate, eaten*; *work, work, worked*. *Work* is an example of a regular verb because its past endings are both *-ed*. The other verbs are irregular verbs because they have different and varying past endings.**

    The meaning here is that the person went to France at some unspecified past point and is still there now; for how long, we don't know.

2 **This is the future perfect simple. The subject is followed by '*will have* + past participle'. You are saying that whatever it is you are doing, you started at an unspecified past time, have not completed it, but definitely will at some point before lunchtime.**

3 **'*must have* + past participle' follows the subject. *Must* is a modal auxiliary verb, and *must have* places the time in the past. It is being used for deduction (informed guess) about a past event, so you think it was a mistake because there is no other likely explanation.**

4 'Subject + *have to* + base verb' is used to state something which is an obligation, usually an external obligation such as a rule or law.

5 '*to put someone up* (*put* + object + *up*)' for a period of time means to give someone a place to sleep for a short period of time.

6 'Subject + *is / am / are* + verb-*ing*' (= present continuous / progressive) here means that you and Zsigi have made an arrangement for lunch – it is a definite future arrangement.

7 '*Could you* + base verb + object' is used in this example to make a polite request.

8 The present simple in the 3rd person singular (*I go, you go, she goes*) is used here to talk about daily routine.

9 Following the time reference, we have 'subject + *will be* + verb-*ing*'. It means here that at a specified future time (this time next week) an action (lying on the beach) will be in progress, but will have begun at an unspecified time before, and will continue for a period after this time as well.

10 'Subject + *used to* + base verb' talks about a past habit or state, no longer true.

We have ten pieces of language with likely levels specified and we have established the form and the likely meaning (**concept**). As new teachers, you may be unsure yourselves of some of this language, but it is important to think of the problems from the students' point of view.

Anticipating problems

TASK 2

For each of the ten examples, consider what specific problems students might have with the form, meaning and pronunciation of the language (NB: aspects of pronunciation were also dealt with in Unit 9).

Example: *I've been working here for two years.*

▶ Students might have trouble with the concept of past, present and future time.
▶ The name of the tense – **present** perfect progressive – may add to this problem.
▶ Students might confuse this with the present progressive.

- Students might be unfamilar with some past participle verb forms.
- Possible confusion with contracted form (*She's*) ... *is* or *has*?
- Confusion with other use of same tense (e.g. *I've been playing tennis* – but not now).
- *been* is pronounced /bin/ in natural speech.

This is not a complete list of possible problems, but it gives you an idea of the types of problems that students might encounter. In many cases we could add 'first language interference', and this certainly applies to this example. There is also a different usage of the present perfect in British and American English, though this applies more to the present perfect simple. So, go ahead now and think of problems for the ten examples. Refer to a grammar book for help if you need to.

Before looking at this task, you may wonder if it is really so important to analyse language in this way before teaching it. It is. Ninety-nine per cent of all trainee teachers that I meet tell me that they are worried about 'grammar'. That is because so few people, in my experience, studied English grammar at school, and this results in the new teacher having to teach something about which they appear to know very little. This contrasts with the typical mid- to high-level student who appears to know much more than the new teacher. They know what a conditional sentence is, what a past participle is, what a preposition is but the teacher 'appears' to know very little, and the student 'appears' to know a lot. In one respect it is true, especially regarding the grammatical terminology, what things are, and rules. However, the nervous new teacher, if her first language is English, has an instinctive awareness of what is right and what is wrong; what is natural and what is not; and what is appropriate and what is not. What this teacher does not have – yet – is a ready understanding of 'Why?' It is this 'Why?' question that teachers fear being asked, as well as the identification of terms.

Of course, many teachers do not have English as their first language. Many trainees that I have worked with have come from many different countries. What these teachers have, usually, is an excellent knowledge and thus greater confidence. On the other hand, their choice of language is occasionally 'artificial' – for example, they might use idiomatic language in the wrong context.

For these reasons, it is essential for the new teacher to analyse the language she is going to teach. Any teacher needs to know the form of the language, the meaning in the context being used in the lesson, the phonological aspects of the language, and the most appropriate way for students to have practice using it. This will give the teacher confidence, and in turn the students will benefit.

When planning the lesson, the teacher needs to anticipate the problems that her students might have, at their level, with the language being covered in that particular lesson. By doing this, the teacher is better prepared to deal with those problems, and will be much better prepared to cope with all aspects of what is to be taught. And the biggest fear of new teachers will be greatly reduced – 'What if someone asks me a question I can't answer?' Again, the main beneficiaries of the teacher analysing the language and anticipating problems will be the students.

In doing the above task there was no specific group of students, no specific lesson plan. Therefore, the points we make are general ones that would not necessarily all apply to any one class; they are not exhaustive. So let's go through the task now.

Key to Task 2

1 She's gone to France.

The tense is called **present** perfect, but it refers to past time.

▶ Confusion with past simple (*She went to France*).
▶ Students may incorrectly add a time reference ('... *last week*').
▶ Students may confuse it with other uses of the same tense.
▶ British and American use of the present perfect is different.
▶ Students may not know the correct past participle verb forms.
▶ Students might confuse the contracted form of *has* with *is*.
▶ In the word *she's* the sound is /iːz/.
▶ In this sentence we have the preposition *to* and this is pronounced weakly.
▶ With this particular sentence, students may confuse *gone* with *been*.

The teacher, then, needs to provide a clear context which illustrates the time reference and to check understanding with concept questions / a timeline. Pronunciation needs to be worked on with the teacher providing a clear model and getting students to repeat it. Any task comparing this tense with the past simple would be valuable. Boardwork could provide a clear record of form.

These points apply to all these examples (but timelines are appropriate only for numbers **1**, **2**, **6**, **9**, **10**).

2 I'll have finished by lunchtime.

▶ It's a complex sentence with a double contraction likely in the spoken form.
▶ The pronunciation of *have* will be weak.
▶ Students are likely to confuse this with other future forms.
▶ The concept of the sentence is difficult (something which will already be finished at a given time in the future).
▶ Students may think of this sentence as only ever applying to future time, when it may refer to something already begun.
▶ The preposition *by* may be confused with *at*.
▶ Students may have problems with past participle forms.
▶ With *she* and *he* students may say *has* rather than *have*.

3 It must have been a mistake.

▶ Students might find the concept of 'deduction' difficult.
▶ Students might confuse this use of *must* with its meaning of obligation (e.g. *You must do your homework*).
▶ Students are likely to have problems with the form (modal + *have* + past participle).
▶ Students will probably think this is present perfect because of the '*have* + past participle', but it's not! If it was present perfect, for example, we would say *he has*, but here it is *he must have gone*.
▶ Students may be unfamiliar with some past participle forms.
▶ Students may be unclear about the time being referred to in this sentence.
▶ The degree of probability (compare with it *might have been*) may be unclear.
▶ Students will think the negative of this is *mustn't* (it's actually *can't*, as in *it can't have been a mistake*).
▶ Pronunciation of *must have* with the weak form of *have* in the contraction. With the negative, if being taught, there is the natural double contraction (*can't've*).

4 You have to pay taxes.

▶ Students may want to use *must* and be unclear of the fine difference between *must* and *have to*.
▶ The concept of 'external obligation' may be difficult.
▶ Students might confuse this use of *have* with the possessive use (*I have a pen*).
▶ The time reference may not be understood (general time in this case, but it isn't always – it can refer to future time, as in *I have to be at work early tomorrow*).

- ▶ The pronunciation of *have* is with an /f/ sound, not /v/, whereas with the possessive use of *have* the sound is /v/ not /f/! There is the weak form of *to* with the schwa.
- ▶ Students may use the incorrect form of *have* (for example, they might say *She have to...*).

5 Can you put me up for the night?

- ▶ Students may try to work out the meaning literally – not possible with phrasal verbs.
- ▶ The time reference may not be clear.
- ▶ The idea of providing someone with temporary accommodation could be difficult.
- ▶ The form is difficult. In this case the two parts of the verb are separated and the object goes in the middle. However, you can also say *Can you put up Marek for the night?*, but you cannot say *Can you put up him for the night?* The form of phrasal verbs is complex!
- ▶ Students can be overwhelmed by the number and different types of phrasal verbs, and in some cases by different meanings of the same verb!
- ▶ In this sentence, the weak form of *can* would be pronounced (kn).

6 I'm meeting Zsigi for lunch tomorrow.

- ▶ The name of the tense (present progressive) conflicts with the time reference (future).
- ▶ Students may want to use the present simple (which would be incorrect here, but correct if you meet Zsigi for lunch every, say, Tuesday).
- ▶ Students might want to use *will*, which they think of as the way to talk about the future.
- ▶ The present progressive has various uses which the students might confuse. The first they are likely to have learnt is for an action in progress at the time of speaking (e.g. *I'm watching TV right now*).
- ▶ The idea of a definite future arrangement, compared with intention, or other possible future function, is likely to confuse students.
- ▶ Spelling forms of the verb could be a problem (e.g. *meet* + *ing*, but not '*shine* + *ing*').
- ▶ Some verbs rarely if ever take the *-ing* form (e.g. *know, hear, like*).
- ▶ If students don't use the contracted form *I'm* and say *I am*, it changes the meaning somewhat and becomes more of an emphatic statement.
- ▶ If saying *he's* students might think they hear *his*.

- Similarly, *you're* may be heard as *your*, and *we're* as *were*.
- With *I'm meeting* the /m/ of *I'm* effectively disappears when spoken naturally.
- Students might be confused by the alternative negative forms (e.g. *you aren't / you're not*).
- Some languages have a single tense covering uses of both simple and progressive in English (first language interference might be an issue with most of these language points).

There are various other possible problems with this sentence / tense, but the above points highlight the complexity of it!

7 Could you help me with my bags, please?
- Students will ask about the alternative modal *can*.
- Idea of a polite request contrasting with other types of requests may be difficult.
- Weak form of *you* in pronunciation.
- Appropriate intonation important to convey politeness.
- Some students might use *to*-infinitive (*Could you to help me...?*)
- Students might confuse this use of *could* with others.

8 She goes to the gym every day.
- Concept of habitual action / routine might be difficult.
- Possible confusion with other uses of present simple that students might have been exposed to.
- Students may try to use present progressive instead, thinking of 'continuity' matching the idea of repeated action.
- Pronunciation of *goes* /z/ – the s can be pronounced /s/, /z/ or /iz/.
- Students may forget to add *-s* for 3rd person singular (*I go, you go, she goes*).
- Students may incorrectly add *-s* to plural form (*they comes*).
- Spelling problems (*play + -s / go + -es*, etc.).
- Students may try to add an auxiliary (*she does go*).
- Some languages have one tense covering the English simple and progressive tenses.

9 This time next week I'll be lying on the beach.
- The form is long and difficult.
- The concept is a very hard one for students (action in progress at a specified future time).
- Linked to the last point, the fact that the action will have started some time before and may continue beyond the specified time, is a difficult one to understand.

- Students will confuse this with other future forms, especially present and future progressive tenses.
- As mentioned in an earlier example, some verbs cannot usually be put into the progressive form.
- The contracted '*ll* is difficult for students to hear, and the contraction is difficult to produce.
- Students may omit the contraction and say *I will* which makes the meaning more emphatic and different from the usual contracted form.
- Spelling patterns, as mentioned before, will cause problems.

10 I used to believe in Santa Claus.

- Students might confuse this with the past simple (*I believed in Santa Claus*).
- The concept of past habit (*I used to smoke 20 cigarettes a day*) might be confused with past state (*I used to live in San Francisco*).
- Either or both of these concepts may be difficult for students to understand.
- Students may be further confused with other forms of used (e.g. *I'm used to + -ing / I'm getting used to + -ing*).
- The pronunciation is difficult – the *d* is pronounced /t/, and the *to* is weak and linked to the /t/.
- Students may pronounce the *s* as /z/ as in the verb (*I use a computer*).
- Students might pronounce *used* with two syllables, when there is only one.
- If the negative form is being taught, students may well incorrectly add -*d*. The correct form is *I didn't use to smoke* and not *I didn't used to smoke*.

Summary

- Analyse the language point you are going to teach. Ask yourself: what the meaning is in the context of the lesson (supplied by a text, CD, internet, MP3, or some other means).
- What is the form of the language?
- What is the correct and natural pronunciation?
- Anticipate the problems that the students might have with this language. Which problems and how many will depend on the level and nature of your class, and on whether it is a monolingual or multilingual class.

- If you don't analyse the language and anticipate problems, you will be 'caught out' – and you will deserve to be.
- The longer you teach, the more you will instinctively know, and the less unsure you will be. Until you reach that point, deal with each language point as it comes up (as you have to teach it) and your language awareness will steadily increase.
- Don't be afraid to ask more experienced colleagues for help as well as consulting reference books.

21 Lesson planning: what would you do if ...?

So, you know your aims; you have planned your lesson; you have analysed any language being taught and anticipated problems students might have with it. However, there is still one more aspect involved when planning – you need to anticipate what might go wrong in your lesson, or any other lesson, and be prepared so you know what you would do. It is sometimes these unexpected problems that panic new or training teachers, especially the latter because they are being observed and assessed. If, however, you can think in advance of virtually any unexpected development in your lesson then nothing can go wrong ... well, almost nothing.

Here, then, are 20 such situations to consider ... and they have all happened to me at some time!

Unexpected problems

TASK

What would you do if ...

1 you planned for an activity where students would work in pairs, but one student was absent and you had an odd number of students in your class?

2 a student arrived very late as you were teaching and had missed an important part of the lesson?

3 you had a student who said your lesson was 'boring'?

4 you had a student who said your lesson was 'too easy'?

5 you were doing a listening activity and the audio equipment didn't work?

6 you had a student who dominated the class and would never let anyone else speak?

7 you had left your lesson plan / materials / book at home?

8 you were asked a grammar question you could not answer?

9 you were teaching a multilingual class which included two students of the same nationality who continually spoke to each other in their language?

10 your class was very big (at least 20 students)?

11 a student(s) always finished tasks well before anyone else?

12 the students found what you are doing very difficult?

13 you had a truly mixed-ability class?

14 your planned lesson finished very early and you had to 'fill time'?

15 the lesson time was up but you still had lots of your planned lesson to do?

16 you had two students in the class who clearly did not like each other?

17 you gave out a task and a student said 'I did this with another teacher'?

18 a student constantly used their dictionary in class?

19 a student's mobile phone went off in class and they took the call?

20 you explained a rule but a doubting student remarked 'but my other teacher said ...'?

There does come a point in your teaching life when you have encountered just about every possible situation (I say 'just about' because you can never be sure!), have experienced every little or not so little problem, and feel completely confident as you walk in to teach. It is good to experience situations like the ones above, because only then will you learn what to do, and your confidence will grow so that you do not fear the same things happening again.

Let's look at these 20 situations and consider some possible solutions – though the precise solutions will depend upon the context and exact circumstances.

Key to task

1 Pair work with an odd number of students

I have seen this situation panic trainee teachers far more than it should, given the relative smallness of the problem. You should not become the odd student's partner because if you do, you effectively become a student in the class and your role as a teacher is lost. You need to monitor the class, help the students as required, generally keep an eye on things – and you can't do that if you are participating in the task. So, depending on the task, two students could act as one. In your instructions you might say 'OK, you're A, you're B, you're A, you're B ... Javier and Ella, you're A together, and Bruno is B'.

Another approach definitely to avoid, and I have seen it happen more than once, is to say to the odd student 'OK, you just watch'. This is leaving the student out of the task completely and is the worst thing you could do.

2 Late arrivals

You should acknowledge this student's arrival ('Hello'), and gesture for them to sit down quickly and quietly. At this stage, do not stop your teaching to tell the latecomer what they have missed – this would annoy those students who were there on time, and effectively send the message that it is OK to arrive late. Carry on, but when the rest of the class begin a task individually or together, go to the latecomer and fill them in on what you have done so far.

If a student is persistently late, have a quiet word to find out why. It could be a case of transport problems or some other simple but genuine problem, but make it clear that they are losing out by missing part of your lessons on a regular basis. Above all, don't let latecomers disrupt your lesson.

3 'Your lesson is boring'

It will happen! If you have been monitoring your students and 'reading their faces' then you may have detected this student's lack of interest. It is usually easy to notice when a student appears bored, then you can do something about it before the dreaded complaint. You also need to think why this student might be bored. In all likelihood, it is because they think the lesson is too easy (see **4**), or maybe they have covered this material before (see **17**). In each of these situations, you can deal with the problem. But maybe they really are bored – perhaps they are reluctant students, sent by their parents. Maybe they have a low interest threshold. Or maybe, just maybe, your lesson was boring! Did you establish interest? Did you adapt the material to suit the needs and interests of your class? Were you displaying some enthusiasm and energy when teaching? Or were you just following the book and not making the lesson come alive?

Whatever the reason for the student's comment, you still need to react properly to it. Don't get angry or defensive or make an issue of the comment in front of the other students. Have a word privately with the student after class and establish the reason for the comment, then try and respond so this student will not feel bored again. However, it needs to be said that sometimes you get a student who will be bored regardless of what you do because they just don't want to be there. Try to include in your lesson topics that you know this student is interested in, maybe involve them actively in some way. Keep them busy.

4 'Your lesson is too easy'

Any of the points made in **3** could apply here. But in addition, it could be that the lessons are too easy. This could be because you are not pitching your lessons to the general and intended level of the class, in which case other students would probably be voicing the same complaint. Or it could be that this student should be in another class. Discuss this student with your Director of Studies and maybe it will be possible to move her to a different class. If it isn't, you will need to give this student extra and more challenging tasks to do.

5 Technology problems

There are a few things that can go wrong when you are doing a listening activity and such problems were discussed more fully in Unit 13. If the worst happens and you cannot use your recording (your CD is scratched, the CD player won't work, there is no internet connection), and you do not have the audio script in the book for students to refer to (thus making it a reading stage), then you will have to lose that part of your lesson and expand on whatever else you have planned. Most potential problems in a listening lesson can be avoided, but if technology lets you down, there is nothing you can do.

6 Dominant students

A student may dominate the class for different reasons. They might be of a good level and know a lot and be keen to show you what they know. Or they might be naturally talkative and outgoing and it is good to have a student in the class who participates well because a class that never speaks is a nightmare. However, you should not let a student 'take over' so that even when you ask another student to speak, the dominating student answers for them. Sometimes, such students like to play the role of the teacher and start correcting other students when you don't want them to. You must, therefore, curb the enthusiasm of this student in a way which is subtle and which does not result in him or her withdrawing from that point on. Using students' names can help (ask an open question and the dominating student will always answer; ask another student by name to speak and the dominant student may keep quiet). A polite gesture to the dominant student to allow someone else to speak, can work. Or, saying something like 'OK, thank you, but someone else'. So you are not telling him to be quiet, but encouraging others to participate more.

7 Missing materials

A nightmare scenario but you still have to go and teach the class! There is no simple solution to this, but the longer you teach, the more materials and 'standby lessons' you will build up, and you can fall back on these in an emergency. You will also become more familiar with resource books and know where you can find a lesson at short notice. Failing that, and if the context allows it, give your class a challenging speaking activity to keep them busy while you think of what to do later. If the class is very low level, give them a task which revises what they have done before (e.g. write the days of the week) which again will give you a bit of time to think. Ask a colleague, or your Director of Studies for help. Best of all, check before you leave home that you have what you need.

8 Difficult questions

The moment dreaded by all new or training teachers. The last unit gave the best advice – if you have analysed the language, and anticipated problems students might have with the language, then you are much less likely to be asked a question you cannot answer.

But if you still get asked a tricky question, there are various possible reactions. If you know the answer but can't think of it right then, throw the question open to the class to see if someone else can answer. Or even throw it back to the student herself – 'Well, what do you think?' While the class / student is trying to answer, you get a valuable minute to collect your thoughts. If this is not going to be enough time, you could set it as a homework task and then make sure you go back to it the next day. If the question is about a point irrelevant to that lesson, say you'll come back to it later but you need to move on. Or, just be honest and say you're not sure but will check. However, don't do this too often or the students will lose confidence in you.

9 Students chatting

Teachers have different views on how best to deal with this situation. Some will make a point at the start of the class to make sure – if possible – that no one is sitting next to another student who speaks the same language (e.g. place names on seats). Others will separate students during a class (but do it sensitively – move several students so it is not obvious that you are targeting particular people). One way to do this, if the class is not too big and it is easy for people to move around, is to say to students in turn 'you're 1, you're 2, you're 3, you're 1, you're 2, you're 3 ... OK, all the 1's sit here, all the 2's sit here', etc.) but if students are sitting in rows behind desks, you can't do that!

Other teachers will let students sit where they want, but strongly remind and encourage them to speak only English. Don't get too strict, make a joke out of it ('That doesn't sound like English!'). Separate them as a last resort but don't forget, as has been said elsewhere in this book, if your class is multilingual you really must try and keep it to English only or else many students will get annoyed. If it is monolingual, as most classes around the world are, all you can do is to minimize the use of first language to an acceptable level.

10 Large classes

It's all very well planning pair and group work, and wanting to monitor students' work, etc. when you have a class of ten students and plenty of space. But if you have 20, 30 or 40 students, sitting in rows behind fixed desks, then what? Clearly you will need to rethink and adjust your expectations, particularly with regards to class management. You will find it difficult to see, or be seen by, students at the back, to move students, to monitor and evaluate progress, and maybe to keep the class in order. There, are, however, some tips to follow. You can still do pair work, it's just that each student will be restricted to working with either of the students they are sitting next to. Maybe, however, they can turn around and pair up with a student in the row behind. If this is possible, then so is group work. A resulting problem is how to get the students' attention back when you want them to stop. Some teachers might clap their hands, or raise one hand, or have some other agreed signal so the students know when they should stop working.

Certain students can help you (e.g. handing out worksheets, acting as a spokesperson for a group, etc.).

You need to project your voice well, and make sure that anything you are showing to the class (including boardwork) is big enough to be seen by everyone.

Finally, give clear ground rules about what is and is not permitted; you have to stamp your authority on big classes so that the class knows what to do, when to do it, and how to do it.

11 Quick students

When students are working individually, in pairs, or in groups, you should monitor their work. One of the things you should look out for is a student who finishes a task very quickly, too quickly for you to be prepared to stop the others. There are various options to deal with this: You could ask this student to help another. You could extend the task ('Think of five more examples'). You could have another task ready for quick finishers. You could, if appropriate to the task, ask the student to review what they have done and look for mistakes. But whatever you do, don't leave this student idle because then she will get bored and frustrated. Keep your students busy and challenged.

12 Materials too difficult

Maybe the student is in the wrong class and they would benefit from a lower-level class, if one is available. Talk to your Director of Studies and see what the possibilities are but don't rush to quick judgements if that student has only just joined your class. Students need time to settle into a class and find their level within it. They often start by thinking the class is too difficult, but are happy enough a few days later.

It could be that the class as a whole is finding the lessons too difficult, so maybe you are pitching the lessons at the wrong level. Sometimes teachers need to lower or raise the level of the lessons to adjust to the students in the class. As you will see in Unit 28, terms such as 'elementary' are very broad and some elementary classes are stronger than others. The teacher has to respond and adapt her teaching accordingly.

13 Mixed ability

To some extent this point is discussed elsewhere in the book. In Unit 28, for example, I suggest that you should avoid ending up teaching groups separately within a single class – it is difficult, and can lead to frustration for all concerned. However, sometimes you might feel this is the only option if you have a student of a very different level, and there is no other class for him to go to. In this case, prepare separate material, tasks for this student to work on, and spend time going over the tasks with that particular student. But I am talking about a student who is genuinely at a different level, not just a little weaker or stronger than others in the class because this happens all the time – after all, no two students can ever have exactly the same level of English.

Another alternative – again time-consuming for the teacher when planning – is to have the same material for the whole class, but different tasks. This is another last resort, in my opinion, simply because of the extra workload for the teacher. You might have the option of letting this student use the school's self-access materials, if they exist. For example, language laboratory work, or reading / listening to graded readers (story books graded for particular levels).

Sometimes a student will gradually adjust, maybe with the help of another student who can work with them. So pairing the student off with a sensitive stronger student might help as well.

Whatever you do don't just let this student struggle alone.

14 Filling time

However well you know your class, and however well you have planned your lesson, you can never be sure that your lesson won't finish early. You will have to fill that time because you cannot just finish early – your students have paid for a certain amount of teaching time and they must get it. My own favourite experience was when, despite having had over ten years' teaching experience at that time, I found myself in a 60-minute lesson having 30 minutes to fill, instead of the 5 or 10 minutes you might expect. I had completely misjudged my students' capabilities with the lesson I had planned, which just goes to show that however experienced you might be, you can still get it very wrong sometimes!

Ideally, you should always have something 'up your sleeve' – an extension to what you have already done, or something quite different. This could be a quick language game, a discussion topic, a review of earlier work, or maybe a quick information exchange ('Find out what everyone had for breakfast today'). Whatever it is, it should be something that does not require any preparation time because you are unlikely to do it anyway. But always be prepared ... just in case.

15 Not enough time

This is the opposite problem, but actually not really a problem at all. For a multitude of possible reasons, there are times when your lesson time is up and you have covered barely half of what you planned to do. This may actually reflect well on your teaching, rather than badly, if you have responded to your students in the lesson and realized that they were having more difficulty than you had anticipated and 'slowed down' as a result. It is much better to do that than finish what you had planned, regardless of your students' needs. Of course, it may be that you have misjudged the level, but as long as you are aware of this and compensate for it in future lessons, no harm is done. Normally, you would be teaching the class again and can continue the 'unfinished lesson' – this has the added bonus of less preparation being needed for the next lesson.

16 Student antipathy

Sometimes a teacher can remain unaware of two students not liking each other, or one not liking the other, because they remain outwardly polite and friendly, and there is no problem but there are tell-tale signs to watch out for in case the problem is more serious. The most obvious is when particular students do not work together when in pairs, when you have seen them working happily with others in the class. Or when a student goes out of her way to avoid sitting next to a particular student. Sometimes it is more open and obvious; sometimes – as sensitive as you might be to such situations – you have no idea until it is too late. This happened to me when I was still a fairly new teacher. I taught a class for three months and remained quite unaware that two young men in the class hated each other – until, that is, they started fighting after a class one day!

All you can do is to keep your eyes and ears open – back again to 'reading faces' – and if you sense a problem, do some tactful class management to keep the pair apart. Maybe talk to them individually if you feel this might help. However, this is a rare problem.

17 'We've already done this'

I hate this but when students are being taught by different teachers, and there are certain materials in the school, available to any teacher, it is bound to happen to you. And at times, you will be that 'other teacher'. Usually, it is impossible to change your lesson there and then – and if this only concerns one or two students, you shouldn't anyway. You could give them different tasks to do, get them to work with students who haven't done it before, or – if possible – give them something quite different to do. If, however, it's a language point ('Oh, I've done the 2nd conditional') be honest with them and tell them that they still won't remember or know everything about it, or tell them that you will be using different material from the other teacher, and that it is important for them to review what they have done before and not think that they have ever 'done' a piece of language.

A more difficult case is when you are doing a particular skills lesson and the whole class did the same text or recording with another teacher. If you can think on your feet and come up with a different lesson on the spot, great. If not, you'll just have to repeat the lesson but make it as individual in style and approach as possible. I'm afraid this will happen to you more than once. Sometimes it is good to ask other teachers beforehand if they have used a particular lesson recently with that class.

18 Over-use of dictionaries

How much you allow your students to use dictionaries, and what kind of dictionaries, is ultimately your decision. My own view is that they are a valuable learning tool as long as students know how to use them properly to get the most from them. However, the dictionary should not become a substitute for the teacher. For example, you write up a new word and immediately a student goes for her dictionary rather than listening to you. You have lost the attention of that student, she is not listening to you, and the dictionary has become a crutch for the student. Or a student checks everything you say, not quite believing you until the dictionary confirms what you have said. In these situations you need to be quite firm – and even more so with noisy electronic dictionaries, especially those that have 'voices'! Tell the students when they can and cannot use their dictionaries, and teach them how to use them. Encourage the use of English–English dictionaries, especially those produced specially for language learners but when the situation demands it, say 'No dictionaries'.

19 Mobile phones in class

This is a particular pet hate of most teachers. It is just polite in any public situation to turn off the phone – whether it's in a concert hall, theatre, or classroom, but when a student not only fails to turn off the machine, but actually takes the call while your class is in progress, this is unacceptable. Gesture to that student to leave the classroom to continue the conversation, but also have a sign to tell the class that all mobile phones should be switched off before the start of the lesson.

20 'But my other teacher said ...'

More often than not the student has misheard or misunderstood what that teacher actually said. It happens a lot, and when you check with the teacher concerned, you nearly always find that the teacher said nothing of the sort! Students worry when teachers appear to have contradicted each other, so always check with the other teacher so you can resolve the issue with the student. Usually this just means clarifying to them what the other teacher really did say.

Summary

In the last four units we have seen that a great deal is involved in planning a lesson. In this unit we have looked at aspects of lessons which can cause problems at any time, mostly to do with the smooth running of classes. Most, if not all, of the problems mentioned in this unit will be experienced by you at some time in your career; and as you deal with each one in the best way according to your circumstances, so you will 'grow' as a teacher. The last four units should have left you with one obvious conclusion ... a successful lesson depends on proper planning. Be prepared!

22 Using course books and authentic materials

When I trained to be a teacher, I remember having to 'create' all my lesson materials (admittedly for only a total of six hours' teaching in four weeks) because we were not using a course book but no teacher could teach on a daily basis without access to resources, either a course book or 'in-house' materials. Yet, there seems to remain some resistance to the whole idea of using a book – usually, I find, among the least expected group – training teachers. This is understandable because we probably all had some experience at school of a teacher just setting work from the book while she proceeded to mark homework, or whatever. And this is the point. Using a course book is only the right option if it is used properly. In other words, teachers need to know how to teach from a book – and this is not as easy as it might sound but if it is done properly, it is an enormous time-saver for the teacher and it benefits the students in a number of ways.

TASK 1

When using a course book teachers need to Use, Reject, Adapt, and Supplement. Later in this unit we will examine what is meant by this, but for now spend a few minutes trying to understand what these words mean, and consider possible examples.

Why use a course book?

As suggested above there are advantages for the teacher and the students. From the teacher's point of view the book provides material, a syllabus structure, and consequently much less time is needed to prepare lessons. Personally, I don't see how any full-time teacher can function without a book. From the student's point of view there is a visual record of progress, easier access to material, the possibility to review work at home, and a feel of greater professionalism (compare this with lots of photocopied worksheets – environmentally unfriendly as well). In theory, then, using a course book would seem to be highly desirable. There is certainly no shortage of books on the market, but there are numerous potential problems with their use, as we shall see.

ESSENTIALS OF A 'GOOD' COURSE BOOK

It is very hard to find consensus on what is a 'good' book – what one teacher thinks is good, another thinks is bad. The truth is that most books are usable. How 'good' one is depends on how the teacher uses it. However, there are some basic requirements:

Ideally, It should have been written by experienced teachers and also be roughly appropriate for the level intended. You can assume both. In addition, though, the book should ideally be appropriate for the country you are teaching in, and this can be a problem. Unfortunately, a great many books are British in content and culture, and if not solely British then European. It's all very well reading an article about British food when you are in London, but less so when you are in Tokyo or Jakarta or New York. Photographs of 'famous people', with some notable exceptions, are often not recognized by students.

Your book, too, should be appropriate not just for the level you are teaching, but for the students you are teaching. We will develop this point later, but enough now to say that just because something is in the book doesn't mean you should use it with your students.

Ideally, the book should be visually attractive and well laid out – clear, and easy to follow. Preferably, the pages won't be too cluttered. It's nice to have a clear Contents page, and the language covered should have a logical progression (starting the book at one level, but finishing it at a higher level).

As for topics, I have to say that most experienced teachers, and a fair number of students, get a bit tired of talking about 'weather', 'food', 'holidays', 'countries', and various other standard topics that appear in most books. However, in defence of these topics, I should say that for lower levels they are 'easy' and 'safe'. Higher levels can deal with more advanced topics such as 'technology' and 'the environment' because they have more language to talk about them. Topics / Units best avoided are topics which include gruesome pictures of suffering people, or contentious issues like war and religion. Teachers, too, sometimes wonder why we are teaching students the vocabulary of, say, crime. Just how useful and relevant is this? I would argue that weather, food, holidays, etc. are in fact, more useful topics, but that much higher levels can, and should, be challenged with more thought-provoking issues.

An ideal course book should have variety and balance – language work, skills work, pronunciation, review units or sections and grammar summaries. In other words, it should be a complete package for the student.

Using a course book

USE, REJECT, ADAPT, SUPPLEMENT

The teacher's dream scenario: you look at the next unit in the book. The topic is interesting, the material is good and appropriate, the 'staging' is logical, the tasks are just right – in short, it's perfect. So, use it as it is. This doesn't happen often, but when it does, make the most of it. There is no need to reinvent the wheel, and new teachers, especially, sometimes feel that they have to create their own materials and do lots of cutting up and pasting. If it's not necessary – don't do it.

The teacher's nightmare scenario: you look at the next unit in the book and the topic is quite inappropriate for your students. Or the material is very dry or difficult or easy or unclear. So, reject it. However, having said that, if you are working in a school where you have to cover everything in the book, you may not be allowed to reject material (i.e. not use it), but if you do have flexibility, don't be afraid to say 'I can't use this with my students'. This is a nightmare because you then have to find alternative material to cover the language you need to focus on, and that takes time. Some teachers are more 'sensitive' than others, for better or for worse. I tend to reject quite often, but some material which I have found 'untouchable' another teacher has had no problems with, so maybe I am too topic-sensitive!

To be honest, **use** and **reject** are the least common courses of action when teaching from a book. Far more likely – indeed, most of the time – you will have material which is OK to an extent, but it needs to be changed a bit. Maybe the listening task is too simple and you want to extend it. Maybe you don't need to use one part of a page. Maybe you would prefer to use your own practice activity rather than the one in the book. In other words, **adapt** (change certain parts as necessary), and **supplement** (use other material – your own, or from other sources). So you are still using much of what is in the book, but you are not slavishly doing everything simply because it is there. If you simply go through the book from start to finish, setting work from it, you are not demonstrating any teaching skills, you are not responding to your students' individual needs and backgrounds and you are not doing your job properly. Even if it's a great book, it still needs exploiting. This takes us back to the comment in the introduction to this unit – teachers, especially new or training ones, sometimes feel it is 'wrong' to use a course book for the simple reason that they had the experience of a teacher at school who simply followed the book. If you do follow the book then your students will indeed be bored and demotivated – and so will you.

There are other considerations, too. A course book will normally come with accompanying CDs, a Teacher's Book, and maybe a Workbook with extra practice tasks. The Teacher's Book is invaluable because it provides answers, and sometimes explanations for answers and some will also have suggested procedure. Either this book or the Student's Book will have the audio scripts. However, there is a danger in relying too much on the Teacher's Book. For a start, any book is liable to have the odd misprint or two – so although a book says the answer to a question is 'A', it might be incorrect. And even if the answer is correctly printed, as it is most of the time, that doesn't mean that it's the answer you would give. So, check the answers beforehand, and make sure you agree with them and know why the answer is what it is.

MAKE THE COURSE BOOK SUITABLE

The authors of your book have written it knowing the approximate level it is intended for but only you know your students. You have to make the book suitable for the people you are teaching.

There are many books available these days, but the chances are that you will be assigned a book to use. You may be lucky and be given some choice; you may be very unlucky and not have a book at all but whatever book you hopefully have, be critical in a positive sense. Don't, as many new or training teachers do, have a quick look at it and say it's no good. I have heard many excellent books dismissed in this way on training courses, partly because of the feeling that 'it's not fun'. Similarly, new teachers are sometimes tempted to describe almost any practice activity as a 'game'. This should most definitely be avoided, assuming you are teaching adults. For many students 'game' = 'not learning' but even if your students do like the occasional game, (and there's nothing wrong with games in the classroom from time to time) it doesn't mean that you have to keep using the word because you don't like what's in the book. You'll be surprised at what students like. In my experience, the so-called 'conventional grammar exercise' is actually very popular, as long as it is balanced with more communicative work and if it is done in pairs or groups, or if students have the opportunity to discuss and compare their answers afterwards, so much the better. In other words, don't be too quick to assume that something is 'boring'. You need to set the activity up in an interesting way, prepare the students for it, etc., but do not ignore lots of good material in the book because it's not 'fun'. The important thing is for learning to be interesting and challenging.

The other general point I would make is about the level. The levels we use ('elementary', 'intermediate', etc.) are very broad and you will always have a mixed-level class to some extent. A common complaint among training teachers is 'They're not all the same level'. Well, what do you expect? How is every student in the class going to be of the same level in all aspects of the language? Of course, there are occasions when, for various reasons, you will have someone of the wrong level in the class, but that is different from having a range of intermediate students in one class. The book, therefore, is for this very general level. Consequently, you will need to adapt, supplement and reject material in order to make it right for the precise level of your class.

TIPS

1 **Critically evaluate the material in the book in relation to who you are teaching.**

2 **Reject the unsuitable and use the ideal. Otherwise, adapt and supplement the material.**

3 **Use the book if there is one (you may have to anyway) – the students expect it.**

4 **Check answers to exercises, and make sure you can justify them if necessary.**

5 **Make real use of the material, don't just say 'OK, do exercise 3 on page 40'. You must use your skills – establish interest, prepare them, clear instructions, etc.**

6 **Don't skip about in the book (Unit 3, then 6, then 14, then 2 ...) – the units are in an order for a reason. You can't just pick the parts you like the best.**

7 **Make sure that the way you use the material in the book is appropriate in every way to the students in your class.**

8 **Teach your students how to get the most out of the book in their free time (assuming they have their own copy). For example, books normally have separate grammar summaries, vocabulary summaries, pronunciation guides, and maybe audio scripts.**

9 **Make it clear to them why you are not using everything in the book (assuming you are allowed not to cover everything), and**

why you are using other material. They are adults and you can involve them in the teaching rationale. Work not done in class can always be done at home.

10 Make full use of the material – new teachers tend to cover in a week what an experienced teacher would cover in a month!

Using other materials

The point has already been made several times that teachers need to supplement the material in the course book with other material. Fortunately, there is a very good range and variety of resource books on the market – look at what your school has – as well as online resources. You also have the 'home-grown' material for those who are creative and have some time to do it, but it doesn't have to be anything special – maybe just some questions of your own to accompany a listening task or just an idea of your own to get the students speaking together.

Also, teachers should make good use of **authentic** material.

WHAT IS AUTHENTIC MATERIAL?

This is real-life material not specially published or adapted for classroom use. Examples include brochures, posters, newspapers (real or online), magazines, leaflets, signs, notices, songs, radio, TV. It is best to use something reasonably up-to-date, at least as far as reading matter is concerned (so, today's or yesterday's news, not last month's). It is good to use authentic material simply because it is real and something your students might be exposed to on any day. However, the value of such material may be more limited when teaching in a country where English is not the first language because the students won't find some of this material quite as easily in English (books, brochures, leaflets, etc.). However, online material is easily accessible for most and students can be encouraged to read online newspapers or magazines or listen to radio online. In fact, it is important in non-English-speaking countries to direct your students to material of all sorts which is available in English (magazines, books, English-speaking radio and TV).

Exploiting it

Units 12–15 covered approaches to skills work so you should read those units for ways to use material for purely skills focus. However, you may want to use the material, at least in part, to focus on language. What we covered in Unit 5 is particularly appropriate for this.

In general, having chosen appropriate material, devise tasks which are graded for the level being taught (and the students in your class), making these as practical, useful and interesting as possible. Decide, too, which aspects of the material you want to focus on. This will be partly determined by the level of the class – what you want an elementary class to do with a newspaper article will be different from what an upper-intermediate class will do with the same article. The level will dictate the nature of the tasks.

Newspaper articles are an especially good source of authentic material. Here are eight ways to use newspapers in the classroom.

1 **You can focus on one article / story for reading, speaking or lexis.**

2 **You can focus on one article for specific language.**

3 **You can compare how different papers cover the same story.**

4 **You can focus on the use of headlines (e.g. prediction of the story to follow).**

5 **You can focus on the different parts of a paper.**

6 **You can use the articles as a springboard for debate with higher-level classes.**

7 **You can give students a headline and they write an article; then they compare their article with the original.**

8 **If you have the facilities, you can compare the TV news report of a story with the newspaper one.**

TASK 2

Think of six different ways to use a holiday brochure in the classroom (say, a brochure advertising holidays in Mexico). I'll give you some suggestions below.

Key to task 2

Here are just a few possibilities.

As with the newspaper articles, you can use brochures to focus on specific language, or as a reading comprehension. You could also focus on the specific vocabulary featured in brochures (e.g. discount, package tour, etc.), or on the style of language used – for example, what 'not far from the beach', and 'cosy room' really mean!

Speaking possibilities are many: students could choose their favourite trip from a selection of brochures and role-play a conversation asking for more information or booking the trip. You might also get the students to imagine that they did go on the trip and to discuss what the reality was. As a writing activity, students could prepare a brochure advertising their home town or a place that they have visited. Maybe you could use your brochure on 'Mexico' as an introduction to a text or recording you have on the country, or as a follow-up to the text or recording.

Summary

▶ Course books are there to be used and they should be used critically by the teacher. You should make full use of the material, and follow the guidelines of **Use**, **Reject**, **Adapt**, **Supplement**. You need to make the material suitable for the students in your class.

▶ But don't be too dismissive of a book or some of its contents. And don't just 'pick out' the parts you like.

▶ Books save preparation time, provide a structure, give ideas and material, language notes and guidance, a visual record, and a daily reference.

▶ British-based books are less appropriate in other countries, but seek out any books which might have been published in the country you are teaching in.

▶ Check the contents of a book, including the Teacher's Book, to make sure you know how something is supposed to work, that you agree with the answers, and can justify the answers.

▶ Yes, a book may be boring, especially if you just go from one page to the next. So make it interesting and stimulating.

▶ Authentic material provides exposure to real English and it can be used in many different ways. It also provides variety.

▶ There is plenty of other material, such as resource books or online material that you can use for alternative ideas. Again, by using other resources you add variety to your lessons.

23 Testing students

Your first thoughts on seeing the title of this unit will probably be 'exams', or 'tests'. These are indeed, part of what is referred to here as 'testing students', but only a part. Teachers test students all the time because testing means to find out what students know and remember. Five examples of classroom testing are:

▶ concept questions; test if students understand meaning
▶ eliciting; tests what students know and remember
▶ language exercises; test what students know
▶ comprehension tasks; test what students understand
▶ drilling; tests students' pronunciation.

However, beyond normal classroom practice, students may take the following types of tests:

▶ placement
▶ diagnostic
▶ progress
▶ achievement.

We will look at these types of testing and at the difference between subjective and objective assessment.

First, though, a test for you!

TASK 1

Complete the following:

1 **Tests are motivating for students.**

 Students _____ (rewrite first sentence)   1 mark

2 **The Cambridge FCE, CAE and CPE exams are: (choose one)**
 a placement tests
 b diagnostic tests
 c progress tests
 d achievement tests   1 mark

3 **We test students informally in class all the time.**
 True or False?   2 marks

4 **The marking system should be _____ (rely)**   1 mark

5 The reliability of the marking system is affected by
   the _____ given to each section.   5 marks

6 When I was at school I _____ tests   1 mark

7 Rewrite the following using all the words:
   be-interesting-do-to-tests-format-and-in-varied-should   8 marks

8 One of the biggest disadvantages of testing
   is _____   10 marks

9 Objective assessment is _____
   Subjective assessment is _____   1 mark

10 Which word is spelt correctly? (no dictionaries)

   accomodation – benefitted – neccesary –
   reciept – bussiness   1 mark

Progress tests are what teachers will give their students from time to time. At some schools they are a requirement; at others, they are strongly encouraged. Typically, they take place once a week / every two weeks and their aim is usually seen as testing what students can remember of what they have recently learnt. This undoubtedly is one aim of such tests, but I also like to present them to my students as an important opportunity for them to review what they have done in class, and to clarify what they are still having difficulty with. Sometimes, I will even let students work together on such tests, but with one important proviso – they cannot refer back to notes or books. Why? Because if they can make themselves remember without such help, they are more likely to remember more easily in the future.

Such tests do not have to be in test format, like the above example (which we go back to shortly). They can be done as quizzes, for example, with students in teams answering questions. You could also get your students to make up the questions for a test, telling each team which language points they need to think of questions about. Or, students could prepare posters which display important points learnt in the recent lessons.

In other words, be varied in how you conduct progress tests. That said, there is nothing wrong from time to time in giving students an authentic progress test. Many students welcome it, seeing it as a 'proper' part of learning but you need to give them notice that they are going to be tested soon (tell them when), and what they are going to be tested on. Some course books will have ready-made 'tests' after every few units, or you can prepare your own.

Let's go back to the task above to make some more points about testing.

Key to task 1

1 The correct answer is *Students are motivated by tests*.

Yes, students are usually motivated by tests, but the great danger, of course, is that they might do badly and be discouraged. This is why I personally prefer students to help each other when doing such tests, because for me the aim is for them to review what they have learnt, rather than to be examined on what they can remember.

As for this question, you were required to write a passive sentence, and using a different tense from the first. Not an easy task ... but only one mark awarded.

2 The correct answer is *achievement*.

An achievement test can take two forms. It can be an internal test given by you at the end of the course, usually done in exam format. And it can be an external exam written and marked by an outside body. The examples given in the question are all Cambridge exams – First Certificate in English, Certificate of Advanced English, and Certificate of Proficiency in English. You are unlikely to be asked to teach an exam class until you have a lot of experience, so this unit will not focus on the exams themselves. However, you may need to administer an internal achievement test. If you do find yourself having to teach an exam class, without much experience, you will work from an exam course book which will tell you most of what you need to know. Beyond this, seek help from your Director of Studies. There is a huge range of public (external) examinations that students can take around the world at all levels. Some are a passport to universities, jobs, promotion, etc. The TOEFL exam, now available to be done entirely on computer with an immediate result, is primarily for entry into universities in the United States. It is, as you would expect, all in American English.

Internal achievement tests, like progress tests, are generally welcomed by students because it gives them what they perceive to be a measure of their progress. If I sound less than convinced by my own words it is because I think exams are limited in their ability to prove to students what they know and understand. Students have to know how to do an exam, how to prepare for it, how to tackle it. Exams have an important place in learning, but maybe not as important as some students believe. How many times have students and teachers been very surprised at someone's result? But, of course, it is a wonderful feeling for both parties when a student does very well in an achievement test.

3 True.

This was a point discussed at the start. Note that two marks were on offer here for a true / false question, compared to only one for the first question which required grammatical knowledge.

4 Reliable (and logical).

The marking system for this test is hardly that! If you are setting a test, award marks (if you are going to award any at all – you don't have to) that reflect the difficulty of the question, and the type of answer required.

5 Weight.

If a test is divided up into different sections (e.g. Reading, Vocabulary, Grammar), does each section carry equal weight? Should it? Do your students know how they are being marked? They should. Five marks on offer for this!

6 This asks for an opinion, it does not test anything and you cannot assess opinions.

As far as the question itself is concerned, most students have negative memories of tests – rows and rows of desks, silence, conditions, invigilators, stress. Should it be like this? Maybe exams have to be, but not internal tests.

7 This should read *tests should be varied in format and interesting to do* (and hardly deserves eight marks).

If you are devising a test, vary the types of question because this will make it a little more interesting. For example, you could include multiple choice, true / false, correction of mistakes, writing sentences, sentence transformation, etc. Make the test as varied and unpredictable as you can.

8 There are several.

The point is that you cannot mark an answer to such a question when there is no obvious answer. How will you award the ten marks? Only to students whose opinion is the same as yours? This type of question has no place in a test.

9 Objective tests are those which have right and wrong answers, with no ambiguity. Example: The capital city of Scotland is a Glasgow b Aberdeen c Edinburgh. Marking is unaffected by the marker, consistent, accuracy based, and easy to assess.

Subjective tests are those which require the marker to assign marks according to a marking scheme.

Obvious examples are composition (essay) writing, and exam 'interviews' (speaking exams). With such testing, it is imperative that students know what the marking criteria are. Marking is affected by the interpretation of the marker and is therefore less consistent and harder to assess.

Many tests are a combination of these two types, and this is probably ideal.

In terms of establishing proper and fair criteria for marking, and conditions for testing, you should consider the following points:

▶ Does it test what you want it to test?
▶ Is the test reliable / long enough to allow students to complete the test successfully?
▶ Is the marking system reliable and fair, and known to the students?
▶ Is it culturally fair?
▶ Is the format varied and interesting?
▶ Is the 'test' going to be carried out in an atmosphere which is not unnecessarily stressful?

Make sure you go over all the answers and reasons with the class.

10 The answer is that none of them are spelt correctly.

It is a trick question – hardly fair. For the record, the correct spellings are: accommodation – benefited – necessary – receipt – business.

We have looked at progress and achievement tests so far – now for two other types.

Placement tests are carried out by a school when students first arrive. They are designed to find out the approximate level of the student in order to place her in the right class. These tests tend to involve grammar (often multiple-choice questions), and speaking (a brief chat with a teacher). Sometimes they are more involved, but when a school has 30 students to test and place in two hours, it is not possible to have a full and proper test. Sometimes, as a result, students need to be moved to a more appropriate class after a day or two. Most placement tests are standard and are used each time there are new arrivals.

Diagnostic tests include placement tests, but also include other types. Teachers give diagnostic tests or tasks on a frequent basis when teaching (as in the 'Test Teach Test' method described in Unit 6). In fact, any time the teacher gives the students something to do with the aim of finding out how much they already know, this is diagnostic testing.

TASK 2

Already we have looked at various types of testing that take place in the classroom when we are teaching. For each of the below, think of two examples of tasks we might give our students, and whether the 'assessment' is subjective or objective.

1 Grammar
2 Vocabulary
3 Reading
4 Listening
5 Speaking
6 Writing

Suggested answers will come later.

Every school I have ever worked at has used placement tests and progress tests. The progress tests are usually left to the teacher to administer because the teacher is in the best position to know what kind of test to give, and what needs to be included.

Some schools I have worked at have had an internal achievement test – a standard one based on the syllabus followed for that particular level. Such a test is sometimes also used to allow a student to go up to the next level and it is also common for students to be issued with an internal certificate and teacher's report on their progress when they leave. This rounds off the course of study nicely and does give the student a sense of achievement with or without an actual test.

Continuous assessment is a type of testing not normally found in EFL/ESL except in the form described above, where teachers write a report for the student on the basis of their work and progress on the course, and also when teachers consider whether a student could move up (or down) a level based on their work in class. External assessment, however, is nearly always done on the basis of exams.

Back to the task ...

Key to task 2

1 Grammar

transformation exercises (see Q1 in the 'test' at the start of this unit) – objective

open-ended sentence completion (more than one answer possible) – subjective and objective since one answer might be considered to be 'better' than another

2 Vocabulary

matching – objective

use of vocabulary in essays – subjective

3 Reading

true / false – objective

questions requiring interpretation – subjective

4 Listening

multiple choice – objective

note taking (e.g. main points) – subjective

5 Speaking

repetition – objective

description of pictures – subjective

6 Writing

gap-filling – objective

essays (compositions) – subjective

Summary

▶ Testing is an integral part of teaching – teachers do it all the time in their lessons. Most tasks we give, most eliciting we do, most questions we ask have the aim of 'testing' our students in some way.

▶ Beyond normal classroom practice, students take placement tests and progress tests, and sometimes achievement tests (internal and / or external).

▶ Teachers most have to concern themselves with progress tests. They should know how to administer tests which are fair, varied, and interesting and which have clear testing objectives and criteria, and which are familiar to the students.

▶ Question types may require either objective or subjective assessment, or a combination of the two.

▶ Teachers should vary the types of test they give, and allow interaction between students if they feel this is appropriate.

▶ Testing should always be seen as part of the learning process and should be done in as pleasant an atmosphere as is possible in the circumstances.

Teaching one-to-one

This book is almost entirely a general introduction to classroom teaching. This unit, however, does look at one specific class type – teaching one-to-one. The reason for this is that I have yet to meet an experienced teacher who has not done this kind of teaching, but training courses rarely prepare teachers for it and as you might imagine, it requires a very different role for the teacher – and for the student. I have done a great deal of one-to-one teaching and I enjoy it; but I know other teachers who avoid it if at all possible but more and more students want to learn this way, and more and more schools are offering specialized one-to-one courses, so it is a type of teaching that cannot be ignored here.

There are different one-to-one contexts. For most teachers, it is a way to supplement their salary; their one-to-one classes are out of school hours and privately arranged; or offered directly by the school the teacher is working at.

For others, one-to-one classes are offered by the school in normal school hours and the teacher is required to teach them.

A minority specialize in one-to-one as their main teaching income, usually supplemented by income from elsewhere. Increasingly common are 'Homestay' courses where the student lives in the teacher's home. The teacher not only gives lessons, but also goes out with the student, cooks for him, etc. It is 'total immersion' on both sides.

If you are a teacher working in a country which is not your own, it is essential that you find out first if you are permitted to teach one-to-one classes. You should check your contract and, if in doubt, ask your employer, because if you are not supposed to teach one-to-one classes, and you do, you may find yourself on a plane home. Even in your own country, there may be something in your contract to this effect, the reason being that you may take potential business away from the school. Schools sometimes prefer to arrange private classes themselves on behalf of teachers, but the problem with this arrangement is that a substantial part of the student's fees goes to the school and not to the teacher.

For my own part, I have taught one-to-one classes arranged by my school, arranged privately, and for a company which sent teachers out to companies to teach members of its staff.

TASK

There are many issues to consider, especially with privately-arranged one-to-one lessons, and not only regarding the actual teaching, but let's begin with the teaching and learning considerations. Consider the following questions.

1 **Why do some students choose to learn this way rather than going into a regular class?**

2 **What are the learning advantages and disadvantages for the student?**

3 **How can a teacher prepare for a one-to-one course with a student when that student has approached that teacher and asked for, say, a month's worth of lessons, four hours a week?**

4 **What are the main differences involved for the teacher when teaching one-to-one rather than a regular class?**

5 **What do you think are the rewards and headaches of this kind of teaching?**

Before looking at these points, it is important to approach a series of one-to-one lessons in a way which is both professional, and which protects your and your student's rights. If you are making a purely private arrangement with a student, follow these points:

TIPS

1 **Agree on a price either for each lesson, or for the series of lessons. Make sure the price is neither significantly higher nor significantly lower than the 'going rate'.**

2 **If you have to travel, travel costs should be included.**

3 **Agree on procedure if lessons are cancelled by either side. This might mean that if the student cancels less than 24 hours before the lesson, they still pay you all or most of the fees. Or if you cancel, the lesson is offered at a later date. Whatever is decided, make sure both sides discuss and agree the terms.**

4 **Agree, also, on when and how you will be paid.**

5 **If the student later asks if a friend can also participate, it is no longer private tuition, so you cannot charge double the price.**

6   Make sure that the lessons will take place in an appropriate setting.

7   If you are being paid for, say, 60 minutes' tuition, that means 60 minutes, not 55. Lessons should be uninterrupted (e.g. don't stop to take a phone call).

8   If you are teaching a student who is also a friend, make it clear when the lesson itself begins and when it ends.

9   Do not arrange very long lessons because one-to-one is tiring for both parties. For most teachers and students, one hour is long enough.

10 Plan as thoroughly as you would for any other class; do not treat one-to-one classes casually.

Back to the task ...

1 REASONS FOR STUDENTS WANTING ONE-TO-ONE

There are many reasons for students doing one-to-one classes, including the following:

▶ Schools usually give total beginners one-to-one teaching when they first arrive until their English is good enough to go into a class.

▶ Students preparing for an exam sometimes feel they need more intensive practice.

▶ Students sometimes feel that they want to have as much tuition as possible to improve their English quickly.

▶ Students often need to improve their English for their jobs.

▶ Students wanting to work in an English-speaking environment will need to bring their level of English up before applying.

▶ Some students just prefer one-to-one tuition over classes.

Whatever the student's reason for wanting one-to-one, you need to know what it is if you are to provide for that student's needs.

2 ADVANTAGES AND DISADVANTAGES

The advantages are obvious enough – the student does not have to 'share' you with other students. Their learning is more intensive and more geared to their own needs, they can ask as many questions as they want, ask you to teach them skills that they need or want, and have lessons pitched at their precise level and desired pace. They will normally cover much more material and language than they would in a regular class. As such, progress is normally faster, and more visible to both parties.

However, the disadvantages are equally obvious. Of course, the student cannot work with other students in the class so there is no pair or group work, or even just someone to talk to. This restricts teacher / students interaction which makes learning hard work for the student, with considerable concentration and attention required at all times. Some students feel the need for interaction and company, while others much prefer the intensive nature of one-to-one learning. For those students with limited time available, and a definite goal, one-to-one can be advantageous but for students on holiday, only wanting to improve their skills, one-to-one makes little sense.

3 HOW CAN A TEACHER PREPARE?

If a student approaches you and asks you to give them private tuition, the temptation can be to think it is a soft option which will bring in more money but the correct way to react to such a request, if interested, is to discuss with the student exactly why they want one-to-one and what their needs are. If it is a student you already know, it is easier but if it is not, then there is much you need to find out before commencing. The best way to approach this is via a **needs analysis**. Students pay for one-to-one lessons because they want a teacher who will meet their needs and accommodate their learning style – and they usually want some control over what goes on in the lessons. Consequently, it is crucial to evaluate the needs, level and expectations of that student.

You need to find out three things:

▶ **The student's current level.** You could use a grammar review test from a course book of the approximate level you think your student is but you need to supplement this with an informal 'interview' to gauge the spoken ability of that student in terms of both accuracy and fluency. If possible, give them some reading, listening and writing, too.

▶ **The student's needs.** How much input does she want? Does she want to follow a set syllabus? Which skills are important for her to study? In what context(s) will she need to use her English? Is she preparing for an exam? Does she require English for her job? Find out as much as you can about what your student wants from you (this could be done in discussion and the 'interview' could form part of your level analysis). You must also be fair to yourself and the student if they ask you for a specialized course which you are not equipped to teach. For example, if you are asked to teach medical English and you have no knowledge of this, nor access to relevant materials, tell the student that you cannot teach him / her.

▶ **The student's previous language learning experience.** This will help you teach the student in the way which is best for him / her.

Having done the above, together you can agree on a specific study course with clear aims. Once the course is under way, be very flexible and adjust the content and approach of lessons as you see fit, or as the student requires.

Beware of students who only want 'speaking'. It sounds an easy option, but it is a vague request and it is hard work for the teacher to maintain nothing but conversation for a whole hour, maybe several times a week.

There is one other aspect which you need to think about before agreeing to teach the student. Do you think the two of you will 'get on'? It is important to have a good rapport with the student you are teaching, and this is another reason for meeting them beforehand.

4 DIFFERENCES BETWEEN ONE-TO-ONE AND REGULAR CLASSES

You obviously can't do pair or group work, and doing reading lessons seems inappropriate because they can do reading at home. The student is paying for tuition, not to be given work to do individually which they could do outside the lesson.

But virtually everything else mentioned in this book applies equally to one-to-one teaching; it's just that it will be very teacher-centred.

▶ You will need to prepare more because material is covered quicker. The material itself can be selected, at least in part, by the student. Have at least 50% more material than you think you need because it is much harder to 'fill time' with one-to-one. Any unused material can be used next time.

▶ You will need to be very flexible.

▶ You will have to concentrate hard throughout.

▶ You should fit in with the student's needs and go at their desired pace.

▶ You can be less concerned with time because there are no other students to teach.

▶ It might be appropriate to use more of the student's own language if you know it.

▶ It is easy to monitor progress.

▶ It is potentially more rewarding because of the last point.

5 REWARDS AND HEADACHES

Most of the rewards and headaches have been mentioned. For me, the toughest aspect of this kind of teaching is the demanding nature of it; you get no opportunity to 'relax' (e.g. when you ask students to work in groups in a regular class). The most rewarding aspect for me is building a unique relationship with the student and giving them what they need, and then seeing their progress if all goes well.

I have had many rewarding one-to-one classes, but let me describe one such class. I was teaching in a school where one of my new students was a near beginner called Zsigmond Sipos, from Hungary. Zsigmond could only come to classes twice a week for three hours a time but he wanted to improve his English quickly in order to take the Cambridge First Certificate exam ten months later. He asked me if I would teach him privately for the remainder of the year and prepare him for the exam. To have gone from his then level to the level required to pass the exam in such a short space of time would have been beyond most students. But Zsigmond knew exactly what he wanted and needed, and he played his part fully in influencing the direction and nature of the lessons. He was the ideal one-to-one student because he had very clear goals and a determination to succeed which was admirable. He worked incredibly hard, asked many questions, did lots of homework, and used English outside our lessons whenever possible. The lessons were intense, but at the same time they were very easy for me because the requirements were so clear, and the student so motivated. By December he was ready to take the exam, and he passed it with an 'A' grade. The credit for this lay almost entirely with Zsigmond, not with me, because he approached one-to-one learning in exactly the right way but when he called me to tell me of his result, I was very pleased and proud. And that is the principal reward of one-to-one teaching.

However, as I mentioned before, some teachers do not like the intensity of this type of teaching, preferring the interaction of a regular class but sometimes you will have to do one-to-one teaching even if you would prefer not to, if only to get some extra money.

TIPS

1 **Keep a record of all work done; particularly important given the flexible nature of the lessons.**
2 **Maybe provide the student with the record, or encourage her to keep her own, to make review of work done easier.**
3 **Keep notes on points that come up as you teach to come back to later. It is too easy to forget otherwise.**
4 **When doing speaking practice, you could record the conversation and then replay the audio for correction work.**

5 Focus more on pronunciation as it is easier to do so one-to-one.

6 Still elicit and encourage learner independence. If you don't, it will be too easy for the student to rely on you entirely and take no responsibility for her own learning.

7 Spend time training the student how best to use reference books, such as dictionaries and grammar books.

8 Review work previously covered. This is always important, but with one-to-one you cover so much more that it is especially important to review progress.

9 If you are using a course book, you will need to adapt a lot of the tasks as they are mostly designed for pair and group work.

10 The student won't mind you finishing late, but you should never finish early.

Summary

The most important points to take from this unit refer to 'being professional'.

▶ The demand for one-to-one learning is growing, but for the student it is expensive. In return for paying high hourly fees, students rightly expect value for money.

▶ Students usually have clear and specific requirements, for which the teacher needs to prepare by doing a needs analysis.

▶ The teacher should not commit herself to a course she is not equipped to teach.

▶ The teacher must also plan thoroughly for each lesson, and be extra flexible in her teaching.

▶ There should be an agreement between parties regarding time, location and fees for lessons as well as travel and photocopying costs, and arrangements if lessons have to be cancelled by either side.

▶ Lessons should begin punctually and not finish early. Nor should they be interrupted by the teacher because of phone calls, etc.

25 Technology as an aid to learning

Here I go with the 'in my day' speech (you might gather that this isn't the first time I have done this!).

When I first started teaching I don't even remember the existence of computers, and certainly there was no internet. For listening lessons I had a reel-to-reel tape recorder that took forever to cue up. There were no mobile phones. No interactive white boards. No social media. Indeed, the OHP (overhead projector) was state of the art technology, and having a whiteboard as opposed to a blackboard and chalk to use was really exciting. Most handouts seemed to be handwritten, unless teachers could be bothered to use the school typewriter. And even when I wrote the first edition of this book, technology in the classroom beyond the familiar and trusted OHP was, or seemed to me at the time, fairly non-existent. Mind you, I'm the person who, when working in the USA in the early 1990s, was asked why I didn't have an e-mail address and I replied, with my usual foresight, 'I don't think e-mails will ever catch on', so perhaps I was just innocently unaware.

Today it's a different world and this is reflected in schools and classrooms all over the world (but to very different extents) with teachers and students using interactive whiteboards, smart phones, tablets, blogs, social media and goodness knows what else to aid their teaching and their students' learning. Is technology in the classroom a real aid to learning, or as I heard one teacher describe it, just 'razzle dazzle'?

For this unit we will read about some examples of how teachers use technology as an aid to learning. I interviewed four teachers at International House London about what they use and how they use it, but also to find out if they had any reservations about using technology. Below is a summary of their thoughts and suggestions for use inside and also outside the classroom. All of the teachers interviewed are experienced teachers and trainers.

Teacher 1 ('Simon') talking about technology generally

'I do think at times that we are going a bit technology crazy and it's probably overshadowing a lot of effective teacher techniques. Balance is very important. Everyone gets very excited about it and for institutions it is a way of showing progression. Students are generally very positive about using technology ('It's great ... we're the iPad generation' said one), but technology is not a magic bullet. Students need an investment of writing things down and thinking about what they've written and asking questions – 'razzle dazzle' can blind people. Teachers are wrong to have the attitude of 'I can't teach without it (technology) – a lot of exploration can still take place with the existing whiteboard – the Interactive Whiteboard can stifle interaction and lead to a presentation style – the whiteboard gives a greater level of interaction'.

Now all this might come across as 'anti-technology', but this teacher does use a wide array of technology when he teaches, but he now uses it less than before for the reasons he has given. For him and rightly so, it's about achieving the right balance. I have observed lessons where technology has been used brilliantly and has aided learning, and I have seen lessons where technology has been overused and got in the way. And I have encountered teachers, usually trainee teachers, who have reacted to a broken down IWB with words such as 'I can't teach my lesson without it'. Technology provides many tools that can really help learning, and they should be used wisely to help our students learn and practise, but those tools need to be used to aid teachers and not to be a substitute for them. That is what Simon does having previously, in his own view, overused it at times. And, of course, technology can break down at the most inconvenient moments confirming my view that IWBs in particular don't like teachers!

'SIMON' TALKING ABOUT THE IWB (INTERACTIVE WHITEBOARD)

So, despite his reservations and welcome call for balance, Simon does use technology to help his students learn, and that includes the interactive whiteboard (IWB). Here's what he says:

'It's a kind of glorified overhead projector. It can be great for showing patterns of language, making feedback more efficient, and for helping to present a more varied diet, and to save time.'

Certainly, time can be saved and feedback made more efficient by preparing your board work in advance on your USB stick, and then showing it at the appropriate time rather than writing everything down during the lesson. You can drag text across the page, write on the board and then with a click of the button transform your dodgy writing into 'typed text', and cover text up and then uncover it by lowering the 'blinds'. And that is just scratching the surface, in time you can discover a wealth of other things you can do with an IWB. At its most basic level, and for me personally, its most useful function is you can use it to project text and images you have prepared before. It can be a real time saver and in exam classes, where time is at a premium, this can be particularly welcome. And when a student asks you 'what is a cabbage?', rather than explaining what it is or trying to draw a picture, by going to Google images you can, in a matter of seconds, show them a picture. For people like me who cannot draw to save their lives, this is a blessing of the highest order.

One more point about IWBs is that writing on them is not easy at first and it takes a fair bit of practice. Along with that, you need to learn the most useful tools of the IWB and to practise using them before trying to use the IWB in class. I have seen many instances of the teacher's lack of confidence using the IWB delay a lesson from continuing. It is you who should be determining the pace and flow of a lesson, not the IWB.

'SIMON' TALKING ABOUT SMART PHONES AND DICTAPHONES

'Smart phones are effectively a substitute for the language laboratory and students respond well to them. For example, a student can practise speaking by rehearsing what they want to say and then recording themselves. Then they can listen back, the teacher can help with correction and reformulation, and then the student can try again and see and hear their own improvement. You can do the same thing with a Dictaphone. At a lower level the student can record their teacher's models of pronunciation and then listen as often as they want to and practise at a time of their choosing. The Dictaphone is useful for providing students with authentic listening. For example, the teacher might record snippets from colleagues in the staffroom in relation to a particular topic and then upload them to their USB stick. Plug this into the classroom computer and play it on the IWB audio and you have a fantastic piece of authentic listening. It is, by definition, more 'real'.'

Of course, all of this assumes a classroom with a computer and IWB but the alternative is to play the recording direct from the Dictaphone. If your class isn't too big, this would still work if not quite so well. As with all this talk of technology, though, do not assume that any school you go into around the world will have access to such resources. You may still find your classroom resources limited to a blackboard and chalk and a small cassette recorder!

Teachers 2 and 3 ('Diane' and 'Josie') talking about tablets

These two teachers are enthusiastic believers in using tablets to aid learning. Here are some of the ways Josie uses them:

'I take pictures of my whiteboard use and review it to use the next day. For example, I see all the vocabulary that emerged during the lesson so by having a visual record of this I can recycle it easily the next day.'

'When monitoring student work I type in examples of language that I hear to use later in the lesson as a delayed language feedback slot. I e-mail it to myself and then copy and paste it into notebook. It is much quicker and I can review it the next day as revision, or an end-of-week test.'

'My students use tablets a lot as a dictionary, for taking notes, for recording the lesson.'

'In the future more and more students (and schools) will use tablets – handwriting is becoming less common and an unnecessary skill, typing is more useful.'

'The industry is taking tablets on board. I use them myself for learning and find them very useful as a student as well as when I am teaching.'.

Diane's department at her school had a trial period of using tablets, and these were the results of that trial which she shared with me.

POSITIVES

The video function was very easy to use, used to record simulated job interviews and presentations, for example.

▶ Use the photobooth function to create visual prompts.
▶ Get students to write to each other and respond on their respective iPads.
▶ Give class language feedback directly to their iPads.

- The poor quality sound issue has been resolved – use the jack (connection) to link the iPad directly to the classroom's sound system.
- Great as an additional resource.
- Can store e-books for homework / exam preparation.
- Upload of personal pictures / videos for class project work.
- Charting of progress through the course – video diary.

NEGATIVES

'We have to wait and see whether students like the device and find it useful in learning, or whether it's a distraction (their heads are 'down' all the time rather that looking at the teacher or each other). We want to hold a student focus group to get their ideas: Do they want tablets in the classroom? How would they envisage using them?'

'Some teachers have reservations about them. I simply ask them to find evidence that satisfies them either way – whether of learning or of not learning taking place – on which to base their classroom practice. I would also urge them to ask their learners and colleagues for feedback and for ideas on how to use them. After all, they are being used in classrooms around the world.'

Teacher 4 ('Liz') talking about using blogs

'I was very sceptical indeed about using blogs – I couldn't see the value of them. I gave it a try and the students absolutely loved it and this inspired me to use them a lot more. It gives them space to communicate in English and the teacher can answer directly. Classmates can communicate with each other in English inside and outside the classroom – there is a real dialogue. It's not just restricted to lesson time, I do the first blog activity in the classroom to set up the blog and show students how to use it and I would put up the first posting – e.g. 'what's your favourite food?' and set the homework of answering the question and responding to at least three posts of others. Occasionally, some students might be less keen initially, and some will write more than others, but early reservations wear off once they see it in operation, and not wanting to feel 'left out'. Privacy is an important issue, especially if they are under 18. I ensure that students provide a minimal profile and the privacy setting is set so that only group members can see posts. Blogs help a class to bond and they provide practice of an important written skill. Blogs provide real and relevant communication. I use them sparingly, usually as a homework task once a week.'

Liz surveyed students about the best ways to use blogs and some of their views are given below:

WHAT DO STUDENTS WANT TO BLOG ABOUT?

- ▶ film reviews
- ▶ storytelling
- ▶ competition – a prize for whoever gets the most comments to a post
- ▶ homework on the blog
- ▶ book reviews
- ▶ favourite places to visit

And, for those in an English-speaking country ...

- ▶ typical food / customs of other students' countries
- ▶ typical weather
- ▶ Christmas / New Year customs

Not every teacher is necessarily convinced, though. For example, one teacher said:

'I've never used a blog in my teaching. I think one of the main reasons is that it's not a way that I communicate with people in my own life. I don't really use much social media – I'm not on Facebook and for me, communicating with people in that way is quite foreign, quite alien, so I think that's part of it, it's just not personal to me. I'm not scared of technology, I use the IWB, and I feel really confident using it. It's just that the whole idea of blogs as a way of communicating seems really odd.'

So what about me? Given the description earlier of how things were when I first started teaching, how easy is it for someone to embrace a whole new set of skills? Well, for a start, keep an open mind. As one of our teachers said earlier, 'I simply ask them to find evidence that satisfies them either way – whether of learning or of not learning taking place – on which to base their classroom practice.' Don't use technology because you feel pressure to do so, or don't believe sufficiently in a particular aspect of it, but investigate how other teachers use it, observe them teaching with it if possible. Draw your own conclusions and listen to the views and suggestions of your students. Then you will be better informed to decide on what will work best with you and for your students. Practise, practise, practise using the technology – it's all part of your professional development.

I use IWBs to a limited extent, but I still find it easier writing on a regular board (one trainee teacher I observed, as he struggled to write on the IWB, muttered audibly 'this isn't like a real board' and to an extent I knew what he meant. This is a good example of the need to practise). I use Dictaphones to record students, but more to set up authentic listening practice. I make good use of the computer in my classroom linked to the IWB (showing video clips, displaying images – 'the cabbage question' – showing websites, etc.). I do a lot of online teaching as well in my work. And my next step is to see how tablets work for me and my students. It's a step-by-step process and overall, my use of technology in the classroom is less than others, and maybe more than some. Overall, though, I see it is vital that I explore, try things out, and then select and reject on a more informed basis. After all, if there is a tool that can be valuable to my learners, I should try and use it.

Summary

So we can see from all of the above that the teachers I spoke to were mostly positive about using technology as an aid to learning, with some preferring certain ways over others. The importance of not overusing technology was made a lot, and of using it in a way that does actually enhance the learning process rather than hindering it. Both teachers and learners need to be confident using any piece of technology, and to be convinced of its value. Technology should be used sparingly as a supplement to the teacher in the classroom and beyond and not a substitute for her (though, of course, learning online and without a teacher is also perfectly possible, but that is a different learning context to ours). And, as every teacher knows to their cost, technology can let you down by not working so there should always be a 'Plan B'.

The tools of technology exist as a means of aiding teaching and learning, so we should exploit anything that is available to us. However, we must be sure of the value of whatever we are using, just as we need to be sure of the value of anything we do in the classroom so that technology truly is a learning tool, and not just 'razzle dazzle'.

26 Transition from course to class

Thousands of people every year complete some kind of pre-service training course in order to teach English, most often in non-English-speaking countries. Many of these courses are either run part time over several months or very intensively over a four-week period. The question I have heard asked more times than I can remember is 'how can anyone become a teacher in four weeks?', and when trainees come to the end of the fourth week, having taught for six hours in the whole of the previous month, is it possible for them to go into a school the next week and teach 15 or more hours in a week? New teachers may also think that all schools all over the world have IWBs, computers in classrooms, Wi-Fi, photocopiers, etc., and that they will teach classes of no more than 12 in big rooms using up-to-date course books, and be given many opportunities for professional development. Are these assumptions realistic?

So what are the answers to these questions, and are those beliefs justified? What do you think? Why not spend a few minutes jotting down your own thoughts and assumptions about this before reading on.

We will look at this in three parts. Firstly, the transition from being a trainee on a pre-service course to having your own class soon after. Secondly, the kinds of different context you might find yourself in. And thirdly, the next unit will focus on finding a job and opportunities for professional development as you embark on your teaching career.

For this unit I interviewed four more teachers. Two of them had recently gone straight into teaching after completing a four-week course the Friday before, and two others were more experienced teachers who had gone on to teach in different countries (Portugal and Russia).

You can't finish a four-week course and be able to start teaching straight away ... or can you?

There is a very simple answer to this question – yes you can. Of course, it's not quite as straightforward as that, nothing ever is, but you absolutely can make that transition. Put another way, yes you can learn to teach in four weeks – at least to an acceptable starting standard that you can and should then build on. For my part, I finished my training course one Friday afternoon more years ago than I care to remember, and three days later I was teaching 20 hours a week, and I survived to tell the story more than 30 years later. And there are many others like me. Let's read about two of them.

I spoke to two teachers who had very recently completed a four-week Cambridge ESOL CELTA course and had then started teaching 15–20 hours a week the following Monday. Here are the tales of Vicki and Harry.

VICKI

I was a tutor on Vicki's CELTA course in 2013 so I was particularly interested to see her progress as she started her teaching career by teaching her first class just 65 hours after finishing her training. Vicki's first timetable involved 20 hours' teaching per week (one class three hours per day, and another class one hour per day).

I started by asking Vicki how she felt the weekend after her course finished knowing she was going to be teaching her own class on the Monday morning.

'I was very happy and also extremely nervous. I had no time to reflect on the course, but it was a good idea to be thrown in with so little time to worry. I planned much less per lesson than I did on the CELTA (which involves six hours' teaching in a four-week period). Instead of planning around three hours for a one-hour class, I spent one hour planning for a three-hour class. The first lesson went without any problem and it felt good not to be watched! I have now been teaching for 12 weeks and I have already taught five different levels. The hardest thing has been not having a 'bank of previous lessons' to use, and trying to pitch my lessons to the right level. My advice to anyone in the same position would be to take it one day at a time and to assess and reflect on each lesson taught when it is finished. I'd say the immediate transition from course to class is completely possible. I did it! It felt hard at the time but it was OK. I had lots of support and everybody asked me how I was getting on and helped with ideas. Following my course I felt quite prepared to teach. I was able to do a good job when I started on the Monday, and now I think I'm doing a much better job.'

HARRY

Like Vicki, Harry had just two and a half days to switch from trainee teacher to real teacher. Harry's first timetable involved teaching 15 hours per week (one class). Here's what Harry had to say:

'It was a pretty rapid turnaround! At the beginning I worried about planning for three hours (as opposed to 40 minutes for most CELTA lessons). CELTA really prepared me and my teaching in the first two weeks has been good because of what I learned on the CELTA. The first two days were a bit daunting, but I didn't feel stressed once I got beyond the first couple of days. It would have been difficult without having had so much support, though. I've been very lucky – senior teachers have helped a lot, especially at the beginning.'

Different teaching contexts

Particularly for those who train in English-speaking countries, the start of a first teaching job abroad provides challenges beyond the already significant one of teaching many hours a week with the responsibility of your own class(es). There may also be issues of a different language, a different culture (sometimes significantly different), finding somewhere to live, working your way round the public transport system, knowing where to buy your groceries, understanding the local currency, and a whole host of other such challenges. Then there's the school itself. Assuming that during the application, interview and contract-signing stages you found out all the information that you needed (e.g. how many hours you will teach, who you will teach, what the facilities are, what resources are available, if you have to teach on more than one site, if you will have a split shift, if you be working on weekends, what holidays you will get, etc.), you still have to settle in to the school itself and get to know your new colleagues. And in class, you will be teaching students who are probably all from the same country – it is you who may be in a country other than your own.

JAMES

Here's Teacher 1's story. This is 'James', now an experienced teacher and trainer in the UK but whose first job was in Russia.

'My first job in teaching was in a small school in southern Russia. I didn't know very much about it when I went there as it hadn't been advertised. Actually it was a friend of a friend who knew of somebody with the school. I went out there on trust, which I can't imagine doing these days. It was a language school set in what had been a primary school so it had a couple of small buildings with about eight classrooms and lovely gardens and a sort of playground. Everyone was very friendly and I was quite well looked after. I had accommodation also on the grounds, which were shared with the school's director. The contract was for 27 hours a week contact time, which is quite a lot. I got my accommodation, flights, visa support, local healthcare and some transport costs all taken care of. My salary was quite good, although I had no experience beyond my one month on the CELTA course which I had completed only a month before. The academic year was nine months and it lasted from September until July. When the school closed there was no work for anybody. That effectively became holiday time and the new contract started in the following September. In the summer I returned to England and worked at a summer school in Cambridge.

I taught all levels of mainly teenage students and my task was largely to help them improve their speaking. The school had limited resources, some activities books and course books. We followed the *Cambridge New English* course from elementary to advanced level and students bought these books. The teachers followed these books. All the teachers were local and experienced school teachers. I was then the only English person so I was given a lot of importance. Each class saw me once or twice a week. I did correct grammar but I didn't teach it much. For each unit of each block I ensured that I had planned my own speaking activities. Some of these came from the three resource books I had taken with me, others from my learning on the CELTA and others I made up. There was no photocopier except during test time so I made sure all my cut up cards and materials were preserved for the next classes. I think a lot of what I did was respond to what students wanted to say as well as practise structures not in a formal way but through speaking.

It was certainly a learning experience and I became very self-sufficient and robust. I developed resourcefulness as a teacher and the ability to make do with little by way of costly materials. I also learnt that students had a lot more to contribute than I imagined and they brought their questions and their eagerness to write and learn about England in the class.

As a new teacher and the only native speaker I found it difficult to say no. At one point I was teaching 36 hours a week and was asked to do more at the weekend. I said 'no', and nobody minded. I think they knew they were working me quite hard already but thought they would give me the option.

Probably the most invaluable help I got from the school was to do with all those things connected with living in the country. The support in finding accommodation, travel, work permits and visas were something which I could never have coped with on my own in provincial Russia.'

JOSIE

Here is Teacher 2's story. 'Josie' had already been teaching at International House, London for a few years and was used to excellent facilities and resources and regular professional development opportunities. She went to teach in Portugal and had a mixed experience there.

Contract, hours and academic year

'Teachers at XXX typically have an 18-hour contract. Although this doesn't sound like a lot, due to the fact that there is a lot of travelling each day from one class to another, it is definitely enough and the day actually felt longer than those I had been used to at IH London, purely because of journeys of up to an hour to get from one site to another. These sites included private schools or colleges, companies or the other site on the other side of the river. Luckily, the school paid for these journeys or provided a driver to take you to off-site companies unreachable by public transport.

The school operates for a nine-month academic year, starting early October and finishing at the end of June. There are some intensive courses run throughout the summer, but these are given to permanent teachers. For new teachers, like me, and most of the staff, a nine-month contract is offered. This is mostly to prevent teachers becoming permanent, for obvious reasons.

You will normally start teaching in the afternoon and continue until evening (as late as 9.30 / 10 p.m.). It is nice to have late starts like these, but it means you miss out on social activities in the evening, which is important when you want to get to know a new city and make friends.

It is also very typical to work on Saturdays, as this is a busy day for the school, with most of the students being children. I worked from 10 a.m. to 1 p.m. on Saturdays, which meant I had a split weekend (Friday and Monday off). This had pros and cons. The advantage was that by Thursday, when you are feeling pretty exhausted, you have a day off and can do nice things like go to an empty beach when the world and his wife are at work. However the drawback is that you don't have two consecutive days to travel to different parts of the country or make a trip home if you need to.'

Levels / ages / groups

'I taught a range of levels and ages. My youngest group were four six-year-olds. This was a completely new experience for me but luckily I was doing the IH Young Learner Celta throughout the first six months of the year, which really helped give me practical ideas for lesson planning and classroom management.

I also had two groups of 10/11-year-olds (maximum class size ten). They were actually my favourite age to teach as they had lots of language already and lots of energy to learn more, plus they weren't moody like the teenagers!

One group was at the main school and the other was at their private school off site.

I had a teenage (14/16-year-olds) group twice a week for FCE and a young adult (16+, mainly university students) CAE preparation class.

I went off site twice a week to teach general / business English to a group of three pharmacists at a major pharmaceutical company. And I had the odd one-to-one general / business English student.

What I noticed about the general level of English in Portugal was that it is much higher than I had been expecting. This is partly due to the fact that, unlike Spain or France, films and TV shows from the UK and USA are not dubbed here. Everyone has cable TV with lots of English speaking channels (the channels here are pretty shocking), so there is much more exposure to English from a young age. It was also nice for me to go to the cinema and watch films in my native language! For this reason, speakers here have far fewer pronunciation issues than French or Spanish speakers have. I was really impressed. There is obviously also a great deal of emphasis on learning English here at the moment as everyone is trying to leave the country due to the economic crisis. The brain drain that is being experienced here at the moment is enormous. The majority of students I was teaching were learning English to try and get work abroad – it was quite sad. But on the plus side, it creates jobs for EFL teachers like us!'

Resources

'The school does not have IWBs and this was a big change for me as I had been used to using them for most of my lessons at IH London. OHPs were also few and far between and we often had to sign them out or liaise with other teachers to share them. Photocopiers were few, old and temperamental. With young learners there was a lot of cutting up to do and the lack of coloured paper and card was annoying. I often bought my own. There was also a lack of stationery like board pens; we were given some at the beginning of each term only.

The course books we were given to use were the choice of the owner and director and depended on the relationship the school had with the publisher and how much they cost. So flexibility was limited and due to tests every term, we had to cover most of the course book material.'

Teacher development, admin and other issues

'There seemed to be a lot more admin required of us than I was used to at IH London. There were detailed reports to be written every term for each student, tests and feedback for each student every term, parents' evening twice a year and work records to upload onto the intranet weekly.

Us new teachers were promised survival lessons in the local language once a week for the first term, but due to timetabling we only had three.

In comparison to IH London, there was much less emphasis on teacher development. There was one session (unpaid) once a term, given by the director herself or the head of teacher training. Staff meetings happened every other week (also unpaid) and didn't encourage staff feedback.

Observations and 'pop ins' were more regular than I had been used to at IH London (three times in the nine-month-period, excluding the four I had for IHYLC).'

Summary

▶ The transition from course to class, even straightaway, is possible – many thousands have done it.
▶ You need to be more economical and efficient with your planning time.

- You need to take advantage of the support available from your colleagues and managers.
- It is important to continue reflecting on your teaching.
- Going to teach in a different country provides a great opportunity for experience of teaching and learning.
- It may not be what you have been used to, though (maybe some parts will be better, others less so).
- You have to adjust to the school, its facilities and resources, and the local culture.
- You may well be teaching different age groups at different times of the day and night, and even at different sites.

So, how do you find that first job, and how can you ensure that you continue developing as a teacher beyond the course you took? On to the next unit ...

27 Finding work and professional development

Finding a job

People go into this profession for different reasons. Many only want to spend a few years travelling and see teaching as the ideal way to earn some money along the way. Others have expectations of making it their long-term career. Sometimes, experienced teachers from the state sector decide that they want to try a different kind of teaching. Many want a career change, to leave their current employment in order to do something completely different. Then there are people like me, who fall into none of the above categories. Having finished university I still wasn't sure what I wanted to do, until one day I saw an advertisement for an EFL training course and thought I would send away for the information. That eventually resulted in my doing the course and starting my first job the Monday after it finished. The rest, as they say ...

This unit looks first at the process of applying for a job, and then looks at ways of continuing your professional development. We saw in the previous unit that the transition from course to class, and maybe to a new country, is all part of this process. So, how can you help yourself get a job?

Increasingly, vacancies are to be found online (e.g. www.tefl.com or www.ihworld.com). You will need to submit an application. This will involve having a résumé (CV), a covering letter and probably your educational and training certificates. Increasingly, though, applications and resumes are submitted online. You will then need to have an interview.

Your résumé needs to be professional in appearance, not handwritten, not too long, and should contain only relevant information.

TIPS
- ▶ Be honest!
- ▶ Don't oversell yourself.
- ▶ Make the résumé easy to handle and to refer to.
- ▶ Include full contact details.
- ▶ Make sure all time periods are covered.
- ▶ List your time in chronological order.

- Include all relevant qualifications and experience.
- Highlight any teaching experience you have.
- Specify which training course you did or are doing.
- Do not include irrelevant details.
- Mention any skills you possess, especially knowledge of foreign languages.
- Include names of referees – at least one of whom should be a professional referee.
- Make sure you do include a covering letter.
- Keep it brief.
- State clearly what job you are applying for and where you saw it advertised.
- Say why you want the job and why you should be considered for it, but don't overdo it!
- Proofread your letter for spellings, etc.

The interview

All being well, you will be invited for an interview. This might be at the institute itself, on the telephone, on Skype, or at a central office which handles all applications. I have interviewed many people over the years, and it has been interesting to see the different approaches adopted by interviewees – from the very formal, well-prepared candidate to the very casual, take-it-as-it-comes candidate. Neither is necessarily better than the other, but it is advisable to 'play safe' and follow certain guidelines.

TIPS
- Arrive on time! It creates a bad first impression if you don't.
- Dress appropriately! At least look as if you have made an effort.
- Don't make it seem as if you are doing the employer a favour by coming to the interview – overconfidence, or even arrogance, do not go down well.
- Answer questions fully and honestly.
- Come ready with questions of your own (see later).
- Know something about the institute you are applying to.
- Be relaxed and friendly in your manner; try to let your personality show through.
- Talk about your previous experience when asked; if you do not have any, talk about your training course and what it included and what your teaching experience was like.
- Show enthusiasm; make it seem as if you really do want the job!

Another important part of any interview is knowing what sorts of questions you might be asked, and what information you need to gain from the interviewer. Yes, you are the one who is looking for a job and being interviewed, but that doesn't mean that you should accept a job offer without knowing sufficient details about the job and the context.

Here are some typical questions that you should expect to be asked:

▶ **What types of class have you taught?** – Include levels, sizes, age groups. If you have no experience, talk about the classes you taught on your training course, if you have done one.

▶ **What materials did you use?** – Include course books and supplementary materials.

▶ **What did you think of the course book(s) you used?** – Give a fair evaluation and avoid 'it was fantastic' or 'it was terrible' because all books have their pros and cons.

▶ **What level(s) do you prefer teaching and why?** – It is perfectly OK to have preferred levels (most teachers do), as long as you make it clear that you would be prepared to teach any level.

▶ **What different nationalities have you taught?** – Be prepared to discuss the particular problems they encountered and how you helped them to deal with these problems. Avoid making any sweeping general statements about a particular nationality.

▶ **Why did you become a teacher?** – It's the obvious question to expect if you are applying for your first job, so be prepared with a good answer.

▶ **Why have you applied for this job?** – Another obvious question to expect, so know something about the institute you have applied to and show an interest in the organization (a few questions of your own about its history would go down well!).

▶ **What are your future plans?** – The only answer to avoid here is something like 'Well, I only want this job for a few months because I want to get a better job once I have more experience!'

▶ **Why do you want to work in this particular country? / Do you speak the language? / What languages do you speak?** – If you do not speak the language of the country you want to work in, show an interest in learning it.

▶ **What do you know about this school?** – As mentioned earlier, do your homework.

▶ **Do you have any questions?** – Have some, but not too many.

So what questions should you ask? Well, a good interviewer should cover all the essential points, if they haven't been dealt with in any literature sent out to you before the interview. However, you shouldn't leave the interview without knowing the answers to the following questions – but if you need to ask all of these then it suggests the interviewer didn't do a very good job!

▶ How many hours a week will I have to teach? (Twenty-five is a standard but it is not uncommon to teach more.)
▶ How will these hours be split? (Maybe a 'block' or a 'split shift'.)
▶ Will I have to work evenings or weekends?
▶ Will all my teaching be in one building or will I have to travel?
▶ If travelling is involved, how much?
▶ What levels will I have to teach?
▶ What age group(s) will I have to teach? (This might mean teaching children.)
▶ Do I have to be in the school even when I am not teaching?
▶ Am I paid for this 'non-contact' time?
▶ How much will I be paid?
▶ Will I be paid weekly or monthly?
▶ How will I be paid?
▶ Are national holidays paid?
▶ What holiday allowance do I get?
▶ When can I take my holiday?
▶ Is it paid or unpaid?
▶ Do I get sick pay?
▶ What's the cost of living? (What seems like a high or low salary might in real terms be different depending on the cost of living. In some countries a little money goes a long way, but in others a lot of money goes not very far at all.)
▶ What taxes do I have to pay?
▶ What length of contract do I get and what notice is required on either side?
▶ Are my flights paid for?
▶ Does the school provide or give help finding accommodation?
▶ If the school provides it, who will I share with, and how far is the accommodation from the school?
▶ Does the school arrange or give help getting work permits, etc.?
▶ How well equipped is the school in terms of facilities and resources?
▶ How many other teachers are there?
▶ What in-service professional development does the school provide?

Do not sign any contract without reading it carefully and checking anything you are not sure about. Make sure you have a copy of that contract. If you do not feel comfortable with any aspect of the job or conditions, don't take it.

But this is a two-way process, and many employers or agencies will tell you of teachers who have agreed to everything, then called at the last minute to say they have taken another job (or not called at all). This is highly unprofessional.

Once in a job, seek help and guidance from your Director of Studies as well as more experienced colleagues.

Professional development

For those who decide that they do want to make this their career, if only for a few years, there are ways to improve your pay and conditions and to do things other than only teaching, but there is more to it than that. You need to develop your own skills and professional awareness so that you keep in touch with developments in the profession, and new teaching ideas and theories.

The majority of teachers start out by doing a 'Certificate' course (e.g. Cambridge ESOL CELTA, or a Trinity College Certificate), but others will do a similar, less recognized course. Some will find a teaching job despite having had no training. After a usual minimum of two years (maybe less) of actual teaching experience, there is the option in most countries of doing a DELTA course. This modular course includes practical and written exams as well as observed and assessed teaching practice. Others might do an MA (e.g. In Linguistics), which helps If you are looking to work in further / higher education especially.

By doing a 'post-Certificate' course and gaining an extra qualification, you are improving your prospects of work outside the classroom, as well as of a permanent contract in your own country. In the UK, for example, it is virtually impossible to get a long-term contract without the DELTA.

So what are the possibilities? Some teachers move into teacher training. To become a CELTA trainer, for example, you need several years of varied teaching experience, and then complete a trainer-training course. The training courses are thorough and carefully monitored but if you are successful you become an approved trainer.

Another possibility is writing. This does not necessarily mean writing books, but maybe articles for specialized ESL publications.

Presenting papers at conferences / conventions (e.g. the annual TESOL or IATEFL conferences / conventions) is a good experience to have.

Teaching Business or other English for Special Purposes (ESP) classes can be more financially rewarding, as well as broadening your experience.

Non-teaching positions within a school are what many people eventually seek. For example, being a an 'ADOS' (Assistant Director of Studies) leaves you equipped to become a 'DOS' (Director of Studies), in charge of the academic direction of the school and its academic staff.

Others, who start teaching adults (16+), choose to move into the field of teaching Young Learners; some go in the opposite direction.

A good move after you have some experience is to become an examiner. This will not earn you a lot of extra money, but it will give you good experience.

For the very ambitious (and brave!) your target might be to one day set up your own school.

Most experienced teachers, myself included, would say that it took them a good two years of teaching before they felt reasonably confident and able in most teaching contexts. Also, it takes this long to gain full confidence about the language itself that you are teaching. If new teachers accept these facts, and do not expect the impossible from the short training courses, then they will have more realistic expectations of themselves. The short training courses described are excellent and invaluable, but only as a starting point.

Employers need to recognize the limits of these courses, too. They need to offer support and guidance to new teachers, whilst at the same time recognizing that no training course providers are suggesting that they are providing you with the 'finished article'. As we all know, you can be teaching for many years but still learning and developing – or you should be!

If we can accept these points, then we can think about how this 'post-training' development can happen; or, in the case of teachers teaching with no prior training, how 'on-the-spot' training and development might occur.

A summary of some ideas for continuous professional development

1 Seek the opportunity from time to time to observe other teachers' lessons.

2 Ask your Director of Studies or an experienced teacher to observe you teaching at regular intervals and to give you feedback.

3 Continue to self-assess your own teaching (as you would have done on any training course you did / are doing) and to develop your strengths and work on your weaknesses (video yourself?).

4 If available, watch DVDs your school might have of lessons.

5 Attend in-service sessions at your school or nearby (often called 'teacher development sessions').

6 Attend workshops and conferences if you get the chance. In particular, the annual conferences held by IATEFL and TESOL (see below).

7 Read new publications and periodicals about the profession, usually available at your place of work.

8 Talk to more experienced teachers and learn from them.

9 Try out new ideas you have read or heard about – don't just continue churning out the same old lessons in the same old way!

10 When you're ready, do further teaching qualifications or online courses (see above).

11 Show an interest and desire to be involved in other aspects of school life, perhaps helping with administration, or social activities, or the design of materials.

12 Join professional organizations such as TESOL or IATEFL if you are working freelance. If you are not, your school is likely to have institutional membership (web addresses given below). IATEFL has SIGs (Special Interest Groups) you can join, such as 'Teaching Pronunciation', if you want to develop your knowledge and expertise in a particular area, and to share with like-minded colleagues around the world.

13 With more experience, write articles for ESL publications and give talks or run sessions at workshops.

14 Start / join a 'reading club' with colleagues – choose a book / article to read, then meet and discuss it.

15 Challenge yourself by asking to teach a different level, or to use a new book, or to teach a different type of class (e.g. an exam class).

16 Create new material for your classes.

17 Experiment and try out new ideas, approaches and resources (including technology).

18 Eventually move into other areas such as writing, training, examining.

19 Recognize that the profession itself develops and moves in new directions. Keep in touch and move with it, maybe even influence its direction in some small way!

20 Keep in touch on the web! There are many useful sites – just do an ESL or EFL search and you'll be given many addresses to explore.

TESOL (Teachers of English to Speakers of Other Languages) has members worldwide. Website: http://www.tesol.org

IATEFL (International Association of Teachers of English as a Foreign Language) has over 30 branches worldwide and over 1,000 delegates attend its annual conference. Website: http//www.iatefl.org

Summary

▶ You need to present your application professionally at each stage.
▶ You need to approach an interview thoroughly.
▶ You need to ensure that you have all the information you need before signing a contract, not just about the school and work but also the area, culture and living conditions.
▶ You need to seek out ways to continue your professional development.
▶ You need to move forward – 'standing still' is the same as going backwards in this profession.

28 A guide to levels

A common question asked by new teachers is 'What does 'intermediate' mean?' (or any other such term). And a common complaint is 'I have a mixed-level class'.

Labels to describe levels of students, such as 'intermediate' and 'elementary' are very broad and a class described as, say, 'elementary' could well include students who seem to be of different levels. It is important, then, to remember that such labels are more guides to the general and approximate level of students in a class, and that students may be better at one aspect of the language (e.g. speaking) than another (e.g. grammar). You do need to pitch your classes to the general level of your class, adapting material as required, bearing in mind that one intermediate group of students may be 'stronger' than another.

A class which is in some way mixed ability – and the bigger the class the more likely this is – will always be more difficult to teach. What you should avoid, if possible, is effectively teaching separate groups within the class, with different tasks, etc. If you do this, you will no longer be teaching and managing 'a class' but separate groups. This is both difficult and ultimately counter-productive. You should give extra support and guidance to the weaker students in the class (for example, when others are working together), but do not pitch the lessons to the needs of the lowest-level students within the class, because if you do that you will frustrate and handicap those whose level is generally higher and who are in the majority.

Do not hesitate, for example, to stop group work even if some people have not finished a task. Students who have already finished something do not want to have to wait every time for all the others to finish. You have to allow a reasonable amount of time for a task, but to be prepared to say 'OK, stop there' and then go through answers together as a class.

Be aware, too, that in some schools a system of 'continuous enrolment' operates. This means that new students can join an established class at any time (often this means any Monday).

So the composition of your class will fluctuate as students leave and others arrive even though you are teaching a fixed course. You will find, as a result, that the overall level of a class can change to varying extents on a fairly regular basis. It is not ideal, but as teachers we have to adjust our lessons and plans accordingly.

The following guide should give you some idea of what a 'typical' student at a given level should be able to do at the end of his or her course. Six labels are defined here, but some schools may have further levels.

(NB: This is an adapted guide courtesy of SKOLA Schools, London.)

Beginner

A student finishing a beginner's course should be able to do or know the following:
▶ the alphabet
▶ tell the time
▶ give simple information about himself / herself
▶ ask other people for simple information about himself / herself
▶ communicate in simple terms in everyday places, e.g. ask for directions
▶ order a meal
▶ make suggestions
▶ buy items in a shop
▶ listen to and understand simple, natural speech and conversation, and complete simple tasks
▶ read some authentic texts such as timetables or brochures and find the information they need
▶ do simple writing tasks such as taking or leaving a message.

Elementary

A student finishing an elementary course should be able to do or know the following:
▶ talk about past time
▶ make future plans or arrangements
▶ describe people using simple adjectives
▶ describe places using simple adjectives
▶ express his / her hopes or intentions
▶ ask people to do something for them

- cope in simple social situations e.g. talk about the weather
- describe simple physical problems
- give advice
- listen to natural speech and conversation, and understand the gist of what is being said
- use authentic newspapers and find specific information required
- write simple letters and be able to link ideas together.

Pre-intermediate

A student finishing a pre-intermediate course should be able to do or know the following:
- talk about more abstract ideas
- participate in discussions and be able to interrupt politely, and take turns in communicating
- give a logical argument to support a view
- converse with relative ease in everyday social situations
- use formal and informal English in appropriate social situations
- help people with problems by making suggestions and giving advice
- listen to natural speech and conversation and begin to understand nuances and subtleties
- read most authentic texts and books for pleasure
- write letters, both formal and informal.

Intermediate

A student finishing an intermediate course should be able to do or know the following:
- express her or his opinion
- agree or disagree with other people's opinions
- express how he or she is feeling and their general emotions
- use conventional social language in greeting and welcoming people
- talk about hypothetical situations in the past and present
- talk about past habits
- speculate about the present and future
- listen to natural speech and conversation, and understand detail
- read authentic texts such as newspapers and magazines and understand the general meaning
- write letters to friends.

Upper intermediate

A student finishing an upper intermediate course should be able to do or know the following:

▶ use all the main structures and tenses in English with a high degree of accuracy
▶ begin to express sarcasm and irony
▶ use appropriate speech in a wide range of social situations
▶ understand and express humour
▶ argue an opinion with confidence
▶ follow lectures and other monologues and be able to take notes
▶ read most authentic texts and be able to understand them with relative ease
▶ write letters, compositions, reports, summaries.

Advanced

A student completing an advanced course should be able to do or know the following:

▶ express himself / herself easily
▶ integrate well with people whose first language is English
▶ vary stress and intonation to affect meaning
▶ follow and understand most forms of entertainment
▶ use a vocabulary of about 3,000 words
▶ study for a high-level qualification in English.

> The Council of Europe has developed a set of common standards in language learning – a Common European Framework for countries and institutions worldwide:
>
> • A basic user of the language is described as being A1 or A2 (beginner to pre-intermediate).
> • An independent user is B1 or B2 (low intermediate to pre-advanced).
> • A proficient user is C1 or C2 (advanced to proficient).

And finally, do not assume that one class of a particular level will be the same as another. All because your current intermediate class found Unit 3 of your current course book interesting and were able to follow does not necessarily mean that another intermediate class will be the same. Levels are broad in nature, and one set of students can be very different from another.

29 Language glossary

This unit is designed to give you as simply as possible a guide to just some language terminology that you will need to recognize and use as you start out teaching, but do treat it as no more than a guide ... for more details, consult your grammar book.

Verb forms and tenses

Here are five examples of verbs, each with four forms.

	a	b	c	d	e
1	to go	to eat	to read	to work	to listen
2	went	ate	read	worked	listened
3	gone	eaten	read	worked	listened
4	going	eating	reading	working	listening

Form 1 = the infinitive

Form 2 = the past simple

Form 3 = the past participle

Form 4 = the present participle

Look first at examples **d** and **e**. You will see that Forms **2** and **3** are identical; the verb ends -*ed* both times. Such verbs are called regular verbs, and they are very straightforward, except for some irregular spellings. For example, a verb such as *cry* in Form **2** and **3** would become *cried*.

Examples **a**, **b** and **c** are different because the 2nd and 3rd forms do not follow this pattern, or even have a separate consistent pattern. These are irregular verbs. There are many irregular verbs and each has its own pattern. Some have no variation at all (e.g. *to hit, hit, hit*), while the example above in **c** has the same form for **2** and **3**, but different pronunciation.

You may wonder what the difference is between the past simple and past participle. The past participle (Form **3**, or 'Verb **3**') is used in conjunction with the auxiliary verb *has / have / had*. For example: *I have eaten, She has gone*, whereas the past simple form would be *I ate (a sandwich earlier)*, and *She went (home yesterday)*.

With regular verbs there is no apparent difference – *I worked (yesterday)* and *I have worked a lot recently* but the first case is Form **2**, and the second is Form **3**.

The infinitive presents its own problems to students. Consider these two sentences:

I like to watch TV.

I may watch TV later.

The first sentence has the full *to*-infinitive form, the second does not (in this case because it follows a modal verb – *may*). Teachers and grammar books vary in how they label this second example. Some call it the 'infinitive without *to*'; others call it the 'bare infinitive'; while others call it the 'base verb'. Just be consistent in whatever terms you use.

Finally, students (and some teachers!) confuse the present participle with a gerund. Both have the *-ing* form, but the present participle (Form **4** above) is a verb, while a gerund is a noun. Look at these two sentences:

I'm eating my lunch.

I like swimming.

In the first case, the *-ing* form is a verb; it says what you are doing. In the second, it is a noun and *like* is the verb, just as in *I like books*, *I like music*, etc.

Higher-level students are usually very familiar with all these terms, but lower-level ones may not be, and you may not want to burden them with such terminology until their level of English is much better. You will find that some students will refer to Verb 3, for example, maybe asking you 'What's Verb 3 of *sleep*?'

You need to know such terms when identifying tenses, and you also need to be aware of the difference between tense and time.

TASK 1

Look at the following sentences and use a grammar book to help you. For each one, identify the tense and the time it refers to.

Example: *I left the country last week* – past simple, referring to finished past action.

1 **I work every Saturday.**
2 **She leaves on Saturday.**
3 **I'm writing this sentence.**

4 I'm meeting Matt later.

5 I was watching TV last night.

6 There was a good film on TV last night but I had seen it before.

7 I've been to Canada.

8 I've worked here for a year.

9 I'm sorry I'm so dirty, I've been working on the car.

10 That's the phone ... I'll get it.

11 I'll have finished by lunchtime.

12 I'll be leaving tomorrow.

Doing this task you should quickly become aware that very often in English the name of a tense does not relate to the time it refers to. This causes many problems as, for example, when a teacher asks 'What's the tense?' and a student replies 'Future' when she means the sentence is talking about the future. As far as future time is concerned, low-level students will often use *will* for any future reference believing that this is the future tense. Here, too, you must be careful. We do not have a single 'future tense' even though we refer, for example, to the 'future simple' tense. There are many different ways to express future time (and present time, and past time) in English and they do not all require the use of tenses. Consider *I used to smoke* and *I may leave later*. One refers to past time and one to future time, but neither is a tense.

That said, tenses are very important, and teachers who refuse to use terms such as 'future simple' are not really helping their students when most course books and grammar books recognize such labels. It is important to be clear when teaching to convey the time reference of any piece of language.

Key to task 1

1 present simple, referring to habitual action – so 'general time'

2 present simple, referring to future time

3 present progressive (also known as 'continuous'), referring to action in progress at the time of speaking – so present time.

4 present progressive, referring to future time

5 past progressive, referring to past time

6 past perfect simple, referring to earlier of two past events – so past time

7 present perfect simple, referring to (indefinite) past time

8 **present perfect simple**, referring to unfinished past state – so past and present time

9 **present perfect progressive**, referring to recent past time

10 **future simple** (or '*will* future'), referring to spontaneous decision (present time) about something you will immediately do (future time)

11 **future perfect simple**, referring to future time

12 **future progressive**, referring to future time

These are merely examples to demonstrate how, sometimes, the name of the tense does not necessarily refer to the time being described.

TENSE FORMS

Present simple is the first form of the verb.

Past simple is the second form of the verb.

Past progressive is the verb *to be* in the past (*was* / *were*) + verb-*ing*.

Past perfect simple is *had* + past participle.

Past perfect progressive is *had been* + verb-*ing*.

Present progressive is the verb *to be* in the present (*is* / *are* / *am*) + verb-*ing*.

Present perfect simple is *have* / *has* + past participle.

Present perfect progressive is *have* / *has* + been + verb-*ing*.

Future simple is *will* + base verb.

Future progressive is *will be* + verb-*ing*.

Future perfect simple is *will have* + past participle.

Future perfect progressive is *will have been* + verb-*ing*.

In each case, of course, there is a subject at the start.

1ST / 2ND / 3RD PERSON

You also need to be aware of the rule regarding verbs in the 3rd person singular.

Ist person	the person / people who is / are speaking (*I* / *we*)
2nd person	the person / people you are speaking to (*you* / *you*)
3rd person	the person / people you are speaking about (*he*, *she*, *it*, *they*)

With 3rd person singular (*he* / *she* / *it*) the verb takes *-s* or *-es*:

I work / you work / she works

I go / you go / he goes

Students at all levels have trouble remembering this rule.

Language terminology

Now let's look at a few other selected examples of language terminology.

Articles – *a* / *an* (indefinite), *the* (definite)

Adjectives – usually modify a noun: *big, expensive, blue, loud*

Adverbs – usually modify a verb: *quickly, efficiently, hard, well, successfully* (but *hard* can be an adverb or an adjective)

Auxiliary verbs – *be, do, have*

Clause – part of a sentence containing a subject and a verb

Common nouns – those that do not begin with a capital letter: *table, chair, pen*

Compound noun – a noun made up of two words: *address book, ashtray, door handle*

Conditional sentences – (see below)

Conjunctions – joining words: *although, but, however*

Contraction – *I am* = *I'm; they are* = *they're*

Countable noun – a noun that can be counted: *pen(s), book(s), car(s)*

Functions – the 'reason' for speaking: *invitation, suggestion, apology*

Modal auxiliary verbs (modals) – *may, can, should, might, would* (see below)

Phrasal verb – verbs with more than one part which do not have a literal meaning: e.g *to look up* (a word in the dictionary)

Possessive adjectives – *my, your, their*, etc.

Prepositions – e.g. *by, on, under, across, through, beside, in, out*, etc.

Pronouns – *I, we, you* are examples of subject pronouns

me, us, you are examples of object pronouns

mine, yours, hers are examples of possessive pronouns

Proper nouns – 'names': *Spain, Thomas, Everest*

Question tags – e.g. *It's cold, isn't it? She's late, isn't she?*

Conditional sentences

Conditional sentences feature in all course books. There are, in fact, a great many types of conditional sentence and not just the three or four presented in most books. But given that you will have to teach the basic types at some stage, here is a simplistic guide to conditionals 1, 2, 3 ... but bear in mind that this merely scratches the surface of this bit of language.

'Look at that sky. If it rains, we'll go back inside.'

The sky threatens rain, so the possibility of this is quite high. We are referring to a possible future happening. The definite consequence of rain would be the speakers going back inside. The first part of the sentence is 'If + subject + present simple', and the second is 'subject + will + base verb'. This grammar with this use is the standard and simple type of **1st conditional sentence**.

'If I won the lottery this week, I'd quit my job.'

We are again referring to future time, but on this occasion, the possibility of the *if*-clause being met is remote, though still possible. Compared with the chance of rain in the first example, the contrast is clear. We have past simple in the first clause, and 'the modal verb (*would*) + base verb, in the second. This 'low possibility' / hypothetical future is one type of **2nd conditional sentence**. Again, this is a simplistic and incomplete definition, but it's a start.

'If I hadn't eaten that undercooked meat, I wouldn't have become sick.'

... but I *did* eat the meat and I *did* become sick. So this sentence is set in the past and you cannot change what has happened. The *if* clause has the past perfect, and the main clause has 'a modal (*would*) + have + past participle'. This is a standard **3rd conditional sentence**.

You need to know this because students often ask about conditionals and, as I said, course books are very fond of these three conditionals, so you will teach them on a regular basis. Once you start teaching higher levels, you and your students will be exposed to the numerous variations of conditional which we use in our everyday spoken language.

Modal verbs

Finally, a further look at modal verbs. There are so many functions attached to modals, which again underlines the importance of illustrating meaning properly, and checking understanding. When students ask 'what does *must* mean?' there is no answer, as the following task should demonstrate.

TASK 2

Look at the modals in these sentences and say what you think the function might be.

> Example: '*You **must** do your homework*' (teacher to student) –
> obligation

1 'Who's that?' 'It *must* be the delivery boy.'

2 '*Can* I go now?'

3 'I *can* speak five languages.'

4 'You *can't* smoke in this school.'

5 '*Could* you help me?'

6 'I *could* play squash for an hour when I was younger.'

7 'You *may* leave if you want.'

8 'It *may* rain later.'

9 'You *may* not go out tonight.' (parent to child)

10 '*May* it always be so!'

This task serves as a taster of the complexity of modals in terms of their various meanings and different shades of meaning. Which functions you teach will depend in part on the level of the class, but virtually all levels of course books feature uses of modal verbs.

Back to the task...

Key to task 2

1 This is making a **deduction** – you ordered a pizza, there's someone at the door, so in all likelihood it is the pizza boy.

2 **Asking permission** to leave.

3 Talking about present **ability**.

4 **Prohibition**.

5 Making a **request**.

6 Talking about **past ability**.

7 Giving **permission**.

8 Expressing **possibility**.

9 Prohibition / refusing a request.

10 Expressing a wish (a rather specialized use of this modal).

Summary

In this unit we have defined just a few common language terms.
Obviously, you should refer to a grammar book and the grammar guides
in any course book for more detailed and contextualized information but
you do need to know terminology, especially when teaching higher-level
students, as they are familiar with such terms. In other words, you need to
have the knowledge before you can begin the planning of how to *teach*
language. This is a gradual learning process. It is often this 'terminology'
that most worries new teachers – all you can do is to learn it yourself as
you go along. It's almost like learning a second language.

30 Glossary of terms

Here is a list of selected terms that you will encounter in the profession, most of which have featured elsewhere in this book. Please note, however, that I could have listed 400 if I had wanted to, so this list is far from exhaustive.

aims Top alphabetically, and top in importance. Your aims are your goals, what you want to achieve and what you want your students to achieve, both in the lesson as a whole and in each part (stage) of a lesson. You can have main aims, and secondary aims. Try to think of your aims from the point of view of what students will do / learn, rather than what the teacher will do / teach.

appropriateness This covers a number of points. In terms of language, what we say may be technically correct, but not appropriate to the context. It may be too formal, for example. In terms of material, what we ask our students to do / read / listen to, etc. must be appropriate according to the culture and background of the group, as well as their age, sex, general interests, the course and the lesson aims.

authentic Authentic material is real-life material, such as a newspaper or brochure. It has not been altered for classroom use, but the accompanying tasks will make it appropriate for the level and needs of the class. Authentic language is real, unscripted and ungraded language, such as a news broadcast from the radio.

clarification This is when you want to check that students have understood meaning (see **concept questions** and **timelines**), or when you need to go over something which has not been understood. It is also the checking of instructions and tasks. Avoid questions like 'Do you understand?' because this is not an effective way to clarify.

closed pairs This is when students work in pairs with someone sitting directly next to them (c/f **open pairs**)

concept questions One of the best ways to clarify / check that students have understood an item of language is to ask concept questions. These are short questions or prompts, usually requiring very short and simple answers. They check understanding of the concept (meaning) of language. When checking understanding of structures within a sentence, avoid using the structure in your concept questions.

contractions When the subject and auxiliary verb are 'joined', e.g. *She's* (*She is*).

controlled practice When students do a practice activity where the nature of the activity means there is a tight control over the language that they use. The teacher restricts the students' language so that the target language is used a lot. Written gap-fills are a good example.

context The context is the situation, and the situation provides meaning. Context could be in a text, a recording, pictures, spoken scenario from the teacher, etc. Language must have context because language must have meaning.

diagnostic A diagnostic test is to find out the level of a student; how much she knows. Within a lesson, a diagnostic task (**Test Teach Test**) is to see how much students already know about a piece of language being focused on in your lesson.

drilling This is when students repeat a piece of language with the aim of pronouncing it correctly and naturally. They do this having first heard a model to copy. Choral drilling is when they all say it together (confidence building), and individual drilling is when they say it by themselves. There are different types of drill, but the basic repetition drill is probably the most common type used by teachers. (See also **front chaining**.)

eliciting Try to get the students to tell you as much as possible, rather than you telling them everything. Ask them questions, find out what they already know, involve them. It relates to keeping the students actively involved in the lesson and participating fully.

feedback (plenary) If students have done a task together, get some reaction afterwards as a class. For example, if they have been discussing preferred holiday destinations, find out afterwards what some of them decided. If students have been working on an exercise together, you have to go through the answers with the class afterwards and clarify as required. **Plenary** is whole class feedback.

front chaining / back chaining When drilling a long or otherwise difficult sentence, it can help students if you 'break it down' from the front or the back. For example: 'I'm getting used to driving on the left' becomes 'on the left'... 'to driving on the left'... 'getting used to driving on the left' ... 'I'm getting used to driving on the left' (**back chaining**).

Each part is drilled in turn with the whole sentence being repeated at the end.

function There is always a reason for saying something – all speech has a function. Examples of functions are invitation, suggestion, apology, refusal, criticism, praise, complaint, deduction, request, offer, giving permission and order. Functions should be illustrated via context.

gist When reading a text or listening to a recording, students can be asked to listen for the gist – what the text or recording is about; the general sense or meaning of it.

illustrating meaning Rather than explaining what something means, teachers should illustrate meaning in some way – via context, visuals, mime, realia, etc. In other words, the teacher should show meaning, not explain it. This is also known as 'conveying meaning'.

L1 The student's first language or 'mother tongue'.

language grading The language teachers use in the classroom must be of a level which will be understood by the students, without it becoming overly simple. Obviously, the lower the level of the students, the more graded the teacher's language has to be. Speaking more slowly is not sufficient if the language being used is too difficult to understand.

lexis not just single words (vocabulary) but the relationship between words (e.g. *to issue a warning, a final notice, a 9–5 job*).

mingling When students get up and move around (as with a 'Find someone who ...' exercise). With very large classes, and especially when they are sitting behind desks, mingling is not a realistic option.

model sentence This is a sentence in context which includes a stucture which the teacher wishes to focus on. It allows the structure to be looked at within a meaningful sentence rather than in isolation. For example: *I'm leaving tomorrow morning on the first flight* contains 'subject + *to be* + verb-*ing*' (present progressive). It is sometimes also known as a 'marker sentence'.

monitoring When students are working together, the teacher should go round as best she can and observe their work and provide help and support. Monitoring also involves 'keeping an eye' on the class, looking to see if someone has finished a task, for example. Even when the class and teacher are working together, the teacher should maintain eye contact with the students and observe reactions and problems. Watching and reacting is a key teaching skill.

monolingual classes Classes where all the students are of the same nationality. Unless you are teaching in an English-speaking country, most classes you teach will be of this type.

MFP The meaning, form and pronunciation of a piece of language.

multilingual classes Classes with more than one nationality.

open pairs If one student interacts with another student in the room, but not one sitting next to them, this is open pairs. This might occur, for example, when one student is asked by the teacher to ask a question of another student in the room.

productive skills Speaking and writing – where the students must produce.

receptive skills Listening and reading – where students receive and comprehend language

rapport Teachers need to build a good relationship with their students, but also foster good relations between the students. This is rapport. A good classroom atmosphere and good relations between all in the class is essential.

schwa The only sound in the language with its own name, the schwa is the most common sound in English. in the word *potato*, for example, the first *o* is pronounced as a schwa.

situational presentation Typically, this is when the teacher provides a situation (**context**) in order to focus on an item of language contained within a model sentence. It is a relatively teacher-centred means of introducing language, but students are involved through the teacher eliciting from them in order to build the context.

scan reading Reading in order to find specific information without needing to focus on or understand other parts of the text.

skim reading Reading for overall gist.

stage A stage in a lesson is a separate part of it. Each stage should have its own aim (objective).

STT Student Talking Time.

structure Some sentences will have a fixed grammatical structure (invariable) which may be a tense (*I'll have gone by 3 p.m.* contains 'subject + *will have* + past participle' = future perfect simple); or maybe not (*I used to smoke* contains 'subject + *used to* + base verb'. When asking concept questions to check understanding, avoid using the structure in the question.

target language This is the language being focused on in a lesson.

task based learning This is when students have to complete a given task. They draft and re-draft language, which the teacher adds to, before delivering the final version of the task.

Test Teach Test This is a way of focusing on language in a lesson which first involves some diagnostic task; then the teacher clarifies meaning; then the students do practice tasks.

timelines The visual representation of time; very useful with tenses.

TTT Teacher Talk Time – which shouldn't be unnecessarily high.

warmers Short activities used at the start of a lesson which are not necessarily related to what is to follow. They are useful to wake a class up, give latecomers more time to arrive, etc. Such activities could also be used as fillers when you have time on your hands at the end of your lesson, or during a lesson to vary the pace. Activities can include simple tasks like 'Think of ten adjectives beginning with *c*'; or 'Find out what everyone in the room had for dinner last night'.

weak forms Typically these are vowel sounds in unstressed syllables. In *Can you help me?*, the word *can* is pronounced with a weak form when spoken naturally and without emphasis.